THE CATHOLIC MODERNISTS

THE
CATHOLIC MODERNISTS

A Study of the Religious Reform Movement
1864–1907

MICHELE RANCHETTI

translated by Isabel Quigly

London
OXFORD UNIVERSITY PRESS
NEW YORK   TORONTO
1969

Oxford University Press, Ely House, London W.1

GLASGOW NEW YORK TORONTO MELBOURNE WELLINGTON
CAPE TOWN SALISBURY IBADAN NAIROBI LUSAKA ADDIS ABABA
BOMBAY CALCUTTA MADRAS KARACHI LAHORE DACCA
KUALA LUMPUR SINGAPORE HONG KONG TOKYO

Printed in Great Britain
by Butler & Tanner Ltd, Frome and London

Contents

Tout ce qui ne va point à la charité est figure

PASCAL

Preface

During the past few years observers of the Roman Catholic Church have sometimes been reminded of the movement known as modernism; for when the Second Vatican Council was being prepared, in particular, and while it was taking place, the Church seemed to be harking back to subjects and problems raised during the modernist controversy about half a century earlier. Modernism was a wide-ranging doctrinal movement within the Church itself, condemned as heretical—indeed, labelled the 'heresy of all heresies'—in the encyclical *Pascendi dominici gregis*; and those who recalled it wondered whether the Church was about to do what it had so often done in the past: that is, salvage the elements of truth from what it had once condemned, years or even centuries before, once these elements had ceased to appear violent or controversial, and those who had proclaimed their truth were dead.

The Church, however, did no such thing, and provided no contemporary example of behaviour known, ironically or otherwise, as 'age-old prudence'. Nor are comparisons between the two occasions likely to be fruitful. The first was inspired mainly by a wish to reconsider the doctrinal order of Catholicism, to free it from the limitations imposed by outdated philosophies, insufficient historical knowledge, and an uncritical acceptance of centuries-old scientific discoveries; and to allow it to take advantage of the discoveries of more modern science and philosophy. Thus, it was felt, the Church would acquire the complete doctrinal authority it then lacked, and to which it undoubtedly had full right.

The second of the two occasions—that of the Second Vatican Council—was inspired by ideas that can best be found in the constitution on the liturgy. This time, it was not a case of reconsidering the doctrinal order of Catholicism, renewing its essentials, and bringing its philosophy, exegesis, dogma, and historical ideas up to date, so that a present-day man—indeed, the present-day world—could accept it as homogeneous with (that is, not contradicting) the ideas of science and of philosophy, of politics and of all the disciplines used in the progress of man. It was, in fact, a case of doing almost exactly the opposite: any definition of a mainly conceptual character relating to the truth of Revelation as 'separate' from an unestablished content of experience was gradually and prudently being eroded.

These, then, if rather schematically expressed, were the motives that inspired the two occasions; and there was certainly no question of a modernistic revival in the second of them. Indeed, the ideas of modernism were rejected, not so much in detail as in a rebuttal of the doctrinal aim. *Pascendi* had condemned it by examining its opinions, ideas, and doctrines individually, whereas the Second Vatican Council condemned it by pointing out, once again, the great conflict between charism and gnosis.

How the Church passed from the doctrinal condemnation of a doctrinal movement to the constitution of the Second Vatican Council, and what were the forces and influences that brought about this change, is outside the scope of this book and cannot be considered in a short preface. I want simply to mention one of the theses that inspired the book, and which seems to have been confirmed by the recent history of Roman Catholicism.

The main thesis of this inquiry is as follows: the modernists wished to restore Catholicism as a doctrine of truth; in order to do this, they felt they should not use the religious experience of small though effective groups of a narrowly political or religious kind, but should rely only on perfecting the doctrinal experience of Catholicism throughout its history—an experience they considered incomplete and therefore ready for further development. Modernism was part of the historicist crisis of culture at the end of the nineteenth century and the modernists cared nothing for the historical order, for historical reasoning, or for any event in the history of the Church, however it was understood; they pursued their own ideal of a kind of doctrinal 'state of perfection', to restore the ineffable, original core of Christianity and to set up against historical Catholicism, which had been discredited by the authority of Rome which lacked, above all, culture; and this meant that they had little or no interest in the great events of the Church's life—matters like the 'Roman question' in Italy or the separation of Church and state in France; more generally and more seriously, it meant that they held aloof from the history of their own time, in which the Catholic Church was playing an influential part (though this is a subject that deserves more thorough treatment). It also meant that they withdrew into cultural isolation, considering themselves prophets whose work was on a level with that of the great creative religious figures; this meant that, like these religious leaders, they were likely to be spurned by the simple and condemned by the priests. But what was remarkable about them was the fact that they kept within a particular circle of doctrine, and a particular kind of culture, as if their original vocation—that is, the fact that they belonged to the Christian priesthood—had helped them and at the same time conditioned them once and for all to make their inquiries or to be fruitful in a particular context, under pain of sterility, like the barren fig-tree of the Gospel. There is also a discrepancy between the breadth of their ideas of renewal and the psychological limitations of some of its aspects, between the apparent intransigence of what they said, and the frail character of those involved; indeed, their history, which is probably the last 'gnostic' effort, in the sense that knowledge took precedence over faith, is also the tragic personal story of a number of priests faced with the authority of Rome.

The inquiry, therefore, has been as it were on the inside of events, and has tried to proceed in a way that is parallel to them, avoiding exterior 'historical' judgements, hindsight and future justifications as much as possible. It seeks to place itself on the inside and to proceed with the painful, imprecise self-awareness of the main movers in the story, taking on the isolation in which they lived and worked. Other events and the history of the time, and, to some extent, the rights and wrongs of the case, are therefore given little prominence.

All this means that there is nothing particularly new in this history of what happened. Most of the material used has already been published (except for Minocchi's autobiography, and a little more besides), and some documents which are now available, although still subject to the discretion of their owners, were not available when the book was first written. It has no revelations, and explains neither the reforming movement, nor the particular actions of its protagonists. In any case, as far as matter published since the Italian edition appeared is concerned, only painful private matters have come to light in the case of the Italian modernists condemned by Rome, and, in Blondel's case, only signs of well-reasoned prudence. Other researches into modernism, both in Italy and abroad, have illustrated important aspects of the subject, sometimes admirably, and more often have given particular interpretations and judgements on what happened. Opinions have been put forward which I should have liked to accept or refute, but I have avoided considering them as alternatives to the central view I myself hold, which I mentioned earlier.

Much could be written on modernism, and on its meaning in the history of the Church and of our own age. In this preface I have merely touched on it, and in what I have said shown that it has been impossible to make comparisons of a doctrinal kind between what was accepted and what rejected, either in the case of single ideas or in that of ideas that inspired the movement. But the story has only just started, and we cannot foresee its developments; in any case, these will go far beyond the still disputed questions of authority and preservation, and not only in so far as concerns the Church of Rome.

I would like to end by thanking Mr. Geoffrey Hunt of Oxford University Press, and Miss Isabel Quigly to whom the English edition of this book is largely indebted.

Florence　　　　　　　　　　　　　　　　　　　　M. R.
May 1969

Publisher's Note

Wherever possible English quotations have been taken from the originals. Translations from the French were made by Miss Carole Burden.

PART I

1. Introduction

'Modernism' is the term used to denote the ecclesiastical aspect of the religious crisis, with its ideas on the reform and renewal of religious culture in general, in the early years of this century. For its understanding, four autobiographies are among the most fruitful sources of information: Alfred Loisy's *Mémoires*, George Tyrrell's Autobiography, Ernesto Buonaiuti's *Pellegrino di Roma*, and Salvatore Minocchi's *Memorie di un modernista*, the first three published, the fourth unpublished.[1] The authors were all clerics, and all suffered at the Church's hands. Other sources are the letters

[1] Alfred Loisy, *Mémoires pour servir à l'histoire religieuse de notre temps*, Nourry, Paris, 1930-1, in three volumes: Volume I (1857-1900), Volume II (1900-8), Volume III (1908-27), 1,860 pages in all. The manuscript bears the final date 27 January 1929, but there are some additions at the end of 1930 and January 1931. Loisy's *Mémoires* use some of the autobiography that preceded them: *Choses passées*, Nourry, Paris, 1913, of which a thousand copies, in booklet form, were distributed by the Union pour la Vérité, in 1912 and 1913. Parts of Loisy's diary, not reproduced in the *Mémoires*, appear in his biography by Albert Houtin, which was unpublished until 1960: *Alfred Loisy, sa vie, son œuvre, par Albert Houtin et Felix Sartiaux, manuscrit annoté et publié avec une bibliographie de Loisy par Émile Poulat*, Éditions du Centre national de la recherche scientifique, Paris, 1960. This is a fundamental work if the *Mémoires* are to be understood and judgements corrected; and particularly important for Poulat's editorial work, and the first complete bibliography of Loisy. On the *Mémoires*, which gave rise to a great deal of polemical writing, see in particular, on the Catholic side, J. M. Lagrange, *M. Loisy et le Modernisme*, Les Éditions du Cerf, Paris, 1932; on the 'lay' side: P. Martinetti in *Ragione e fede, Saggi Religiosi*, Einaudi, Turin, 1942, pp. 229-69, and A. Omodeo, *A. Loisy storico delle religioni*, Laterza, Bari, 1936. In Loisy's *Mémoires* a great many letters are quoted from laymen and priests with whom Loisy discussed his plans for reform, especially in the early years of his religious formation; among his most frequent correspondents was Baron Friedrich von Hügel, on whom see Michael de la Bedoyère's *Life of Baron von Hügel*, Dent, London, 1951, in which other letters and diary extracts are quoted: Maurice Nédoncelle, *La pensée religieuse de Friedrich von Hügel* (1852-1925), Vrin, Paris, 1935, and Jean Steinmann's *Friedrich von Hügel*, Aubier, Paris, 1962.

Autobiography and Life of George Tyrrell, Volume I: *Autobiography* (1861-84) *arranged with supplements*, by M. D. Petre; Volume II: *Life of George Tyrrell from 1884-1909*, by M. D. Petre, Edward Arnold, London, 1912.

Ernesto Buonaiuti, *Pellegrino di Roma. La generazione dell'Esodo* (Darsena, Rome, 1945, 2 ed. Bari, 1964, ed. by M. Niccoli). The introduction is dated Pentecost 1944. It is not Buonaiuti's only autobiographical work—he often wrote 'autobiographically'—but it sums up his religious experience far better

3

of Baron Friedrich von Hügel, either published or quoted in the autobiographies, a number of Fogazzaro's letters, and Blondel's correspondence. Together these provide a basis, first of all for the understanding of individual events and of the intellectual relationships between the movement's main exponents, and secondly for the establishment of a new philosophy of religion.

Among the autobiographies, Loisy's *Mémoires* is undoubtedly the most important. Written about 1930, the book takes its author from birth until nearly the end of his life. Loisy neither recreates his own times, nor sees the past in the light of his present feelings; he does not even give a detailed portrait of it. What he does, using an enormous number of documents (not a note or a cutting appears to have been lost or neglected), is follow the day-to-day progress of a young priest who realized that his own story would be immensely valuable, both humanly and ecclesiastically, and

than many narratives which stick more closely to the facts or to particular incidents in his spiritual progress.

Salvatore Minocchi, *Memorie di un modernista*, typescript kept at the Biblioteca Nazionale in Florence, in two volumes bound in boards, and, in a slightly different version, by his family in Florence. This book has so far been unpublished, but a critical edition is now being edited by Professor Attilio Agnoletto, author of a monograph on Minocchi. Among Minocchi's papers, which the family had the courtesy to show me, and for which I thank them here, there are many notes for the revision and correction of his memoirs, apart from drafts of different versions; I have borne these notes in mind in writing this book, as well as many letters to Minocchi (among them some important ones from Loisy, Tyrrell, and von Hügel).

The letters of Fogazzaro, the great layman of the reformatory movement, are found in *Lettere scelte*, edited by Tommaso F. Gallarati Scotti, Mondadori, Milan, 1942; in *La vita di Fogazzaro*, also by Gallarati Scotti, Baldini e Castoldi, Milan, 1925; in *Fogazzaro nel suo piccolo mondo. Dai carteggi familiari*, by Ottorino Morra, Cappelli, Bologna, 1960, apart from those in Loisy's *Mémoires*; some unpublished letters are among the Minocchi papers, and refer to the Fogazzaro Lectures; others have been left out of Gallarati Scotti's edition, for the sake of prudence.

Blondel's correspondence is in course of publication; so far the following have been published: his correspondence with Auguste Valensin, in two volumes, Aubier, Paris, 1957, edited by a priest who may be identified as Fr. Danielou, a model critical edition, with very full and always necessary notes; the letters exchanged between Blondel and Laberthonnière, edited by Claude Tresmontant (Éditions du Seuil, Paris, 1961); a selection of *Lettres philosophiques* (to Boutroux, Delbos, Bremond, Le Roy, and others), Aubier, Paris, 1961; and, edited by René Marlé, a selection of letters, *Au cœur de la crise moderniste (le dossier inédit d'une controverse)*, also published by Aubier, Paris, 1960. In 1961 Les Éditions du Cerf published the first volume of Blondel's *Carnets intimes*, which relates to the years 1882–94. This volume, like the correspondence on the modernist crisis, bears the imprimatur.

who therefore compiled an enormous dossier of irrefutable evidence that would help towards an understanding of the religious history of his age. At the very moment in which he entered the religious life Loisy assembled the evidence, setting down beliefs and doubt as impartially as a judge who, seeking to understand, neither absolves nor condemns, yet without even really believing that a life could be understood and justified in the light of such scrupulous self-knowledge. Loisy's objectivity is clearly suspect, if only because of the complete self-absorption of his memoirs, as Catholics, many of whom had suffered unfavourable criticism at his hands, not unnaturally pointed out—in particular Lagrange; yet his distortion of the facts has as much interest as the facts themselves, since it is always prompted by excessive zeal in getting at the facts of religious psychology, and then airing them in the light of critical reason. Philosophical and religious subjects of the kind clearly belonged to the age he lived in, and Loisy dealt with them in his *Mémoires* with deliberate, courageous lack of prudence, as well as a fair degree of critical awareness.

If, as an old man looking back on his youth, Loisy had felt as patronizing as a man normally feels in the circumstances, or if, as an adult, he had felt the usual impatience of one faced with his own uncertainties, mistakes, and failures of understanding, his *Mémoires* would not have given us, as they do, the portrait of a mind whose special quality lay not in its judgements but in the way it built up, piecemeal, a work of religious psychology (philologically and religiously certain, even when shakily truthful, Loisy maintained that this was the result of an essential intellectual process), and gave us a living example of his theme in both the outward events of his life and in his inner development.

And indeed, Loisy's slowly developed wish to sum up the fundamental themes of both modernism and the religious thought of his time in his own spiritual life is on the whole justified. His exactness in expressing himself, his critical alertness and the remarkable vigilance of his mind meant that he saw what was developing around him, indeed thanks to him; while his moral curiosity, his intellectual ambition, and his way of summing up the motives of others, within his own limitations, meant that he was in fact an official exponent of the movement of renewal; so much so that his attitude towards the authorities influenced that of others—his sometimes unintelligent imitators—and had its effect on the reasons for, and even the personal and private nature of, resistance and prosecution. Besides this, Loisy corresponded at length with those who were active in the movement at every level; and he uses and quotes letters that bring alive the figures of von Hügel, Duchesne, Houtin, Monsignor Mignot, Hébert, Tyrrell, and Blondel, often in their own words. These are always marginal figures, however, never determining Loisy's thought and behaviour; indeed, they seem to urge him to express it, and in one case at least, that of von Hügel, the main correspondent and the medium, as it were, of the new religious spirit, throw light on his intellectual processes by failing to understand them, in his particular, individual case. They have, too, a kind of collective conscience for which Loisy feels responsible. Occasionally one of them, for personal reasons or through a difference of intellectual development, seems to leave the communal womb where new religious thought is gestating; and then Loisy abandons him to his fate, pretends he no longer understands him, and passes immediate sentence on him. The *Mémoires* therefore show us, through a number of Catholic laymen and clerics seen in their letters to Loisy and their personal relationships with him, the origins and development of the religious crisis; and the very fact that Loisy never had the doctrinal or philosophical equipment with which to accept or reject the thought of others on the basis of his own convictions (he always pressed his own critical intentions and the discoveries in exegesis), meant that his study of ideas and characters was as rich in detail as it was inadequate in wider fields or in matters of exact doctrine. Indeed, though he felt involved in the broad sweep of European historicism, and, in his own field, seemed to think he was expressing it, Loisy's flaw lay in his sense of history, at least in so far as his awareness of motives, his own and other people's, was concerned; a fact proved by his almost total lack of understanding of what inspired the most important event in the history of the church in his day: the Vatican Council. This lack of an historical sense was found in nearly all the modernists and religious philosophers who came after him.[1] And this very fault means that his autobiography has a particular quality: it

---

[1] The identification of the 'relative' value with the 'historical' aspect of truth implies an interpretation of the modernistic movement as a particular aspect of the historicist crisis of the Church which, although interesting, we cannot share. See, to support this thesis, G. Martini, *Cattolicesimo e storicismo. Momenti d'una crisi del pensiero religioso moderno*, Naples, 1951.

isolates the personalities of the innovators just as it isolates itself
and sees them freed from the shackles of belonging either to the
Church of Rome and its doctrinal body or, to a certain extent,
to its history and even to their own national histories; while only
partially aware that this is one of the most traditionally heretical
and schismatic attitudes, as the Vatican Council made clear.

In his *Mémoires* and *Choses passées*, Loisy writes the religious
history of our age within the carefully documented framework of
his own spiritual history and that of others like him. George
Tyrrell's autobiography, on the other hand, is first and foremost
an attempt at a philosophical synthesis, or at least a doctrinal
reconstruction. An attempt at this appears, indeed, in all his work,
as his critics rightly pointed out.[1] Tyrrell wrote his autobiography
not for publication but as a private document, sent privately to
another to make what spiritual use of it he could; he stopped at
1884, not because he felt he had come to a suitable stopping place
but, according to M. D. Petre, because he found it impossible to
continue after writing about his mother's death. This means that
his narrative ends with an event that posed the question his whole
autobiography propounded, sometimes explicitly: the validity of
unnatural experiences and efforts as compared with the natural
truth of earthly affections. What happened to Tyrrell both humanly
and doctrinally after 1884 is told by M. D. Petre on the basis of
the many papers left her by Tyrrell at his death, and told in the
same spirit as his autobiography. Letters and documents connected with those concerned fill in the gaps and throw light on
the reasons for Tyrrell's behaviour in the decisive years; and Miss
Petre's comments are so tactful that the reader who may seek
to justify what happened by looking beyond what was actually
said and done will very rarely go astray.

If Loisy was the exegete whose discoveries might revolutionize
Catholic doctrine and apologetics, Tyrrell was the master von
Hügel held up to his correspondents, and in particular to his
Italian friends, as a model of spirituality, and as a thinker. Now
his autobiography immediately shows us a characteristic that the
Italian modernists, for instance, and Buonaiuti in particular, seem
to have failed to ponder, but which was to influence both his

---

[1] See in particular: P. Martinetti, 'La filosofia religiosa di G. Tyrrell', in
Ragione e fede, pp. 135–74.

outlook and theirs. Tyrrell, who was rightly called the only intelligent continuator, was, like Newman, a convert to Catholicism who knew, through having practised it, the spirituality of other faiths. His autobiography, his letters, the very facts of his life, cannot be understood without taking into account the determining fact of his conversion, which was a discovery not of the faith, or not only of this, but of a form of worship and of a tradition recognized as true by comparison with other faiths. Tyrrell's violence in his later writings, his famous indictment of Rome, his 'wholesome excommunication', cannot be fully justified if the events of his life are seen in terms of a simple opposition between philosophy and religion. Behind him, in fact, was the Anglican truth and the traditions in which he had been brought up as a child, there were Dolling's pious practices, which persuaded the young man to admit the need for faith; just as, when he accepted orthodox Catholicism, he was powerfully drawn to the most militant religious order, the Society of Jesus. All the same, whether it was fully understood or unconsciously absorbed, Tyrrell's 'conversion', like his experience of other traditions of thought and culture, influenced the development of the innovators' religious thought; indeed his intransigence, though its personal reasons may have been unknown, played a determining part—for the Italians in particular—in making clear the value of authority, which Tyrrell freely and voluntarily accepted, and others, thanks to his example and his preaching, recognized as a fundamental element of Catholic belief. Besides, unlike Loisy, both in his *Mémoires* and in his other writings, Tyrrell's autobiography and letters show that his constant wish was to found a new philosophy of religion, different from the teaching of Rome yet within the Church and through the truth of the Church. To this new philosophy the various Christian sects, which Tyrrell knew better and more critically than his imitators and pupils, would contribute, just as the modern philosophies he used intuitively would do. Some of the contributors to *Rinnovamento* and *Nova et vetera* used this religio-philosophical syncretism as a perfect doctrine; and it might, in fact, have been the one way in which the innovators could have been united, doctrinally speaking. But, just as happened in Loisy's case, Tyrrell's personality—which was clearly a more religious and a mystical one—was often used, by both leaders and followers, to serve as an example rather than for any doctrinal purpose, while his quarrel with Rome and his death inflamed both supporters and enemies to unreasonable excesses of praise or blame.[1]

Of the two Italian autobiographies, Ernesto Buonaiuti's *Pellegrino di Roma* is undoubtedly the more important; not so much an accurate account of the age of modernism as a reappraisal of it. Buonaiuti did not develop homogeneously, though an inner coherence can easily be found in every aspect of his life and thought. What is more, the years of *Nova et vetera* and of the *Letters of a modernist priest*, that is, his years of polemics and revolt following *Pascendi* but preceded and stirred by the critical and spiritual developments here examined, seem to him a 'youthful mistake'.[2] Unlike Loisy, who betrayed no

[1] Tyrrell was involved far more than Loisy in the formation and development of the Italian modernists groups. He wrote for *Rinnovamento* and even more for *Nova et vetera*, Buonaiuti's modernists' review in 1908, and he corresponded with many of the Italian modernists, among them Buonaiuti and Minocchi. Yet it seems that the trust they felt in him was not returned; in fact, Tyrrell shows in many letters (see, in particular, the letters in de la Bedoyère's biography of von Hügel), that he did not share Buonaiuti's areligious extremism and that he feared his thought might be radically distorted if he wrote in *Nova et vetera* with others whose inspiration was definitely anti-ecclesiastical. For this reason, the letters from Tyrrell which Buonaiuti quoted in his history of Catholic modernism give a rather false impression.

[2] See a similar judgement in *Una fede e una disciplina*, Campitelli, Foligno, 1925. 'The modernistic crisis, it is true, caught me up completely and swept me into its explosive centre. But I was quickly disabused, and all that was paradoxical and untimely and eccentric in the—admittedly very noble—programme, of the movement which thought it would all at once make the Church irresistibly effective, thanks to a basic renewal of its attitudes and outlook, soon fell away like dross. No one around me believed this, and I was left to the risks of my solitary pilgrimage.' See Minocchi's retort to this repudiation, 'A Ernesto Buonaiuti, Una fede ed una disciplina', in *Giornale d'Italia*, 17 February 1925: '... I could not without a friendly word ignore the pages in which you briefly look back and, to please implacable enemies, today repudiate your modernistic past and confess that the distant and, I feel, best forgotten time of modernism was for you a time of error and betrayal. You are wrong. That time, which I lived through with you, or even before you did, was in fact the solemn moment in which our young souls rose to a higher faith, with a wider vision of the Christian principle, leaving behind them the dross of a theological tradition that was destined to vanish from civilization. And yet I believe, in fact I am certain, that many, perhaps all the modernists of that time, who are silent and will carry their hapless silence to the grave, keep pure and firm in their hearts the conviction that, with their modernistic attitude, they helped the Church in the world and the universal Christian religion that is so much greater than any church. Are you the only one to regret this? Are you the only one to believe that what was and will be, in the pure enthusiasm of our souls, still unused to human malice, your boast and your highest glory, was an error? ... The first error into which you fell was your repudiation of modernism; a great error on which all the others depended.'

uncertainty, perhaps because he never had anything but intellectual impulses,[1] Buonaiuti is a generous writer rather than an accurate self-examiner; so, in his book, his angry outbursts against those he considers betrayed a religious vocation (for instance, in his account of the modernist meeting at Molveno, and the 'portraits' of Alessandro Casati and Tommaso Gallarati Scotti) are possibly more useful than the doctrinal points he makes, and he seems to deny or reduce to a minimum the meaning and value of modernism. It is not the anonymous editor of *Nova et vetera* but the official editor of the *Rivista storico-critica*, which appeared contemporaneously in 1908, that seems to live on in the Roman priest—though certainly not through posthumous approval of *Pascendi* and denial of the *Programma dei modernisti*—and to grow in doctrinal knowledge and spirituality; and this in homage to immortal Rome, to whose truth, which rose clear of all heresy, he claimed he had borne witness. As far as the crucial years of modernism are concerned, then, Buonaiuti's autobiography is almost valueless; and he makes no reference to persons or situations that might throw light on what happened, or clear up what has been uncertainly interpreted. He had got over those early years of his, and had no wish to write a religious history of our time; his autobiography is of value for what it shows he considered vital at a distance of many years—which means precious little—and for the way it recalls, in a hurried but lively way, his religious vocation. Unlike Loisy the historian and Tyrrell the philosopher, Buonaiuti had become involved with many spiritual, philosophical, and critical ideas, which he always cast off once he had taken the pith of them (just as he sincerely absorbed the personalities of those he asked to collaborate with him, but did not follow them to their doctrinal or practical consequences); he was also, as his autobiography shows explicitly, an active organizer, an active researcher, and sometimes a popularizer. For all these reasons his

---

[1] At least in the public version of the *Mémoires*. Other extracts, suppressed in the published edition but communicated to Houtin and mentioned by him in his biography, revealed a suffering, buffeted inner nature. Anyone who could have read the memoirs in their old exercise books, later destroyed, would have found 'instead of a peaceful mind, one which was profoundly troubled, instead of an arid and narrow heart, a whole world of passionate, tender feelings, instead of a life filled only with the search for truth, an existence tortured with every kind of doubt, ambition . . . and deception'. See Houtin, op. cit., p. 57, where disciplinary action taken against Loisy when he was a seminarist, on account of an affectionate relationship of his, is also mentioned.

memoirs provide a valuable record of a religious feeling that was widespread in his age; and in his human courage and generous, vigorous personality, people saw, in spite of all uncertainties, the image of a persecuted religious vocation.[1]

Minocchi's unpublished *Memorie della mia vita* (or *Memorie di un modernista*) betrays its author's age.[2] Written in 1936 (June to September), and more faithful to the original documents than Buonaiuti's autobiography, with appendixes containing passages from letters, and notes on gaps in the text, it is strewn, unlike the other autobiographies, with lyrical outbursts, painterly visions, poetic effusions, and literary meanderings that are often useless, and nearly always irrelevant. His interpretation of a great many things, and his constant dissatisfaction, hang on the contradiction between his two vocations, literary and religious; yet this contradiction seems to have moved from secondary to primary importance because Minocchi, as an old man, could find no other means of expressing himself, except through this all-important distinction or choice in his life. As a young man he had felt the two values were antithetical, and indeed throughout his whole life and profession of faith he believed them to be so; and it was on this contradiction that his 'non-modernism' was based. That is, he sheltered behind the idea of a vocation *manqué* as opposed to a vocation forced on him, apart from instantly and officially submitting to the religious authorities' disciplinary action, for which he was so bitterly reproached. Yet Minocchi was the first to gather young Italian clerical scholars round a periodical, first the *Rivista bibliografica italiana* (1896–1899), then the *Studi religiosi* (1901–1907); and it was through these publications that the names and ideas of Loisy, Houtin, Harnack, Tyrrell, and Blondel became part of Italian culture; and in spite of the brisk, popular air Minocchi tried to maintain in his publications, and the way

---

[1] Much has been written and argued about Buonaiuti's ingenuousness and candour, or about his duplicity and cunning. But as this refers to Buonaiuti's whole religious experience, and not so much to his modernistic 'error', they go beyond the terms of this book, just as comparisons and judgements on the value of the historiographical activity that followed *Pascendi* are outside its scope.

[2] Some extracts from Minocchi's memoirs have been published: see 'Memorie di un modernista di S. Minocchi', an extract edited with an introduction by F. Gabrieli, in *Ricerche religiose*, XIX, 2, Rome, 1948, pp. 148–67, and 'Uomini e cose di ieri e di oggi. Dalle "Memorie di un modernista" di Salvatore Minocchi', edited by Giuseppe Martini, in *Itinerari*, nn. 47–8, Geneva, March–April 1961, pp. 29–52.

he kept urging moderation on his writers—though his memoirs show this was not part of his policy—he published the new ideas and organized the new critical outlook in a way not unlike Prezzolini's in *Voce*, some years later. In his memoirs Minocchi is a moderate; this is shown by the way he judges Semeria, Buonaiuti, and Loisy; and a moderate, it would appear, on the Catholic side at that. He is well aware of the newness of the philosophy expressed in his review, of the way a movement is forming, of the need to renew the clergy's culture and to fight scholastic theology; but he fears the danger. He wants reform, but not a break; he has a fairly critical and almost totally unphilosophical mind. His masters are Loisy and, to some extent, Renan, he knows Harnack's thought, can discover a new apologetic in Blondel's work, but he reproaches Loisy for forgetting he is a priest, and confines Tyrrell to the role of mystic. To him, Rome's refusal to allow the new discoveries in biblical exegesis is something transitory, the result of religious diplomacy, not a doctrinal necessity; just as he finds inconceivable the idea of a new philosophy of religion that goes beyond the reform of the doctrine professed by Rome. Personally he may break with the authorities, but not through any spiritual and intellectual differences: only because he has another vocation, and one that is no longer religious. His *Memorie* is also interesting for what it tells of the relationship between him and the Italian intellectual groups, in particular the *Voce* group, but his meetings with the Giubbe Rosse[1] philosophers and his invective against Gentile, whose boast of having provided doctrinal ammunition for (and even the actual phrasing of) the draft of the encyclical *Pascendi* he refutes, seem to show no special awareness of what idealism contributed to Catholic restoration. The fact that he accused Gentile of dishonesty was something much more personal than ideological or doctrinal, and the anti-idealistic line taken by *Nova et vetera* was not supported by anything Minocchi had previously known.[2] As

[1] From the name of a well-known café in Florence, where philosophers and literary men used to meet in the first decade of the century.

[2] The relationship between Minocchi and the Giubbe Rosse philosophers, the fact that he took part in the meetings of the Philosophical Library in Florence, and in particular his relations with Gentile, date from his suspension *a divinis*; that is, they all show that he was trying to participate in the philosophical movement he thought he had helped to turn towards problems of faith. For some years he was often a welcome, respected guest at meetings and debates (as his contributions to *Voce* show, and his name in the indexes of the 'Bulletin of the Philosophical Library'), but this did not last long, and was a sort of parenthesis

for personal relationships, Minocchi mentions those he met in an appendix, and gives a number of letters, but all from the time of the decree of suspension *a divinis* (except for one, from Loisy, in 1903); and so, although they show the clergy standing together, they reveal little about the actual state of affairs between Minocchi, Loisy, Tyrrell, Semeria, von Hügel, Fracassini, Casciola, the *Rinnovamento* group, and Buonaiuti. Lastly, *Memorie di un modernista* is a sad account of Minocchi's efforts to enter university life. In Loisy's case, this was offered him, after the religious and disciplinary crisis, as a natural outlet for teaching that was unacceptable to the religious authorities in their own institutions; and Buonaiuti was able to teach until the coming of Fascism, and so had a relevant part to play in the development of religious culture. Whereas Minocchi, once out of the priesthood, refused or was unable to make any contribution to the religious culture he had so actively promoted; nor did he produce anything important in his scientific work, either.

Apart from their autobiographical writings, the other works of Loisy, Tyrrell, Buonaiuti, and Minocchi express their strength, their new ideas, their awareness of what they had to do in the matter of renewal, and in the break within the Church, and what their position was in relation to the culture of their day. But one thing they seemed unaware of, in particular Minocchi and Buonaiuti: that they were part of a process moving towards freeing reason from authority, that they represented the religious aspect of a movement towards freedom of thought that was taking place in fields outside their own as well, although they felt that everything to be replaced and re-established was to be found in theirs

---

after his dismissal by his superiors. Neither Minocchi nor the 'philosophers' found any common ground. Understanding was impossible, too, because the pragmatistic phase of Italian modernism did not coincide with the pragmatistic phase of Florentine culture, which had then already gone beyond it. The idealistic restoration, that is, the philosophical movement promoted by Croce and Gentile, and its alliance with the Catholic restoration, may have confused Minocchi and many others with him, but neither he nor those in the small Florentine group were especially aware of the need to put up a conceptual resistance. Papini, vulgar as ever, or rather more so than usual, who had asked the undisciplined *Nova et vetera* group: 'What are you doing to morality?', might well sneer at the priest who was about to marry; others were simply unaware of him. That, after frustrated efforts to get a university post, Minocchi wasted his mind is shown in the pathetic biography of his son Sigieri, who was killed in East Africa and commemorated by his father in a painful effort to restore religious values to a Fascist death.

alone. They had been brought up on religious philosophy and could not get away from theological writing. They had seen the crisis in the Catholic clergy, tried to find a way of transcending their profession of faith and their scholastic background, and when critical thought was applied to dogmatic truth they confused it with the actual law of truth, or with truth itself. As members of the clergy, they acted for their colleagues, whose teachers and persuaders they became, while laymen, who were automatically in a position subordinate to the clergy, looked up to them; or they learnt from laymen who, like Blondel, supported the orthodoxy that, in matters of discipline at least, maintained this subordinate position. The way the movement spread only in countries with a Catholic tradition, in particular in France and Italy, and the small amount of interest it aroused outside the field of Catholic religious philosophy, shows that, both in its origins and in its results, it was essentially a controversy within the Church of Rome. This is something far more obvious from this distance than it was at the time, when public opinion, and the efforts at self-justification both by those who had been condemned and by the authorities, made ideas and proposals quite foreign to the modernist movement seem to have contributed to it, and when people looked far for its origins and suggested, as likely, influences it could not possibly have had. Indeed an historian seeking out the causes, near and far, of a movement that in its early days seemed likely to provoke a revolution far beyond its own field, finds it very hard, indeed actually impossible, to go back beyond the second half of the nineteenth century—unless he seeks out isolated forerunners who seem to have hit on similar ideas haphazardly, by guesswork. Impossible, too, to go outside the Catholic Church, or indeed outside the circle of a few 'promoters' recognizable as representative of the movement, since they knew just what they were doing and where their speculations were leading them, within the Catholic Church and in the face of Catholic doctrine. They were, of course, influenced by a climate of opinion they themselves recognized; but they were 'modernists' only in that they saw what it meant in relation to Catholic doctrine, only in that, as practising Catholics, they sought a reform in doctrine, only in that they suggested a Catholic alternative to Rome. To quote Kant or to recall the positivism that dominated philosophy and science, to weigh up influences with suitably matched quotations, or recall how so-and-so put forward similar ideas in such-and-such a year, is perfectly possible, but not very useful. The new philosophy is better understood, and understood in its truest sense, perhaps, through what its accredited exponents said. Besides, through them critical thought was applied to Catholic doctrine, and in this they were both its heirs and also innovators. Thus, these four autobiographical writers are important to any study of the movement's origins; and, from this distance, we can see how their varying cultural and historical backgrounds meant that they formed intellectual subgroups, such as those of the *Rinnovamento* and of *Nova et vetera*. In these, ideological and doctrinal ideas that were quite foreign to them combined with the group's original character in order to achieve a synthesis or work out some sort of action; but both these possibilities foundered on the Church's theological declarations and disciplinary measures.

2. Loisy

To take Loisy, then.[1]

Theology, as such, is finished, the old style of exegesis is disappearing. These days, when I reread the first three gospels in a critical frame of mind, I realize that there are, in fact, many discrepancies of detail. . . . But two things stand firm: first, the general impression made by Jesus Christ . . . secondly, these divine discourses. . . . It is enough. . . . It may seem that one is launching the ship at the height of the storm, but because Jesus is there, there is no danger.

[1] Alfred Loisy was born at Ambrières (Marne) on 28 February 1857, the second son of a small farmer. 'Of a relatively delicate nature,' Houtin wrote (op. cit., pp. 7–8), 'Alfred was brought up like a little girl and with little girls. He played with dolls which he dressed himself. He could spin [with a bobbin], sew, and knit. He made stockings and socks, hats and dresses for his sister's dolls. Some twenty years later, when he was already teaching at the Institut catholique, he would make clothes for his nieces' dolls during the holidays. He liked tapestry and could embroider. He also knew something about cookery. In short, he deserved the unsmiling remark once made to him by one of his great-aunts: "My father would not have allowed a boy to lead the life of a young lady." A young lady in an agricultural village of 300 inhabitants, where they spoke patois, where the patriarchal customs still lingered on, destroyed after 1870 by the spread of republican ideas.' Educated to respect tradition ('There is something in me that hates anything new,' he wrote later, 'that hates changes; yet in thought I have broken all the fences down'), he left primary school top of his class in 1868 and the same year won a prize for scripture and history in a regional competition. At the prize-giving, he was applauded in the presence of the civil and academic authorities: 'All the empty show of such occasions escapes the notice of a child. On that day I had a vague premonition of the glory to which the work of the mind could lead,' he remarked in his autobiographical notes in 1884. In 1869 and 1870 he was at school at Vitry, then from 1872–4 at Saint-Dizier, and in October 1874 he entered the large seminary of Chalons-sur-Marne. In June 1879 he was ordained priest. For two years he was a country parish priest, then in May 1881 he returned to the Institut catholique where he met Louis Duchesne again, who showed him Tischendorf's great edition of the New Testament, with immediate results: 'My attentive reading of the Gospels immediately destroyed the idea I had been given of them. Faith told me that these writings were wholly divine; reason showed me that they were wholly human, in no way exempt from contradictions, and bearing clear traces of the individual leanings of their authors. The authenticity of Matthew and John seemed to me to be very suspect. This is as far as I went. I did not have time to look for a theory of inspiration which would reconcile faith and knowledge.' See *Autobiographical notes of 1884* (quoted in Houtin, op. cit., p. 30), but also in *Choses pensées*, pp. 56–7, and in *Mémoires*, I, pp. 97–8.

This is part of a letter from Duchesne to Loisy in August 1881, that is from the head of the Institut catholique in Paris (founded a few years earlier, in 1875) to his pupil. The letter's intention lay not in what it said, but in the exhortation that followed, which Loisy quoted in his *Mémoires*:

Allow me this freedom too. As I see you becoming aware of these serious problems and rejecting sacred tradition, I feel the need to warn you against feelings of doubt and discouragement. Having been through difficult times myself, I am in a position to help you in the light of my own experience. In fact, it is my duty, for nothing would be more painful for me than to think that you might suffer anguish from following a path I had helped to show you.[1]

But Loisy remained unmoved by this exhortation: he used the letter to point out, though 'bien rudimentairement, bien vaguement', the modernist programme, and to maintain at this early stage that Duchesne, although he foresaw that 'modernism' was both possible and necessary, purposely avoided going into it more fully in order to avoid the consequences, and kept out of argument and revolution to maintain his mandarin position.[2] So Loisy could

---

[1] Quoted in *Mémoires*, I, pp. 98-9.

[2] Louis Duchesne (1843-1922) is a difficult figure to interpret, and we cannot hope to throw light on his inner feelings because his papers, notes, and correspondence were burnt after his death, on his orders. Professor of Church History in the Faculty of Letters at the Institut catholique in Paris in 1876, and in the Faculty of Theology in 1878 and 1880, he founded the *Bulletin critique*, which was the first to carry out critical research within the Church, and served as a model for later efforts. In 1895 he was appointed Director of the French School in Rome and remained there until his death; in 1900 he was appointed Apostolic Protonotary by Leo XIII and in 1911 he replaced Cardinal Mathieu at the Académie Française. In 1912 the Italian translation of his fundamental work *Histoire ancienne de l'Église* was put on the Index, together with the critical edition of *Liber Pontificalis*. All we know of his relations with Loisy is unfortunately what Loisy tells us; and Loisy was a pupil who refused to admit the debt and deference he owed his master, and acknowledged only his advice and irony: 'The Voltarian manner which he assumed even more readily in conversation than in his books ... An excellent sailor, he took in his sails as the storm grew wilder' (*Mémoires*, I, p. 98 and pp. 105-6). Duchesne's irony must have been unbearable to Loisy, because, apart from anything else, it struck at his ambition to be a 'Father of the Church'. A particularly cruel blow was Duchesne's answer to Loisy when he commiserated with himself and with the Church—the one soon to die of bleeding from the mouth, the other deprived of a great reformer: 'Your death', Duchesne wrote to him, 'will certainly be an irreparable loss to half a dozen people.' On Duchesne, see d'Habloville, *Grandes figures de l'Église contemporaine*, Paris, 1925; in order to correct Loisy, see Lagrange, op. cit., pp. 19-26 and *passim*.

no longer regard Duchesne as his master, the master he was seeking in those years, who could strike the right balance between faith and science:

Line of conduct.—On one side, routine passing itself off as tradition; on the other, innovation passing itself off as truth. The former is no more an indication of faith than the latter is an expression of knowledge. These two attitudes are in conflict in the biblical field, and I wonder if there is anyone in the world capable of holding the balance between faith and knowledge. If there were, he would be my master.[1]

This was written between 1881 and 1882. Loisy, appointed Hebrew tutor at the Institut catholique, at Duchesne's suggestion, began to attend Renan's lectures at the Collège de France. For three years he attended them; and there, in the textual criticism of the Old Testament, he acquired a method which he claimed he simply applied; there, too, as early as 1884, according to the *Mémoires*, he was inspired to formulate what was to remain his fundamental proposition: the idea that all general theories of theology and of science were only relatively true, and therefore always imperfect and always perfectible.

Loisy kept this idea of relative truth to himself. All he did was mention it in personal notes which remained unpublished, because, as he says straight away in his *Mémoires*, they would have been misunderstood and found shocking. In the meantime he told himself that the time would come when, after many years' teaching, his pupils, spread about France, would find these ideas more acceptable, 'because the way had been prepared'.

The time would come, and Loisy was working for it. But—and it was characteristic of his self-centredness—the fact that he kept this truth in reserve, and even his assertion that truth was merely relative, showed at once how he meant to stand aside from and avoid involving himself in the official teaching, and wished to develop a doctrine whose inevitable success he foresaw, in order to be one of the few depositories of the truth. This, Loisy felt, was his right; and in the meantime he made a clear distinction between what the Church was officially teaching and what he was secretly working on and intended to bring to light. Certainly he still meant to stay within the field of Catholic doctrine; but already he saw a split between the two aspects of doctrine: one, for general

---

[1] See *Mémoires*, I, p. 102.

use, was official, traditional, and in a rough and ready way true; the other, which was nearing completion, and was in fact developing of its own accord in the minds of the more intelligent priests, was for the learned. In the case of this latter aspect of doctrine, what was needed to fight the Church's enemies was weapons like their own—rational and historical, not religious and scholastic. And the more intelligent priests realized, of course, that these attacks on the Church were far more solidly based than, officially, they could admit.

Loisy was not the only one who then believed that time would mature all this, and who foresaw, with growing clarity, the need for reform, both in seminary teaching, where the methods and discoveries of the historical school would be used, and in apologetics, in the actual concept of the entire Catholic doctrine. These were the years that followed the Vatican Council. First had come all the ill-will and argument over the proclamation of the dogma of Papal infallibility, and the serious crisis precipitated by Dollinger's opposition. Then the reasons for the Pope's attitude were reconsidered, by Protestant liberals, rationalists, historicists, Anglicans, and Catholics, especially in relation to liberalism. Meantime the new Pope, Leo XIII, seemed to want a wider share in what was happening in the contemporary world. For centuries the Church had prudently been condemning the thought developing outside it, and at the same time, to avoid a complete split, questioning it.

Leo XIII's first encyclical, *Inscrutabili Dei consilio*, of 21 April 1878, which considered the possibility of the Church coming to terms with modern civilization, might have appeared to be overturning his predecessor's policies. *Aeterni Patris*, in 1879, restored Thomism, set up Catholic university faculties, and opened the Vatican archives to scholars—all of which was part of a plan of renewal (or, it was then said, revolution), which seemed to open up the way for further, more decisive steps.

In fact, watchfulness rather than confident expectancy seemed called for by the fact that many of the proposals of the *Syllabus* of 1864 reappeared in the Vatican Council's *De fide*, and by the part played by the Pope in the preparation of the *Syllabus* text. But the violent eruption of the Roman question, which suspended the Vatican Council itself, and the rise to power in Italy of men like Ricasoli, showed that things were going in a new direction, that there was a chance of renewal. For such men had already, in their early political days, obviously been anxious to see religious reform, and thought themselves responsible for it almost in the way that they thought themselves politically absolute. This meant that the kind of reform envisaged would be the expression of a new political class, which would above all settle the relationship between Church and State by reforming both institutions, and not merely by distinguishing between their two spheres of competence, considered, on the whole, juridically. Both politically and doctrinally, therefore, particularly in the sphere of the Pope's authority, it no longer seemed a simple matter of two perpetually warring sides coming together—the lay 'truth' and the clerical 'truth'—but a question of a possible intermingling, a political and doctrinal unity that might be followed by unity in practice. Hope of renewal was justified, then; but it was general optimism rather than an objective evaluation of what the new Pope said and did that was responsible for an atmosphere that was intellectually on the alert: the atmosphere that inspired the meetings of Catholic scientists in those years, for instance. Admittedly, as the scientist Loisy, who did not attend them, noted, these meetings were enfeebled from the start by their plan to avoid dogma, and to confine themselves to studying Catholic science; and a study of Catholic science that never touched on the problems related to theology was 'a pretty disputable notion'. But what is equally true, though Loisy does not stress it, is that Catholic scientists, lay and clerical, from all the countries of Europe, came together and exchanged opinions; their learning was something living and moving; varying situations at varying stages of development were compared; and all this might have led to the founding of the Catholic science they imagined existed—which in fact did not.[1]

Loisy notes:

My basic belief, which I was careful not to make too explicit, was that in the Catholic Church there was no such thing as a scientific approach to the study of the Bible. I believed that it was necessary to introduce it by underpinning (so to speak) both the introductory study of the Bible and exegesis itself, in order to remove them from the theological level,

---

[1] The International Scientific Congresses of Catholics took place in Paris (1888 and 1891), Brussels (1894), Fribourg (1897), and Munich (1900). A sixth Congress was to have been held in Rome in 1903. In 1892 the Italian Catholic Congress of students of the social sciences took place in Italy, and on its initiative the International Review of Social Sciences and Auxiliary Disciplines was founded, edited by Mgr. Salvatore Talamo, to which Semeria contributed.

where they are viewed dogmatically, to the historical level, where they are viewed rationally and critically.[1]

This policy of gradualness corresponds to Duchesne's idea, which Loisy took over, that a scientific evolution in the field of the Bible was morally impossible within the Catholic Church. Loisy wrote this in 1889. The following year the Dominican Lagrange founded the *École pratique d'études bibliques* in Jerusalem. In 1892 the first volume of Loisy's personal review *Enseignement biblique* appeared; and, in the same year, Lagrange's *Revue biblique*.[2] Although the two reviews appeared at the same time, their programmes were very unlike; and when Loisy mentions the dates he cannot fail to mention the enmity his work, however successful, was arousing.[3] Loisy could be accused only subjectively and

[1] See *Mémoires*, I, pp. 172–3.

[2] J. M. Lagrange (1855–1938), Dominican, founder of the Biblical school in Jerusalem, author of commentaries on the Gospels considered to be 'classics' by both Catholics and laymen, admired by Loisy (which caused him ironical surprise in the preface to the work which rebutted the *Mémoires*), unreserved supporter of Leo XIII's programme and member of the Biblical Commission, he was in a sense Loisy's orthodox counterpart, the orthodox aspect, as it were, of Loisy's doctrine and his behaviour, or at least its boundary line. Although Lagrange respected Loisy's talent and some of his critical attitudes, in *M. Loisy et la critique dans le crise moderniste*, in particular, he refuted a great deal that Loisy said in his *Mémoires* and reacted unfavourably to his exegetical findings. In fact—though this is outside our present subject—Loisy's 'relative truths' had only a brief success in Old and New Testament exegesis; and in studies on the canon, on the dating of the Gospels, and on religions and myths, very little remains of all his efforts and research. On Lagrange, see J. Chaine and others, *L'œuvre exégétique et historique du Père Lagrange*, Paris, 1935, and F. M. Braun, *L'œuvre du Père Lagrange*, Fribourg, 1943.

[3] In the programme of *Enseignement biblique*, published in the January–February 1892 number, and in the first edition of *Études bibliques* (1894), but suppressed in the later editions and mentioned only partly in the *Mémoires*, Loisy said: 'Certainly nobody will be surprised to see us applying the historical and critical method to biblical knowledge. It is not because we are losing sight of the supernatural character of the Scriptures, or of the dogmatic principles which are the infallible guideline of exegesis; we are only complying with the exigencies of the present time. E. Renan writes, "It is something a theologian could never be, by that I mean an historian. History is basically impartial. The historian has only one concern, art and truth. . . . The orthodox theologian has perhaps one interest, his dogma. Reduce this dogma as much as you like, for the artist and critic it remains unbearably heavy. The orthodox theologian may be compared with a bird in a cage: any really independent movement is denied him. The liberal theologian is a bird who has had several wing feathers cut off. You think he is his own master, and in fact he is until the time comes for him to take flight. Then you see that he is not entirely at home in the air" [*Vie de Jésus*, preface to the 13th edition, pp. ix–x]. This passage from the preface to the *Vie de Jésus* contains many errors, but they are very widespread and ones which cannot be

psychologically, of moral faults—curiosity, pride, ignorance—faults mentioned in the encyclical *Pascendi*. But the fact that a critical review existed at the time, very likely promoted by the Pope himself and certainly approved by him, because he agreed with its ideas, meant that these accusations were all the easier to make. For the benefit of posterity, who would thus see clearly what he intended doing, Loisy set down in the first number of his review six points in a kind of doctrinal questionnaire, which, as a Catholic scholar, he promised to answer in the course of his researches.

Therefore, the first question for study would be this:
How was the idea of divine inspiration born, how was it proclaimed, and how has it perpetuated itself; how did it come to be defined, how does it continue to be defined, and how should it be assessed from the point of view of historical and philosophical criticism?

The second question would be this:
Given that such books are inspired and thus form a divinely authorized body of writings, known as the canon of the Scriptures, in what circumstances (whether we are speaking of the Jewish Scriptures, those of the Old Testament, or of the Christian scriptures, those of the New Testament) were these writings produced and preserved, and what is the historic and actual authority of these writings, known as canonical and deemed to be normative?

The third question:
In which languages were these books written and into which were they translated, and how? What are the circumstances in which they have been preserved and passed down to us, and how far can we be certain that the text has been correctly transmitted?

The fourth question:
When, how, by whom, and with what end in view were they first written, or, in other words, what character and authenticity may properly be attributed to them?

The fifth question:
What information can be extracted from these books regarding the

---

effectively refuted with syllogisms. It is postulated where biblical history is concerned that a theologian cannot be an historian in the full sense of the word. It is for us theologians to prove the contrary by showing that we are as capable as anyone of practising criticism, sincere criticism, and even in the truest sense free criticism, because in the field of biblical history, as in any other subject, faith guides the investigations of knowledge without restraining them, and because the indisputable conclusions of criticism cannot be in opposition to what faith has revealed to us as certain.'

history of the religious institutions of Judaism and primitive Christianity?

The sixth question, which I could just as well have placed after the third:

To what account have these books been turned and how and according to what principles have the Jews interpreted the Hebrew Bible; how and according to what principles has the New Testament interpreted the Old, how has the Christian Church interpreted, and how does it still interpret, the two Testaments in such a way as to support its faith; how, recently, has scientific, that is to say, critical and historical, exegesis gradually detached itself from the traditional, theological exegesis and became autonomous in its methods and conclusions?[1]

It is clear that Loisy knew a formula could be found to avoid having the whole project blocked by orthodox opinion; and obviously he had worked out the formula himself:

The sacred writings are inspired in order that they might be true; they are inspired in order that they might be what they are; we should study what they are to know what part of the truth they may contain[2] . . . There was in the texts both an historical and a traditional sense, the former by virtue of their origin and nature, the latter having been grafted onto them by the workings of faith in the subsequent development of Judaism and Christianity.[3]

Loisy knew, then, that the first category involved the historian critic, for whom it was the only thing that mattered, while the second was concerned with exegesis and belief. But he knew very well that

the great—it could be called the only—difficulty, and the one which was to break me, was real, substantial, alive: that is, the authority, or more accurately the tyranny, which in Roman Catholicism has supplanted Scripture and even tradition, and which aims at dominating everything—thought, history, and politics.[4]

Then the authorities struck. First the students at Saint-Sulpice were forbidden to attend his lectures; then an article by Monsignor d'Hulst on the biblical studies of what he called the *école large*[5]

---

[1] See *Mémoires*, I, pp. 173–4.   [2] See ibid., I, p. 177.
[3] See ibid., I, p. 178.   [4] See ibid., I, p. 179.
[5] Mgr. d'Hulst's article on the biblical question appeared in *Correspondant* on 25 January 1893; in it were described two schools of apologists: 'that which accepts as history, infallible by virtue of being inspired, everything which is not obviously a parable, and that which, after having put the dogmatic and moral teaching on one side, thinks it can make a selection of biblical writings according

provoked Loisy's dismissal from the Institut catholique. Loisy always maintained that, although he was trying to be helpful, d'Hulst had in fact made the authorities hasten to take action against him.

Loisy makes no attempt to justify himself in the *Mémoires*; on the contrary, he confirms what he said before, refuses to recognize himself in d'Hulst's description of the exegetes' school, and mentions another aspect of his thought, as if to justify his own condemnation. The Bible is a book written by men for men, and therefore bound by the laws that condition every human book, even in matters of faith and morals; it can therefore be completely in touch with the truth of only one age—the age in which it was written. The Old Testament ideas of God and human destiny, of the concept and arrangement of salvation, do not conform at all with those of the Church, since throughout the centuries biblical belief has been subject to changes, and this elaborated belief is now the Church's ordinary teaching.

Here again we have the theme of relative truth: neither in the Bible, nor in the Church's teaching—its best human interpreters—has religious truth found an absolute and immutable form: it keeps indefinitely becoming.

It was the year 1893. Loisy was close to being condemned and his review was in danger (Cardinal Richard was to ban it at the end of the same year). It was then that he received his first letter from Baron Friedrich von Hügel, who wrote from London, asking for two copies of his book on the Caldean myths of the creation and the flood, 'for propaganda', his photograph, to put on his desk beside Duchesne's, and the right to translate into English from *Enseignement biblique*, 'lorsque la chose pourra se faire prudement'. Von Hügel also asked Loisy to come to England as soon

---

to the methods of historical criticism', and it was clear that the author's sympathies lay not with the right-wing, conservative school, but with the left wing, with what he called the 'école large', whose most official representative everyone considered to be Loisy (who, in fact, went well beyond the 'école large'). On Maurice Lesage d'Hautecœur d'Hulst (1841–96), secretary, then Rector of the Institut catholique in Paris, from 1880, and promoter of the International Scientific Congresses of Catholics, see A. Baudrillart, *Vie de Mgr. d'Hulst*, two volumes, Paris, 1921. Of Loisy, d'Hulst used to say among friends: 'C'est un petit Renan.' But if he had really thought this of him, his biographer adds, he would hardly have kept him on his staff. See Baudrillart, op. cit., I, p. 476. See also J. Bricout, *Mgr. d'Hulst Apologiste*, Ancienne Librairie Poussielgue, Paris, 1919.

as he could, and said he would introduce him to his friends, among them Robertson Smith.[1]

Loisy quotes this letter fully in his *Mémoires* and through it we meet the remarkable figure of the main modernist layman. A man used to giving inspiration and spiritual advice, von Hügel was to become—perhaps without fully realizing it—the movement's organizer and, as it were, go-between, visiting the exponents, introducing them to one another, either personally or by letter, keeping them in touch and sometimes making them agree, in spite of or beyond their personal differences. He was a friend to them all, and revered by them all for his spirituality rather than his thought—indeed it is hard to disentangle his thought from that of his correspondents, except perhaps in his most important work, on the mystic Catherine of Genoa; and it was through him that many modernists came to see that they were inspired by something more than a common aim, that the idea of 'relative truth' appeared at the beginning of their relationship—or, more generally, the idea of the historicism of truth. And von Hügel was able to bring to bear on the development of this idea the thought of other laymen he knew and plunged into the intellectual world of modernism—men like Troeltsch and Eucken.

In one of his first letters to Loisy (18 November 1893) von Hügel wrote:

I find it very difficult now to tell you the history of my views on the Bible. They were formed over a long period. However, it was the contradictions in the gospels which opened my eyes, and I came almost immediately to the conclusion that it is necessary to accept the idea of relative truth in the Bible, since it cannot be maintained that what it contains is the absolute truth. Furthermore, I am no metaphysician,

---

[1] Friedrich von Hügel (1852–1925), baron of the Holy Roman Empire, son of the Austrian Ambassador to Florence, where he was born in 1852. His mother was Scottish, a convert to Catholicism. After a cosmopolitan education, he settled in England in 1867. An attack of typhus in 1870 left him deaf. He was converted through the influence of the Dutch Dominican Raymond Hocking. In 1884, in Paris, he first met the Abbé Henri Huvelin, who played a large part in his religious formation, and Duchesne. In 1893 he wrote his first letter to Loisy, and thus began the most painful phase of his life. (Huvelin, confessor of Charles de Foucauld, is known only through letters and some lectures printed in 1912, after his death, but von Hügel collected a series of his maxims that show Huvelin's spirituality, so much like von Hügel's own; see *Selected Letters*, pp. 58–63.)

and if I admit a large part of biblical truth to be relative, how much more must I acknowledge the relative truth of my own system.[1]

It was therefore natural for Loisy and von Hügel to feel they were allies, and the extent to which they agreed was made clearer than ever by the complete agreement between von Hügel and Mgr. Mignot[2] when they met on 22 November 1893. In his *Mémoires* Loisy says that this meeting might be considered the date when modernism was born, or at least a memorable date in its history. And indeed, from this meeting onwards the two priests and the layman were to be in constant touch: consulting one another, exchanging opinions, agreeing in brotherly friendship and already unconscious accomplices who knew they would have to speak out to the authorities. Indeed at their first meeting Mgr. Mignot told his friends that, fearing the Pope was about to put out an encyclical on biblical studies, he had written beseeching him to leave the critics free, and neither to halt nor to precipitate anything.

The encyclical *Providentissimus Deus* on biblical studies was in fact dated 18 November 1893, two days before von Hügel's meeting with Mgr. Mignot. A few days afterwards Loisy wrote to von Hügel:

The method of exegesis prescribed by the encyclical is as follows: take the Vulgate and interpret it by the *consensus Patrum*. I could still escape by saying that the Pope regulates theological exegesis, but not historical exegesis, to which the method indicated does not apply. What I say is correct; but the encyclical has not even touched on historical exegesis. This is not enough to give it a right to exist.[3]

So my first impression [Loisy writes in the *Mémoires*] was that Leo XIII's encyclical, drawn up by theologians, signed by a Pope without the first idea of criticism, was strangling criticism and at the same time believing that it was allowing the exegetes the measure of freedom to which they were entitled.

---

[1] Note the remarkable similarity between von Hügel's letter to Loisy and Duchesne's, quoted earlier. See *Mémoires*, I, p. 292.

[2] On Eudoxe-Irénée Mignot (1842–1918), Bishop of Fréjus in 1890 and Archbishop of Albi in 1900, called the Erasmus of modernism, see Louis de Lacger, *Notice et Sovenirs*, Albi, 1918, and Mgr. Mignot, Paris, 1933. Mignot's *Journal*, together with letters and accounts by other people, all still treated with extreme discretion, await publication.

[3] See the letter of 6 December 1893, in *Mémoires*, I, p. 297.

Time was to confirm this impression. But Loisy in those days thought he could and should deal freely with all the problems of philosophy and religious history not outside but within the Church, although it was already fairly clear to him that in doing so he would come up against official orthodox opinion. 'What I wanted was impossible: freedom of thought in the Catholic Church to examine the claims of the Catholic religion,' he wrote later in his *Mémoires*; but back in December 1893 he sent the Pope a report on exegesis, to inform him what the true position was, since he felt the Church did not know it, and attributed the doctrinal attitude of Rome to this ignorance. But Rampolla's answer, on 19 December, could not have given him any hope;

Nevertheless, having taken into account what has happened, His Holiness believes it to be more expedient and beneficial for you, if, following your generous inclination to use your talents to the glory of God and the benefit of your neighbour, you would apply them more particularly to the cultivation of some other branch of knowledge.[1]

So all his early hopes were dashed; and his review, *L'Enseignement biblique*, ended with the December 1893 number, in which his commentary on the synoptic Gospels appeared. Having left Paris, Loisy went to Neuilly as chaplain to a convent of Dominican nuns. There he stayed for five years (1894–9).

Von Hügel also sent the Pope, through Cardinal Rampolla, a report on the biblical question and on the way the encyclical had been received at Oxford and Cambridge (10 January 1895). In it he suggested that, as far as English Catholics were concerned, the biblical question should be interpreted in a broad and liberal way. In the same report he also dealt, in an equally liberal spirit, with the validity of Anglican orders, and suggested that conditional reordination should eventually be adopted.

In the same spirit he had published, in those same months, a series of articles on the Church and the Bible ('slightly overloaded, crammed with metaphysics and quotations', Loisy called them), in which he made a distinction between the Church's indirect disciplinary authority in matters of critical research and its direct disciplinary authority in matters of faith, but concluded that the difficulties the Bible presented had their definitive solution in Catholicism, and only there. In this von Hügel differed from

[1] See ibid., I, p. 317.

27

Loisy not just out of prudence, but from real conviction. Alone as a convent chaplain, and in direct touch with the faith of simple nuns and schoolgirls, Loisy felt more strongly the need for a philosophical foundation to Christianity. 'I go even further, I dream. My sermons on perseverance have given me the idea of a general statement of Catholic doctrine for use at this time, this turn of the century, something sound for everyone and reconciliatory for those outside the Church,' he wrote to von Hügel on 15 September 1896. In the same letter he first mentioned Newman:

It has occurred to me that I might find support and good ideas in some of Newman's writings, which I do not know. I have extracts from a book on doctrinal development containing sound principles. What do you think of him? If only my rheumatism would leave me another four years of life, I should like to die a Father of the Church. ... I am sure you have all Newman's books [Loisy went on], and could tell me which would be useful to me from the theological-apologetic-polemical-pastoral point of view.

'These were the circumstances and the frame of mind in which I embarked on the studies which were to lead to my so-called modernist publications,' he remarks.[1]

Von Hügel sent him the *Grammar of Assent*, the *Essay*, and *The Idea of a University*. Loisy explained some time later that he wanted to broaden Newman's theory of Christian development, to apply the idea of evolution not only to the history of Christianity after the Gospel, but also, and especially, to the biblical revelation in the two Testaments, since these two collections were themselves the product of a historical evolution unnoticed or unstressed by Newman himself.

Loisy had not given up his dream of an intelligent theology; and Newman, together with Schell, and with Harnack's *Dogmengeschichte*, helped him to establish his new Catholic doctrine, which denied all supernatural mechanism, and even the existence of exterior revelation (this was exactly what *Autour d'un petit livre* was to be condemned for in *Lamentabili* and in *Pascendi*).

---

[1] See *Mémoires*, I, p. 410. The article on Christian development according to Cardinal Newman, signed Firmin, was published in the December 1898 number of the *Revue du clergé français*, and Thureau-Dangin (*La renaissance catholique en Angleterre*, I, 1889, p. 308) said it gave 'all the material needed to reply to the objections that anti-Christian knowledge claims to draw from recent discoveries made by historical criticism concerning the origins of our religion'.

All the same, it must be considered above all in relation to what it was opposing. It was, on the whole, aimed at correcting, or providing an alternative to, the current doctrine of the Church, whose special and important error Loisy maintains is its wish to keep as its own a branch of learning (what is called 'sans rire', theological science), while in fact it was forced to submit to a scientific movement taking place outside it. Loisy felt, on the contrary, that theology itself should, like philosophy, take note of contemporary science, because the main task of philosophy (which meant philosophy in Loisy's rather ingenuous meaning of the word), like theology (by which he still meant philosophy), was to provide a general concept of the world and of man which fitted in with the state of science at that particular moment.

'Official' theology, on the other hand, saw anyone who failed to accept Catholic science absolutely as an innovator and a rebel, and so it tended to push out of the Church those it hoped to keep away from science. All a scientist need do to lose his faith was take literally what most theologians taught; in order to continue believing, he must either avoid thinking deeply about the object of his belief, or else set up as a theologian himself, whatever the danger, deriving from symbols the true meaning that ordinary theology hides under its completely material ideas. The idea of 'relativeness', already applied by Loisy to the Holy Scriptures, should be applied to the Church's teaching as well, if the past was to be accounted for and the future, to some extent, foreseen and planned. The formulas of dogma always accorded with the science of their particular period, and so, meanwhile, these formulas would be fixed in accordance with the traditions of Christianity and with present-day science. But tradition itself was an interpretation of the faith in the language, and using the intellectual idiom, of a particular time and milieu. So this 'relativeness' was in fact based on what was in itself relative, with nothing absolute about it but the indescribable depths, the ineffable object of the soul's deepest perception, as the prophets, and Christ, and the Apostles expressed it.

These are notes for a theory of dogma Loisy wrote about 1897, and never published, although some of the same ideas appear in *L'Évangile et l'Église* and *Autour d'un petit livre*. From what he says in the *Mémoires* and from the spirit of what he writes, which is quite clear, it can all be reduced to the idea of 'relativeness' and the idea of development, neither incompatible with a doctrine based on the indescribable, or on the ineffableness of revelation. Loisy's rough idea was not, then, a theory of knowledge alternative to the *adequatio*, nor is the yardstick of pragmatic verification even mentioned—this was something Loisy had always rejected and opposed when it seemed, as it did in *Nova et vetera*, to ally itself with doctrinal elements he knew and loved; in particular with the idea of development as he derived it from Newman. Rather it was a way of religious research that could complete traditional apologetics; and for this reason he was to remain, with his accurate mind, within the range of Rome's authority, in matters of doctrine. In a way the whole line of argument can be seen in his final summing up:

To finish this book as it should be finished one would need the accents of a Paul, of Paul explaining to Peter in front of the community at Antioch how one should live in order to gain the whole world for the gospel. But who today would dare talk to Peter? The faint sound of the kiss we humbly deposit on his foot does not rise as far as his ears. . . . Yet Peter is no greater now than he was then. The stay in Rome has perhaps changed his character, but his mission has not changed. . . . It is time the Catholic Church stopped looking for subjects and confined her thoughts solely to making all men more like Jesus Christ.[1]

But the book that might have contained all Catholic modernism was left unpublished. This means it was left in that hidden part of the truth which Loisy kept to himself and gave his friends only piecemeal. These friends were, with Loisy himself, mounting a religious, doctrinal opposition to the authorities, and among them the ever-alert von Hügel found 'a young English Jesuit, a convert . . . [who] thinks, speaks and writes on the Anglican question with an open-mindedness both admirable and amusing. . . . This Father Tyrrell also admires you,' he wrote to Loisy in October 1897.

[1] *Mémoires*, I, p. 477. Loisy considered he was neither methodical nor philosophically gifted enough to express his thought in dogmatic theology; instead, he wanted a permanent platform on which to express himself personally, to show his friends, followers, and the authorities how his studies were progressing, how his critical method was developing. The *Revue d'histoire et de littérature religieuses*, the first number of which appeared in 1896, officially edited by a committee of seven members, if not the 'organe scientifique du modernisme français', as people tried to define it and Loisy himself refused to consider it, was in fact the platform from which he expressed his personal ideas. In it his critical writings appeared, first under pseudonyms, then, after 1900, under his own name; later these were collected and published in book form, often more correctly and less violently written.

Thus Loisy came to hear of Tyrrell, 'le futur martyr du modernisme', who at that time had been removed from Stonyhurst, where he was teaching young Jesuits, because of his particular Thomism, a Thomism in which Loisy instantly recognized a kind of modernism.

Other friends, in those years, joined together to form the initial Catholic opposition. Henri Bremond, Giovanni Semeria, a Barnabite (who read von Hügel's memoir on the Hexateuch at the Friburg Congress—on which occasion two French and an Italian priest struck up the Marseillaise), Father Laberthonnière of the Oratory, the Protestant Paul Sabatier, Father Genocchi of the Missionaries of the Sacred Heart, who taught at the Apollinare, Marcel Hebert, Albert Houtin, all those whose names are linked with international modernism, were gathered here at its French source, around Loisy.[1] But one of them, Duchesne, who was more

---

[1] Henri Bremond (1865-1933), Jesuit, educated in England, friend of Blondel from 1897, then of Tyrrell, Loisy, and von Hügel, made Newman's thought known in France. He left the Society of Jesus in 1904 without any known conflict, and was punished for giving funeral rites to Tyrrell (1909). A delicate writer, his fundamental work is *L'Histoire littéraire du sentiment religieux en France* (Paris, 1916–33), in eleven volumes. He was elected an academician of France, following Duchesne; and was a friend of Fogazzaro, and, like him, of Klein.

Giovanni Semeria (1867–1931), Barnabite, friend of Loisy and Paul Sabatier. considered by his adversaries the leader of Italian modernism, preacher, student of biblical problems, friend of Murri (who wrote him the letters on the education of the clergy which were later published in *Battaglie d'Oggi*), and less friendly with Minocchi (with whom he travelled to Russia on the trip that culminated in a visit to Leo Tolstoy). Author of many works, among them *Scienza e fede, Il primo sangue cristiano* (1901), *Dogma, gerarchia e culto nella chiesa primitiva* (1902), he was the only one allowed to take the anti-modernist oath with reservations. After a violent campaign against him (for which see A. Colletti, *La divinità di Gesú Cristo impugnata dal modernismo nei libri del P. Giovanni Semeria*, Spoleto, 1912), he left Italy and all his studies, then returned to Italy during the First World War, in which he was a chaplain.

Lucien Laberthonnière (1860–1932), editor of *Annales de philosophie chrétienne* from 1905–13 (the date on which they were put on the Index), Blondel's great friend, confidant and almost 'secular mind', author of the *Essais de philosophie religieuse* (1903), *Le réalisme chrétien et l'idéalisme grec* (1904), and many other works in course of publication, all put on the Index.

Paul Sabatier (1858–1928), author of a famous biography of St. Francis (1893), which had remarkable sales and brought him honorary citizenship of Assisi, friend of Minocchi and Fogazzaro and an active member of the modernist rebellion, was severely criticized by some of his friends (who reproached him for having forced the modernist cause in an anti-ecclesiastical and Protestant direction), but not by Loisy.

Giovanni Genocchi (1860–1926), of the Congregation of the Sacred Heart, consultant of the Biblical Commission of 1903, was the liberal moderator of the

directly in touch with the Roman authority which the others were reforming in their minds and letters and friendships, was very much less hopeful than the rest. His letter to von Hügel, which Loisy quotes, shows a man who was highly intelligent, both critically and psychologically. Loisy always stressed Duchesne's scepticism, making it appear that he was more a mandarin than a faithful member of the Church; yet the letters he quotes in his *Mémoires* shows that Duchesne was a far more radical and aggressive opponent of the Curia than his pupils and friends were, for the very fact that he was in a position to see both its strength and its lack of intelligence from day to day; but that he never opposed it doctrinally, on a theological basis. The actual political presence and disciplinary firmness of the Church Duchesne speaks of makes it seem much more real and alive than the Church whose doctrines Loisy and his friends wished to reform. Duchesne was not a realist out of caution, or because he wanted to avoid being disciplined himself (in any case, his works were attacked, even if he personally was not, a few years later). He wrote as an historian, not as a man interested in ideology; certainly not as a reformer, or even as a heretic.[1]

Americanism was condemned, and so was Schell. To Loisy and his friends, Americanism did not exist. Modernism too, would exist to them only from a disciplinary point of view, as something

modernists in Rome, friend to all, confidant of many, and attacked by both modernists and anti-modernists.

Marcel Hébert (1851–1916), teacher and then principal at the Fénelon School in Paris, philosophically learned, author of the dialogue *Souvenirs d'Assise*, left the Church in 1903. An important personality, called by Houtin in his biography a 'symbolist priest', he was venerated by his pupils, among them Roger Martin du Gard, who dedicated his *Jean Barois* to him.

Albert Houtin (1867–1926), teacher at the Little Seminary of Angers, was in touch with all the modernists in Paris from 1901 onwards, in particular Loisy, whose biography he wrote—a work as profoundly hostile as it was knowledgeable. In 1912 he left the Church. Author of *Histoire du modernisme catholique* (1913) and of many other well-written but rather superficial works (*L'américanisme, La crise du clergé*, 1908) and biographies of ex-priests (*Marcel Hébert*, 1925, *Le père Hyacinthe*, 1920–4); also of an autobiography (*Une vie de prêtre*, 1926, and *Ma vie laïque*, posthumously edited by Felix Sartiaux, 1928).

[1] In Loisy's rebellion, what is immediately clear—quite apart from values and reasoning—is the fact that he demands the right of personal choice, the right to decide what most matters, that he acknowledges no disciplinary authority in the field of scientific knowledge, and believes that freedom must be fashioned first within authority, and then in opposition to authority, thus involving all the aspects of heretical psychology even more than those of heretical doctrine and procedure.

with which to stand up to the authorities, not as an ideological movement. Loisy had Schell's book on his desk, but did not understand it. After these two condemnations, Duchesne wrote:

It has been proved yet again that the Church does not wish to extend her role in any field; that she is satisfied with her past and is quite determined to carry as much of it as she can into the future. . . . The Roman Church governs itself according to the views of the masses, whether manifested directly by a display of their aversions and preferences or indirectly by the attitudes of governments. For neither peoples nor princes are interested in the reconciliation of intelligence and religion. It is a long time since intellectual development concerned anyone apart from theologians; and they are not expected to be reasonable. As for religion: one makes do without it, or if it is kept one admits that perhaps it cannot be better ordered than by the traditional method. It will not make any difference to the general position if the Pope changes or if one or other of his counsellors disappears or if one is counteracted by another. Here there are no intellectual needs and it is considered bad enough for other people to have them. Your little sallies will be tolerated, or rather ignored, if you keep quiet about them, or rather, if you have no enemy who will denounce them. They are talking of putting Kraus's book on Dante on the Index, of forcing Semeria to leave Italy; all the devils have been let loose.[1]

Some years later, Duchesne was to repeat the same ideas, again comparing the Cardinals' Rome with Loisy's exegesis:

No one will ask you to say that at His first meeting with Saint Andrew and Saint Peter Our Lord gave them a visiting card which said, 'Jesus Christ, the eternal Word, consubstantial with the Father'. Considerable development may be, and is, allowed[2]. . . It will take time for an exegesis like this to be accepted. However, as you have noticed yourself, things which only fifteen years ago were considered sacrilegious are now in the process of being assimilated. . . . In spite of this, I am uneasy. On the whole I do not think that Catholicism is irreconcilable with the type of criticism you practise—I mean that criticism which results inevitably from the present state of our knowledge. But, to move from the realm of possibilities to that of concrete happenings, I cannot see theologians and cardinals presiding over the feast you will serve up to them. . . . If people pay attention to what you say, quite a number of questions in the catechism will have to be suppressed as being indiscreet. The faithful will wonder what this new religion is. . . . In fifty years' time, so I am

---

[1] See *Mémoires*, I, pp. 514–15.
[2] See letter from Duchesne to Loisy, 15 January 1903, ibid., II, pp. 191–2.

told, everyone will find these ideas natural. Possibly—but will this 'everyone' still be Christian?[1]

This shows how unusually clear was Duchesne's view of the problems. Loisy was to be struck (and at the very time Duchesne was writing) by an authority he considered merely unintelligent, an obstacle to all his plans. But Duchesne, though his letters seem to indicate that up to a point he shared Loisy's opinion, saw more in the authority of the Church than that. More important, to him, was its role as described in *De ecclesia*, as the summit of the living organism which the Vatican Council had dealt with, and had altered far more radically than Loisy and his friends seemed to realize. Loisy had the traditional idea of authority and of truth, an idea that fitted the medieval Church and so preceded the Vatican Council. He failed to understand the origin of all that had happened recently and merely heard the scholastic uproar on the subject; he failed to see how *De fide* meant something quite new, how *Aeterni patris* put forward an official philosophy but one based on the new concept of the truth as settled in the Council's decisions. At the end of the nineteenth century the Church assimilated the philosophy of the positivists before its exegetes had understood it theoretically;[2] indeed, through Newman, the Church had already clearly welcomed, or at least considered, the theory of development and could almost come to a pragmatic concept of truth. Of course there were two sides to all this: on the one hand, there was the unintelligent way the authorities behaved, and on the other the problem of how much that was new could still be called Christian in what to Loisy seemed like freedom (here was where Duchesne was uncertain). The Church was split down the middle, and the struggle between traditionalists and those who accepted a doctrinal development that had not been religiously conceived could not fail to destroy the very people, who, in an imperfect way, were part of the Church's living truth.

[1] See letter from Duchesne to Loisy, 26 October and 17 November 1903, *Mémoires*, II, pp. 276, 277.

[2] See A. Omodeo, *Alfredo Loisy*, p. 16: 'The pragmatistic outlook, which should have pervaded the modernistic movement, was born of the very fact that the Church in the 19th century was steeped in pragmatism, until it was improved at the time of the Restoration. In reality, the least pragmatistical was Loisy himself, whose cultural and scientific education meant he followed—and still follows—the austere cult of veridicity, of the hard affirmation of what thought and science have conquered, against all passion and illusion, in the second half of the 19th century.'

At the end of the first part of his *Mémoires* Loisy mentions this coming struggle, but clearly saw it as something of minor importance, almost a private affair. Unlike Duchesne, he saw the fight and the reason for it in the freeing of humanity from religious tyranny, and in the birth of a new moral conscience, quite independent of a basis of historical revelation: those taking part would come from among the new critical intellectuals, whose outlook was, indeed, formed by historical exegesis, and once more Loisy's task was to be the conscience of the rest:

My two friends and I never suspected that we were on the eve of a Seven Years War, that in the eighth year I would be expelled from the Church, that in the ninth year, with Tyrrell dead, von Hügel would remain alone, unbeaten, on the battlefield, determined to serve the Church in spite of herself through knowledge; 'our archbishop' watching from afar, sadly and thoughtfully, the wrecking of our hopes. And it was I who, in all innocence, was to open fire in the first battle by taking a public stand against the adversary who had just killed Firmin.[1]

[1] See *Mémoires*, I, p. 578. Firmin was one of Loisy's pseudonyms. On 2 October 1900, Cardinal Richard, Archbishop of Paris, maintaining that the proposition set out in an article signed by Firmin on the religion of Israel, which appeared in the *Revue du clergé français*, was in contradiction to the Vatican Council's statute *Dei filius*, forbade its continuation.

3. Blondel

The first round fired in the battle which Loisy deals with towards the end of the first part of his *Mémoires* was the publication of the first of the 'petits livres rouges' in November 1902, *L'Évangile et l'Église*;[1] but here again, Loisy assumes the right to set himself up above the others, a right which could be justified only in the strictly ecclesiastical sphere, and in particular where it was a matter of personal quarrels between clerics and where the disciplinary side of the controversy was concerned. For about that time many others in the small rebellious group had expressed themselves far more violently and precisely than Loisy, who had left his statements of 1897 undeveloped and, at the very moment when he was taking up lay teaching, decided, quite willingly it would seem, to confine himself to learned research, the sort of free, critical exegesis on which he was in future to concentrate. To himself and to the press at the time Loisy seemed the most official exponent of the movement for reform, the doctrinal enemy *par excellence* of the Roman hierarchy; whereas from this distance he appears an isolated case of a researcher who was justified in writing that he felt he was 'not the stuff of which the reformer or the heretic is made'. Admittedly in the *Mémoires* he sees himself as taking a decisive part in the movement, and, rightly enough, as being an example in it of a

[1] *L'Évangile et l'Église* was published by Picard in Paris in November 1902; 1,500 copies were printed. It was the first of the series of 'petits livres rouges'; their name came from the colour of the covers, but in fact *L'Évangile et l'Église* had a red cover only after the second edition, published by the author at Bellevue in 1903. The second was *Autour d'un petit livre* (Picard, Paris, 1903); the third, *Simples réflexions* (published by the author, Ceffonds, 1908); the fourth *Quelques lettres sur des questions actuelles et des évènements récents* (published by the author, Ceffonds, 1908); the fifth *Choses passées* (Nourry, Paris, 1913); the sixth, *Guerre et Religion* (Nourry, Paris, 1915); the seventh, *Mors et vita* (Nourry, Paris, 1916); the eighth, *La Religion* (Nourry, Paris, 1917); the ninth, *De la discipline intellectuelle* (Nourry, Paris, 1919); the tenth, *La morale humaine* (Nourry, Paris, 1923); the eleventh, *L'Église et la France* (Nourry, Paris, 1925); the twelfth, *Religion et humanité* (Nourry, Paris, 1926); the thirteenth, *Y a-t-il deux sources de la Religion et de la Morale?* (Nourry, Paris 1933); the fourteenth, *George Tyrrell et Henri Bremond* (Nourry, Paris, 1936); the fifteenth, and the 'achèvement d'une longue expérience religieuse', *La crise morale du temps présent et l'éducation humaine* (Nourry, Paris, 1937).

particular sort; but, from then on, his example was to be of a moral kind: he was to stand as a member of the clergy who, on a matter of principle, carried through to the end and to his own cost a course of action that was outside, if not foreign to, the morality of the Church that disciplined him. It was not so much that he was setting up one truth against another, or science against faith (paradoxically, it was contrasts of the kind that he claimed to be aiming at), it was not so much a matter of where he stood in the historical quarrel between critical and dogmatic thought, as that his whole personal and intellectual development, his entire religious experience, were marked by an irrevocable refusal to obey: a refusal that extended to the Church and his colleagues as well, even those who, like von Hügel, urged prudence, or, like Blondel, asked him to elucidate his thought. Loisy was remarkably uncritical, and for this reason remarkably intransigent; nowhere in the *Mémoires* is there the slightest doubt or uncertainty, either intellectual or moral, nowhere are his own convictions even reconsidered; only, just occasionally, is regret shown for not having expressed them explicitly enough. Priest and thinker were swallowed up by the moralist, who put his own outlook above all else; thus ethical and theoretical thought was narrowed to such an extent that science, freedom, free investigation, relative or absolute truth, all the bases of judgement, were no longer critically dealt with but were used to prop up Loisy's own attitudes.

The others, meanwhile, were also getting ready for battle. Loisy's friends, though perhaps better armed than he was, were ready to follow his image and made no claims on the leadership of the movement.[1] Two of them in particular, Tyrrell and Blondel,

---

[1] The only one to put forward a right of precedence was the strange Fr. Hyacinthe Loyson, a married priest; on whom see A. Houtin, *Le Père Hyacinthe dans l'Église romaine* (Nourry, Paris, 1920), *Le Père Hyacinthe reformateur catholique* (Nourry, Paris, 1922) and *Le Père Hyacinthe, prêtre solitaire* (Nourry, Paris, 1924); and also Houtin's *Autour d'un prêtre marié* (published by the author, Paris, 1910). Father Hyacinthe Loyson was referring in particular to a letter he wrote on 20 September 1869, to the Reverend Father General of the Discalced Carmelites in Rome (see the text in Houtin, op. cit., I, pp. 319–22), in which he protested 'against the practical doctrines which are called Roman, but are not Christian, and which, pressed ever more boldly and ruinously, are trying to change the constitution of the Church ... against the division, which is as irreligious as it is stupid, between the Church, who is our mother in eternity, and the society of the nineteenth century, whose sons we are in time ... against the sacrilegious perversion of the Gospel of the Son of God himself, the spirit and the letter of which are trampled underfoot by the pharisaical new law.' Fr.

had established a kind of ideological basis for religious renewal. Both were in touch with Loisy, Blondel in person and by letter, Tyrrell by letter only, and, thanks to von Hügel's constant and sometimes tactless intervention, were already thought of, together with Loisy, as possible spiritual leaders of the younger clergy. Blondel indeed was already taken seriously by lay philosophers as the author of *Action* (1893), and was (as he remained) the only one to be taken so by the laity, and from the point of view of academic philosophy. His relations with the modernists were always 'private', his voice and his authority were never officially connected with the movement,[1] and attempts on both sides to blacken his reputation were always defeated by the fact that he was, ungenerously but prudently, extremely reserved. It is only recently, when some of his letters have been published, that any light has been thrown on his views and feelings; and other letters, kept among his papers at Aix, will help to clarify his relationships with others and to show where responsibility lay. In what might be termed the official history of modernism, Blondel was the only important person involved who was never directly attacked, the only believer never condemned or silenced, and never made to retract. He was not, of course, indifferent to the sad fate of his friends—indeed, his silence might be interpreted as sympathy; but, and in this he resembles von Hügel, he never thought he had gone outside the limits of ecclesiastical doctrine or discipline, he was unfailingly respectful towards the authorities, and he continued to behave as a pious churchman without appearing to notice any discrepancy between his own ideas and the Church's truth—even though a careful study of his work sometimes shows such a discrepancy.

Hyacinthe Loyson was one of the first priests to marry, thus inaugurating a practice which it was hoped would be considered a right and a fundamental problem in the modernistic controversy—which in fact it was not. See what Loisy wrote on the subject: '[Fr. Hyacinthe] saw very clearly and very far in this matter of marriage seen in relation to an ideal of human morality. But where he was completely mistaken was in thinking that, by getting married himself, he was starting Catholic reform at the point where it could best be initiated. It might have been one of the points which needed reforming, but it was also the point at which immediate reform was impossible in morally satisfying conditions.' (*Revue d'histoire et de littérature religieuses*, 1922, p. 589.)

[1] 'No, I have never been reprimanded by any representative of the Church; I have not received any advice to remain silent or to wait,' he wrote in *L'itinéraire philosophique de Maurice Blondel. Propos recueillis par Frédéric Lefèvre*, Paris, 1928, p. 96.

In 1927, when there was a possibility of *Action* being reprinted, Blondel wrote to Alcan, the publisher, and thus described and made clear 'the first inspiration of this thesis which was conceived and started in my second year at the École Normale':

My original intention was to establish a philosophy which was autonomous and which from a rational point of view nevertheless complied with the most minute and rigorous demands of Catholicism. I was amazed to establish that, both in the development of doctrine and in the outlook of those around me, philosophical speculation proceeded as though man's real state was a purely natural one, onto which, like a wig, a Christianity would be thrust which would not succeed in gaining a hold even in the minds of those still faithful to their baptismal vows, and even less in the minds of those who, although steeped in Christianity, benefit from it only by breaking with it or even opposing it. The former showed only a sort of artificial harmony and the latter indifference or even hostility, which their way of looking at the religious problem prevented them from overcoming.

Christian philosophy seemed to me to have been treated too much as a compromise or patchwork. It seemed to me that now one should start again, whether by taking from the ancients or 'separated' philosophers those seeds which prepare the ground and provide the sap for Christianity, or from the Christian philosophers themselves a preoccupation with homogeneity which has sometimes been integrated, often misunderstood, and occasionally exaggerated, as it was by St. Bonaventure and Malebranche. Not Concordism, Dualism, or Monism. Distinguished from one another and yet in harmony. It seemed to me that one could do more than simply draw up a rationalist, self-sufficient doctrine—a closed system which would leave no openings for religious scruples; and from then on my primary aim was to discover by studying human activity and thought the points of intersection which not only makes it possible for Christianity to strike roots deep in our consciences, but also for it to make demands in the name of inner integrity as well as in the name of divine authority and of the outward manifestations which authenticate the revealed truths and prescriptions.

I came to the conclusion, when looking for the cause of the vice of speculation for which I wished to find a cure, that our habit of confining philosophy to the field of ideas and abstract theories was the reason for the abuse of the differences between instinct and thought and action and even between action and faith and inquiry. I became intent on finding the exact point at which these things meet; it was no doubt right to distinguish and discriminate between them, but it was wrong to separate, isolate, or even set them in opposition to one another. Human action seemed to me to be in fact that point on which the powers of Nature, the light of intelligence, the strength of the will, and even the benefits of grace, converge—not to merge into one another, still less to fight and destroy one another, but to combine their efforts and bring about the magnificent unity of our destiny.[1]

And about the same time he replied thus to Lefèvre, who had asked him about the teachers and friends to whom he may have felt grateful, as sources of his thought:

... With regard to them, as to the other thinkers from whom I drew sustenance, becoming as it were the contemporary of those whose ideas are immortal, I think that, without any sort of duplicity, I was leading a double life, one of loving docility and at the same time inalienable independence. ... I felt that they did not share the standpoint I was searching for and which proclaims it our duty to find our own answers to the eternal and eternally renewed questions; and what was more, having freed myself of a tendency to think in abstract terms and tacit assumptions, I felt the need to underpin, to place myself squarely in front of the real issues, to satisfy at one and the same time all the requirements of criticism and the continuing demands of human destiny. The secular attempt to reconcile ancient philosophy with Christian knowledge, necessary and fruitful though it may have been, appeared to me to remain as far as it could an attempt at concordism. I had the impression that, on both sides, they had stopped short of doing everything possible, at the risk of exposing themselves to misunderstandings or causing offence by not braving the meetings that were necessary and by not preparing for the beneficial union.[2]

In both cases Blondel is remarkably revealing, considering his usual obscurity. Both passages show a change of attitude, and, for this very reason, their ideas and character seem the more revealing. And they are particularly interesting and revealing because in the one case they are preceded, and in the other followed, by statements more directly concerned with Blondel's position in the field of modernism, as it appears in the work that, more than *Action* even, and before the 'reactionary' arrangements of 'Histoire et dogme', vindicates and clarifies the relationship between Loisy and von Hügel, Laberthonnière and Tyrrell, Semeria and Sabatier and Bremond and Duchesne: the *Lettre sur les exigences de la pensée contemporaine en matière d'apologetique et sur la méthode de la philosophie dans l'étude du problème religieux.*

[1] See M. Blondel, 'Lettre-préface pour une réédition de l'Action' in *Études blondeliennes*, I, Presses Universitaires de France, Paris, 1951, pp. 16–17.
[2] See *Itinéraire*, pp. 39 ff.

In 1927 Blondel wrote:

In order to protect myself from dangerous incriminations, I have been led at too great length into controversies which have diverted my originally exclusively philosophical aim into the sphere of apologetics. For the present it had become necessary to establish that, without venturing into the theological field, without aspiring to take part in historical and exegetical arguments, without the least assumption that conscience was capable of discerning grace or that reason could call on, recognize, or grasp the supernatural, philosophy poses certain questions, specifies certain attitudes and a certain kind of concern, lays down certain fundamental premises which religious teaching could profitably use as a basis for its authority and to introduce its invigorating activity into the innermost depths of man's soul.[1]

In 1927, Blondel might say that his famous *Lettre* was seeking only to clarify matters. This may have been part of his intention, but it was certainly not the whole of it: the fact was that his proposals were a great deal more revolutionary than even his friends seemed to realize. (And incidentally, in its day, what a fuss he made of it: how many letters to Valensin, how many appeals for prudence to Laberthonnière! And throughout it all, Blondel keeps appearing in his favourite pose—that of the oracle reluctantly agreeing to settle an argument, to straighten things out because he alone knows the truth of it; and knows it not rationally or theoretically but purely through the light of faith: not that this prevents him using the terms of reason on the highway of immanence, the only middle way between Loisy's arrogant disbelief and the vulgarities of the uncritical supporters of what was most doctrinaire in Rome.)

What Blondel in fact proposed—and this was what made his teaching 'modernistic'—was that Christian doctrine and spirituality should both be reconsidered from within; and while he claimed to support and revere the faith, at the same time he claimed the right to examine its concepts and question its truths. Here, as with Loisy, it was, in a sense, a case of refusing to obey, but Blondel's refusal was based on a difference of understanding, and not, like Loisy's, on the historical facts of revelation. Loisy made, as it were, a sidelong attack, from his historical researches; but Blondel attacked the very foundations. The distinctions Blondel claimed to respect in this latter passage were in fact

---

[1] See *Lettre-préface*, pp. 17-18.

brought in surreptitiously in order to protect his own independence as a philosopher. His *Action* in 1893, and more directly his *Lettre* in 1896, had to some extent undermined the validity of the techniques on which this independence was based. Theology, the supernatural, formal reasoning on historical or exegetical lines— all these are unhurt in the latter passage; but it is a case of saving what is traditional after attempting a radical, destructive revolution. Blondel (as Gentile himself showed quite clearly) always misunderstood himself and refused to face what his own ideas involved.

. . . I studied *Action* without the slightest intention of setting up one idol against another, or of refusing to think, of belittling intelligence, undermining fundamental theology, or of introducing any innovations whatever in dogma or Christian practices. Far from travelling to the Left, as has so often been asserted, I placed myself in opposition to the minimizers, on the extreme right wing, in reaction against Renanism, ephemeral symbolism, and modernistic neo-Christianity, aimed at glorifying the word, the literary approach, and safeguarded all the most positive and concrete demands of that type of Catholicism which is essentially a belief in incarnate truth, as opposed to an ideology or idealism which looks down on action.

And elsewhere, but about the same time, and meaning the same, he wrote:

. . . Whatever certain people have said, it has not then been the search for apologetics, not an interest in ethics, nor a desire for reform or innovation, that has guided me during the long itinerary of my intellectual adventures; and these have not been without suffering and danger. Most of all I have always wanted to turn philosophy into a technical and autonomous exercise, in line with present trends and the traditional approach, my only ambition being to explore patiently the whole area accessible to reason in questions common to both philosophy and religion, to define and stretch to its utmost limits the validity of philosophy, to recall or bring to the attention of all critical minds some of the first, or last, problems, from which they had turned away or which, in the absence of a suitable method, had not been placed expressly in the rational sphere.[1]

Here his own words might be used against him: for it was not 'a search for apologetics', but a 'new' apologetic, not an 'interest in ethics', but a 'new ethic', not 'a desire for reform' but an actual

[1] See *Itinéraire*, pp. 44–5.

reform that guided him as a thinker; because, in fact, he wanted to take up an independent philosophical position as audacious as any then being attempted collectively. This would give a new meaning to tradition and use the method of immanence which was no less suspect, no less worthy of the modernists' attention, because it was hard to understand (von Hügel, for once as prudent as he was intelligent, in fact suggested he should 'keep it dark').

Thus conceived, Blondel continued, his ideas could not fail to lead to an integral doctrine of Thought, Being, and Action, to a philosophy neither separate from Science and positive Religion, nor dependent on them. Essentially though not accidentally religious, and with a set purpose into the bargain, this philosophy went hand in glove with the boldest criticism and the most authentic Catholicism—by which he meant a Catholicism that would agree with him in finding three distinct meanings of that much-discussed term Immanence, in the *Pascendi*: the first meaning, which was condemned, referred to the doctrine of Immanence; the second, also condemned, sought to remove the supernatural from nature; and the third, which was allowable and *traditionally* used, referred to a grace in man, either originating or implanted in him, without which he is helpless in matters of faith and salvation, and which involves conversion and the Christian life; a grace deeply infused by our 'immanence', and coming only from above, *desursum*.

In any case, there was no need to wait for *Pascendi* in 1907 to establish his orthodoxy; long before, von Hügel had made efforts in Rome to forestall any attack on Blondel.

'As long as eight years ago, before he became Master of the Papal Household, but when he was already very influential, I approached him [Lepidi], about the fate of my dear good Maurice Blondel,' he wrote to Hébert in 1902. In 1897 he had again approached Lepidi and Rampolla, and Cardinal Perraud had approached Leo XIII. Another intermediary was Ollé-Laprune. In January of 1897 Albert Cufourq was able to reassure Blondel thus:

. . . Two pieces of good news, which I can confirm are from a reliable source: 1. Father Frühwirth, General of the Dominicans, requires Father Schalm to cease from any criticism of your ideas that might be harmful. 2. If ever the *Lettre* or *Action* is referred to the Index, Cardinal Serafino Vannutelli—who was once Prefect of the Index—will put all the weight of his authority into defending them, for he is sure that 'the remedy would be worse than the evil, if evil there is'.

And in fact Leo XIII, briefed by Cardinal Perraud, 'recognized at once that the accusations were malevolent and gave precise orders to the commission of the Index to refuse even to examine the *Lettre*'.

So, there was to be no condemnation. Why?

Certainly the way von Hügel, Ollé-Laprune, Lepidi, and Perraud had defended Blondel would not have been enough to suspend, delay, or cancel any action taken against him. Their help would not have been useless, but neither would it have been enough. Duchesne is quite explicit on this point, and it is impossible not to notice that many minor breaches of prudence, many far less revealing attitudes or remarks, were speedily condemned. Blondel was held in high regard, by both clergy and laity, since the appearance of his *Action*; his *Lettre* was hailed as the manifesto of a new school, and as soon as it appeared was considered and criticized as a very important document in its field. So it was not a case of ignoring some abstruse, often unintelligible, work (quite harmless to most people, for this very reason), which deserved to be discussed because, in spite of what its author said, both previously and at the time, it took a stand in the very centre of the argument on the new philosophy, and on the problem of the relationship between science and faith, philosophy and theology, the natural and the supernatural. Besides, the Catholic critics who found traces of subjectivism, monism, and rationalism in it (enough to '*énerver la certitude du dogme catholique*', as one of them rightly put it, though not in their pure state, or in really significant amounts) even from this distance appear to have struck home enough, at least on the face of it, to justify some disciplinary action. Von Hügel did everything possible to defend his friend's orthodoxy; the clergy, above all the young and including the Italians (in particular Semeria), found a new breath of spirituality in him, something that restored confidence in the recurrent crises in religious thought, and was upheld by a renewal of scholasticism, the point of which, apart from any disciplinary value it might have, probably none of them stopped to consider. But was this new orthodoxy and this new spirituality obvious and recognizable enough to account for the fact that he alone out of all the new theorists, and all who followed his methods and popularized his thought, escaped censure from the Holy Office? Was it that Laberthonnière, in becoming the 'translator into French' of Blondel's

ideas, betrayed his master's thought? Might it be that Laberthonnière's neater, homelier, and less vibrant prose failed to put
across the tone and meaning that alone justified Blondel's thought
and method? Or did the very fact that he was a layman, and a
practising Catholic at that, make Blondel stand out? That a layman
should assume the right to play a leading part in religious controversy was in itself something new and remarkable; years later,
the laity's right, in fact need, to take part in the Church's life was
to be put forward as something capable of renewing it. But were
Blondel's good faith and good intentions admitted, right away?
Were his diaries, confessions, and letters carefully considered?
Was the 'inspiration to be true', to use Loisy's fundamental phrase,
recognized in the concept he expressed with so much effort and
concentration?

Certainly Blondel never stood up to Rome, never gauged his
'personal' truth, never sought a 'personal' alternative to Rome.
All that he said about his teachers, whether at the time or earlier,
his constantly repeated wish to stand aside from the fray and not
be involved in argument, meant that, like Achilles, he kept out
of the battle itself. And it cannot be said, either, that he cheerfully
used his underling Laberthonnière to fight his small rows, and
settle minor differences.

But there is another reason, perhaps the most important one:
by opposing Loisy, by answering the Loisy of *L'Évangile et
l'Église* with his *Histoire et dogme*, Blondel broke the reformers'
front, came—or tried to come—between Loisy and von Hügel,
united Loisy's enemies and provided a useful doctrinal weapon
against him. It might be argued that Blondel, by refusing Loisy's
help, and sometimes his very suggestions, turned the condemnation away from himself and on to others, by allowing 'modernism'
to take shape.

4. Tyrrell

Tyrrell, on the other hand, was always a violent modernist, decisive, open-minded, and imprudent; the only one of the group who made a coherent profession of faith. His statements were explicit, all he wrote—and he wrote a great deal—was clear; so were his letters, talks, and private conversations; he never refused to face an accusation, never sought to avoid his responsibilities, never agreed to be silent or prudent or to compromise. It was only towards the Italian modernists of *Nova et Vetera* that he showed any doubt and uncertainty—justified, as it happened—during his last years. But towards the end of the century, he seems more confident than von Hügel, Loisy, Bremond, and even Blondel, more anxious than any of them to go ahead, more enthusiastic in what he says and does. He met von Hügel in 1897; the baron had asked him to give his daughter spiritual guidance, for the girl was upset by the degree to which her father had confided in her, discussing his spiritual doubts and his hopes of a change in Catholic doctrine. Their friendship lasted until Tyrrell's death in 1909, and, in spite of many misunderstandings, was a remarkable example of spiritual and emotional collaboration. Tyrrell's devoted friend Maude Petre was right in saying that his death was a liberation for von Hügel, who feared Tyrrell's courage and lack of prudence, but this does not mean that he deliberately tried to separate his own convictions from those of his friend in order to avoid incurring the same disciplinary measures. Among the reformers, Tyrrell was convinced more than anyone of an error in the Church, an error that, for very love of the Church, must be cut out; for he loved the Church fervently, vibrantly, and considered it always, as he wrote to Bremond, his Beatrice, his *donna gentile*,[1]

a possible answer to a problem which I had been made to feel, and whose solution was the governing motive of my life; whereas to the Catholic born and bred the problem is to conceive a living interest in

[1] See *Autobiography*, II, p. 72.

any other possible view of the matter. I was as one suddenly cured of congenital blindness, marvelling how indifferent others seemed to the world of light and colour.[1]

Tyrrell, the only convert among the modernists, was also the only one who had been religiously active before being ordained a Catholic priest; he had been a follower of Richard Dolling, whose religious experience has characteristics remarkably like those found later among the worker priests. And not only this: when he was converted to Catholicism he chose to enter the Society of Jesus, which meant he chose the most radical 'state of perfection', the most perfect and exposed society in the Catholic Church; and at the time he was censured he studied scholasticism with a new-broom fervour that involved him in arguments over his orthodoxy with the Roman hierarchy, in order to gain approval. His religious progress was therefore exemplary, and he carried straight on to the end, reaching positions the hierarchy thought heterodox and often in error. He was removed from teaching, in fact, the very year before he met von Hügel, because of his excessive strictness in interpretation, a strictness upheld by the new Jesuits led by Cardinal Mazzella. This logical vigour, and a certain schematic method derived from his scholastic training, appear in his writings, particularly the early ones, although always supported by a remarkably able style. That he was proud of this is shown by what he wrote in his autobiography (1900):

Whatever order or method there is in my thought, whatever real faculty of reasoning and distinguishing I have acquired, I owe it to St. Thomas. He first started me on the inevitable, impossible, and yet not all-fruitless quest of a complete and harmonious system of thought.

I no longer accept as adequate, or as more than ingeniously illustrative, the simple categories of form and matter, purpose, pattern, by which scholasticism seeks a mechanical explanation of things spiritual and celestial, in the terms of the works of men's hands; I see that scholasticism is saturated hopelessly with principles whose development is materialism and rationalism; that the realism it defends plays straight into the hands of idealism; that it really has no room for such conceptions as *spirit* and *life*, since it explains these higher things—thought, will, love, action—mechanically and artificially, in the terms of those that are lower. Hence it is too opaque a medium to admit the full light and beauty of Christianity to shine upon the eyes of those who think and

[1] See ibid., I, p. 188.

speak in terms of experience higher than those of the workshop or the sculptor's studio. Yet it is perhaps not a more gross thought-system than that which Christ had to use as the vehicle of his revelation; and by dint of many manipulations it has become a sufficiently flexible medium of expression to suggest the main outlines and chief prominences of the world of spiritual and intelligible realities—a sort of musical notation, meaning much for musicians, though little or nothing for the unmusical.

Unlike his friends and correspondents, that is, he did not reject his training; on the contrary, his thought was guided by the Thomistic system. Tyrrell felt that Aquinas might be 'historicized'; his ideal, in those years at least, was a kind of critical Thomism. The way to arrive at this—as he wrote to his friends—was to re-estimate, or rather make use of, Newman's thought, and assimilate its spirit: thanks to Newman, they could pour the Catholic truth from the scholastic into the Catholic jar without spilling a single drop. Tyrrell spent much time studying Newman's thought—unlike Loisy, and more deeply than von Hügel; and was more deeply and directly inspired by it than the others, so that he could recreate both what was called the modernist Newman of the 'progress of Revelation', and the Newman who, he wrote in December 1893, like Ward recognized

the fluctuating character of science and criticism, [and aimed] at a more lasting and wide-reaching utility, namely to make the preambles of faith in some sort independent of, and indifferent to these very fluctuations; to relieve the majority of believers from the mental disturbance inseparable from the erroneous impression that their faith is in continual jeopardy at the hands of scientists and critics.[1]

Here his intuition went far beyond Loisy's critical intelligence. 'Hence a detailed encounter with German Criticism would have been beside the mark until the preliminary question had been settled,' he went on to say, sounding prophetically correct in Loisy's case; for, in fact, this was the task Loisy chose, whereas Tyrrell, and in another field Blondel, agreed at least on the need to set up a critical basis for faith, religion, and truth, either opposed to official theology, or independent of it.

Through von Hügel, and before him through Bremond, then a Jesuit, Tyrrell read Blondel and Laberthonnière: 'To put it more truly he [Blondel] reaches by a methodical research what I

[1] See *Autobiography*, II, p. 58.

stumble on by luck, or, at best, by instinct. Hence it is a great strength to me to discover that I have been unconsciously talking philosophy . . . I found I had simply to translate it into explicit English as I went along,' he wrote to von Hügel in 1900,[1] but even earlier, in a letter in December 1897, only a few days before his first meeting with von Hügel, he had written:

Thank you very much indeed for the pamphlets. Blondel I had already received from Father Bremond, and had read without much profit, for his style is most obscure, especially to me whose language is scholastic though my thought is mystic. But Le Dogmatisme m oral was a great joy to me as giving a clearer insight into the 'Philosophy of action' or rather the Philosophy of the heart and concrete to human nature. I felt at home in nearly everything, and doubt not but I shall be able to fit it all into my own mind without any violent revolution.[2]

The fact that Tyrrell, Laberthonnière, and Blondel are to some extent in agreement is really quite fortuitous. They had common interests and sometimes shared a way of expressing themselves, but Tyrrell's background was quite unlike theirs, as were his traditions of thought and even of spirituality. It was natural enough that Tyrrell's thought, which, as he himself admitted, evolved through intuition and direct religious experience, should meet parallel developments; von Hügel, more firmly convinced than his friends of the need for intellectual agreement or a common consideration of things, was anxious to point out these parallels. At the time, von Hügel appears in a way to be the 'true' modernist, that is the man who, out of the various ideas and religious and philosophical experiences he met as a worried, ever-curious believer, tended to make a philosophical and religious syncretism that could be justified only if it was meant to act in disciplinary and doctrinal opposition to Rome. In fact, however, von Hügel himself diverted this syncretism from the end it was clearly leading to, and withdrew into personal suffering or private, irrational spirituality.

I think that in what strikes me as its two main doctrines,—the unconscious or variously obscure, but most real and, when favoured, powerful presence within us of an inward Christ pushing us upwards and outwards with a view to joining hands with the outward Christ Who

---

[1] See Tyrrell's letter to von Hügel (7 September, 1900), in ibid., II, pp. 91–2.
[2] See Michael de la Bedoyère, Life of Baron von Hügel, p. 102.

is pressing inwards, these two as necessary conditions for the apprehensions of Faith and Love; and the illuminative character of action, which makes the Christianity of the individual soul continually to re-begin with an experiment, and re-conclude by an experience,—that in these two main points it is entirely Blondel and Laberthonnière, but, of course, with all the sound and sane mystics generally,

von Hügel wrote to Tyrrell, when *External Religion* appeared in 1899,[1] and, as if to improve his education, he urges Tyrrell on to biblical criticism, and to the study of German, in order to read Troeltsch and Eucken, besides von Harnack and Döllinger. But, von Hügel did not 'pervert' Tyrrell. Tyrrell's desk might be deep in philosophical works and letters from anxious Catholics, his talks with von Hügel and his correspondence with the sensitive Bremond might urge him to reflect further and to clarify his personal position; but it was the attitude of the Church, and the needs of his own personal commitment, that moved him, far more than anything his friends might do.

Certainly, in those years at the turn of the century, letters and articles still show him to be a moderate, a 'mediator', as he defines himself in a letter to Ward; but this same 'mediatorial' position, which he shared only with his teachers—Newman in particular—underwent a profound change, that was to lead him, even before Loisy, into fighting openly.

The Church may neither identify herself with 'progress' nor isolate herself from it. Her attitude must always be the difficult and uncomfortable one of partial agreement and partial dissent. ... We must not shrink from the paradox that contemporary science and history is always wrong; not wholly wrong ... but mingling so much extravagance and excess with its reason ... as to make it invariably safe to hold back and wait. It is truth 'in solution', but not attainable apart and in its purity till it has long ceased to be a theme of discussion and excitement.[2]

In this very important letter to Ward, two years later, Tyrrell confirmed his position:

I should prefer 'mediatorial' to 'moderate' or to *Juste Milieu*, were I anxious to brand myself; for these latter imply a definite programme (e.g. with regard to the Index, Inquisition, Higher Criticism, Church Government), whereas all I want is a conciliatory spirit on both sides, each wishing to yield all that can rightly be yielded to the other in a

[1] See *Selected letters of Baron von Hügel*, p. 78.
[2] See *Autobiography*, II, p. 102.

spirit of true liberty. But since this can never be (seeing the one-sided character of the human mind, which ever lurches to port or starboard), I think the function of the mediatorial party, which, of course, is always relatively a small one, is to try to interpret the extremes to one another; to act the part of heat in chemical combinations; and so it is through its instrumentality that the process of modification is gradually forwarded (i.e. forms are interpreted and new matter selected and assimilated).[1]

In the Roman authorities' refusal to recognize this very process, and to accept and even absorb and assimilate Newman's thought, which subtends his, Tyrrell had already singled out the error that was to take him outside the Church, a martyr for resisting that authority.

The first serious and in a way definitive controversy with the authorities, either Jesuit or Roman, came about through the publication, in 1899, of an article in the *Weekly Register* entitled 'A perverted devotion'. In it Tyrrell put forward not only his personal views on the dogma of Hell, but also his own definite rejection of the scholastic position; Loisy's parallel work must have contributed to this:

It would almost seem from many indications [he wrote] that the same rationalism in religion which occasioned the defection of the sixteenth century has, like a fever, worked itself out and brought about its own cure by an experimental demonstration of its insufficiency as a substitute for faith. In a saner spiritual philosophy born of a revolt against materialism—the last and lowest form of rationalism—a basis is found for a certain temperate agnosticism, which is one of the essential prerequisites of intelligent faith; the attempt to build up and interpret the lower by the higher is definitely abandoned; the essential incapacity of finite mind to seize the absolute end which governs and moves everything towards itself, the natural necessity of seeming contradictions and perplexities in our estimate of God's thoughts and ways are accepted as inevitable. This sense of our mental insufficiency is no reason for credulity, nor does it relieve the 'apologist' of his burden of establishing the fact of revelation; but it prepares the way for Christ by showing that something equivalent to a revelation is as much an exigency of our nature as religion is. Thus God's spirit working outside the Church is preparing for himself an acceptable people; and we within must co-operate and go forward to meet his movement by purging out of our midst any remnant of the leaven of rationalism that we may have carried with us from earlier and cruder days, when faith needed the rein more than the spur.[2]

[1] See ibid., II, p. 10. [2] See ibid., II, pp. 117–18.

This article, which the general of the Jesuits defined as 'offensive to pious ears' ('I wish Rome would either define pious ears, or give a list of them so that one might know,' Tyrrell wrote), and which the Baron considered 'his finest work, so profound and so full of the mystery of faith and of the invisible world', shows that Tyrrell was beginning to be convinced that it was impossible to agree in any way with Rome. Once convinced of this, he abandoned moderation, and wrote thus to a friend:

The best policy, I half think, would be not to oppose but to fan the flame of this 'Authority-fever', and to get them to declare the infallibility of every Congregation, of the General of the Jesuits, of every Monsignore in Rome; to define the earth to be a flat plate supported on pillars, and the sky a dishcover; in short, to let them run their heads full tilt against a stone wall, in hopes it may wake them up to sober realities.[1]

The truth was that Tyrrell was as uncertain as he was angry:

As to faith, it is my one hope that there is a solution yet to be discovered; and that not very far hence. I think there are crises in human thought comparable to those in evolution when life, sense and reason first come on the scene; and that after such crises there are seasons of great confusion pending readjustment. . . . Naturally we do not know where we are just at present; and it will take time to translate faith into that language, yet I believe faith will reappear, though I am not so sure that it will be Roman faith—yet even that is to me the more probable issue—in some sense a certain issue. How far away even Newman seems to one now! How little he seems to have penetrated the darkness of our day! His method and spirit are an everlasting possession; but of his premises and presuppositions hardly one has escaped alive.[2]

Tyrrell assumed the right to speak because he was uncertain and at the same time convinced that a new religious certainty could be found only through profound meditation on faith and truth; into this new certainty would flow the thoughts of many— philosophers, plain laymen, unknown teachers of other creeds. His voice was no longer to be that of a teacher, it was often to assume the tone and characteristics of prophetic writing. One thing only was never in doubt: the error of Rome, an error obstinately maintained and restated, consisting in refusal to take account of a changed situation, to recognize the need to introduce into the concept of infallibility modifications like those already made, from

---

[1] See *Autobiography*, II, p. 146. [2] See ibid., II, p. 144.

acknowledged and vital necessity, in the concept of biblical infallibility, and to maintain the distinction between the *Ecclesia docens*
and the *Ecclesia discens*: 'it is not, as they suppose, about this or
that article of the creed that we differ; we accept it all; but it is the
word "credo"; the sense of "true" as applied to dogma; the whole
value of revelation that is at stake'.[1]

[1] See ibid., II, p. 197.

5. Von Hügel's Hopes

And I am having the strange, very sobering impression that God is deigning somehow to use me—me, in my measure, along with others who can and do do more, and much more—towards making, not simply registering, history. And, dear me, what a costing process *that* is![1]

Who were the friends on whom he was to build, with whom he was to make history? Tyrrell, to whom he wrote this letter from Rome, towards the end of 1901, Blondel, Loisy, Laberthonnière, Bremond, Duchesne himself?

Yes, von Hügel maintained that theirs were the ideas which could renew Catholicism. These ideas were still undeveloped, still haphazard, still piecemeal, and must be allowed to grow within the framework of Catholicism, without being set up against other ideas temporarily professed by the Catholic hierarchy. They must wait for the right moment, put up with obvious misunderstandings, intolerance, and even disciplinary measures: they must sometimes be silent before justifying themselves, and believe there was good faith on both sides, and that the right moment was not far ahead. The great Pope Leo XIII was old, which meant that the Roman hierarchy was too rigidly entrenched in its old positions; the Pope, who had done so much to make Catholicism a current reality, 'a catholicism of his own time', as tolerant and free as an eternal truth can be, was too weary to carry on his work; and so it was natural that, in waiting for the new Pope, who would carry on and perfect his great predecessor's work, the hierarchy of Rome and elsewhere preferred to stiffen in their old positions, not to accept anything new for fear of rashly anticipating a development that must naturally, logically, and necessarily come. The important thing was to avoid being condemned: if the forces von Hügel counted on and thought he belonged to could state their case exactly and stand together within the Church, or at least without the Roman hierarchy taking any definite stand against them, the Church could get over its failure of authority and of doctrine,

[1] Quoted in *Selected Letters*, p. 103, and in Michael de la Bedoyère, op. cit., p. 128.

provoked, in the last years of the century, by the slackening of the old Pope's power. Within the Church these were living forces; whereas outside it they were only isolated doctrines, which could merely provoke crises of conscience among the younger clergy. As long as it could count on a group of Catholic philosophers, theologians, exegetes, and scientific researchers who could argue without accusing, and discuss without bitterness the hierarchy's mistakes, anti-historical incomprehension, and misunderstanding of contemporary needs, and could find in God and in themselves the vigour and devotion needed to carry on their work, the Church would be saved; and at the same time, as long as these philosophers, theologians, and exegetes worked on behalf of the Church, generously handed over to it the results of their research, combined with it in verifying what was only partially known, and admitted their own mistakes, they would be saved too. As part of the *Ecclesia docens*, they would, even if kept out of its present work, be forging the Church's tools for the future; whereas outside the Church, or kept out of it deliberately, they would only add to the errors of their day.

This was what von Hügel put forward, his hopes nourished largely by his natural optimism, which made him find a religious basis and object in the doctrines of his friends and correspondents, and at the same time made him see the Roman hierarchy's position as temporary, or else as justified in some religious way. He was delighted when he found evidence of what seemed to him a parallel development of ideas on the two sides, and never failed to point out occasions when they seemed to be saying the same thing; others, more critically minded, realized that the very writings he cited were either in opposition, or at least in contrast, to one another. In much the same way von Hügel attributed an absolute value to the doctrines of Tyrrell, Loisy, and Blondel. It was not that he accepted them uncritically (his own works show that he did not), but that he considered they had an intellectual weight and importance the Church could not neglect. Indeed, some of the compromises and uncertainties on either side were due to his direct personal efforts.

On the other hand, what he hoped to achieve was in another way justified. He may not even have realized this himself, but from this distance it seems the more apparent. His friends, and those with whom he sought to ally himself, stood not so much for any new or original thinking, as for the way in which a movement of thought contrary to the Church was going: that is, they were trying to turn the crisis of religious thought into a movement for the liberation of thought from theology, dogma, and Revelation.

Loisy's exegesis, Blondel's apologetics, Tyrrell's religious pragmatism—they might be absorbed, as Newman's doctrine of development had already been absorbed, by the Church. But the Church stood out against the breakdown of traditional theology, against autonomous criticism, against the naturalistic evolution of religion, against the non-dogmatic character of Revelation. Or else these men's doctrines partly expressed an ideological process that was developing outside the Church, rather than contrary to the Church. The Church could make use of them to oppose ideas that were quite alien to it, but which they, on the other hand, had some connection with—this was what Tyrrell called the 'religious solution'. The Church would then be in a position to get the better of its enemies. Supported by these doctrines, it could behave as *prima inter pares*, with an eternal right to pronounce on truth, as it appeared in contemporary cultural life. The alternative was for it to withdraw altogether from the world of history, from the 'concrete development of truth', from the 'progress of Revelation'. And if it did so, the faithful, without the critical support of these exegetes, apologists, and philosophers, would turn from the 'eternal truths' which could not be communicated in scholastic terms, to the 'relative truths' of science, evolutionism, and historicism. In such a case von Hügel's friends, instead of being in the vanguard of cultural life, would fall behind.

So they must be part of the Church, and be seen to be part of the Church, in particular of the *Ecclesia docens*. The actual position taken by the Vatican encouraged von Hügel's friends to hope. But these hopes were dashed by an official document on 29 December 1900, a pastoral letter from the English Catholic hierarchy on *The Church and liberal Catholicism*. This document claimed to re-establish—though according to von Hügel's friends it introduced it for the first time—a precise distinction between the *Ecclesia docens* and the *Ecclesia discens*, and thus made clear the opposing points of view.

Optimistic as ever, von Hügel interpreted the pastoral letter hopefully: supported, perhaps, by Duchesne's opinion; but Tyrrell's reaction was immediate, violent, and public:

As an analysis of facts the current theological doctrine of the functions of the *Ecclesia Docens* involves at first sight a theory which could in no way be regarded as a legitimate development of earlier teaching, or escape the charge of an almost abrupt innovation, nor could it be defended as a necessary or even valid deduction from the Vatican decrees. It would cleave the Church into two bodies, the one all active, the other all passive, related literally as sheep and shepherds—as being of a different order with conflicting interests; it would destroy the organic unity of the Church by putting the Pope (or the *Ecclesia Docens*) outside and over the Church, not a part of her, but her partner, spouse, and Lord, in a sense proper to Christ alone; it would shear the bishops of their inherent prerogatives while restoring to them a tenfold power as the delegates and plenipotentiaries of the infallible and unlimited authority claimed for the Pope.[1]

In his article, 'La méthode de la théologie', which had previously been published in the *Bulletin* of Tolosa and then in the *Revue du clergé français*, at the end of 1901—and which, Loisy said in his *Mémoires*, was one of the first manifestos of Catholic modernism —Monsignor Mignot, Loisy's friend and adviser, made the same point as Tyrrell, in direct opposition to the pastoral letter: that is, that the teaching Church learnt from the work of the rest of the Church. But von Hügel wrote and begged Loisy to be prudent, not to express such an opinion publicly, for fear that, suspect as he was in the eyes of the Church, he might spoil the high hopes of collaboration between the two sides—and for something von Hügel considered of minor importance.

In fact, von Hügel's *'lucide candeur'*, as Loisy put it, seemed to have had its hopes confirmed when, early in 1902, it was announced that an international commission was to be set up to re-examine the entire biblical question. In that case, Loisy would be safe: von Hügel was as exultant as if he had engineered the whole thing himself. It all now seemed an accomplished fact; Blondel

---

[1] Quoted in *Autobiography*, p. 396. See also letter of 17 February to the Editor of the *Weekly Register*: 'It seems to me that the joint Pastoral . . . makes a distinct line of theological cleavage with Jesuitism, for lack of a neater term, on one side, and Newmanism on the other. It fixes a programme of a policy on which we so-called "Liberals" should be able to unite, sinking all minor and less fundamental differences. It is just a question of the constitution of the Church; of the relation of the Pope and the Ecclesia Docens to the Ecclesia Discens . . . We should not fight as to whether we are to accept more or less of the results of criticism until we have established the place of criticism with regard to ecclesiastical teaching' (*Life*, pp. 153–4).

congratulated him and called him the Commission's 'adviser and president', and von Hügel wrote to Ward:

I think it plain that *the authorities here feel and see, that they cannot, as a matter of fact, stop us from serious, scientific method and working*; and that as long as we ask for no kind of approbation or authorization, and as long again as the others do not press them too much on the point, or are counter-worked by us, so long shall we be able, *if we can continue to find in God and ourselves the vigour and devotedness necessary*, to continue to work. And I am very sure that in the minds of at least the majority of the Commission, this continuance of this our (simply tolerated but thoroughly independent) work is an absolute necessity of the situation. We—I think of such men as Loisy, Touzard, Lagrange, myself, etc.—cannot, ought not to attempt the work of the Commission, but neither can the Commission do our work; and without our work the Commission loses its true subject-matter, its special occasion, its driving force.... I think we should try patiently and perseveringly in all sorts of ways (direct but chiefly indirect) to make our public feel and apprehend:

(1) That here is a body of learned Catholic theologians and scholars, appointed by the Church as a no doubt permanent institution, with a practically inexhaustible subject-matter, the science to be considered being so rich in its contents, and as yet constituted only in its principles and general methods, and but a few of its conclusions—hence that neither *Roma actiona* (Padre Lepidi told Mgr. Mignot that *Rome* in this matter wished to spell *mora*), nor the good sense of Catholics generally, nor their respect for the deep things of God, could permit them *even to wish for any early*, or simply final, or complete report, let alone decision. (2) That here is a body to which they can refer, in all times, possible anxieties as to the tenableness of this or that, the orthodoxy of this or that person; or (much better) as to how to meet and what to think as to such and such apparent facts or difficulties; and that, since the Pope himself has appointed it, although possessed already of the ordinary congregations, *we shall be following his initiative and the evident trend of his action, if we henceforth treat the Commission as the presumptive and primary authority and tribunal for the slow threshing out of these questions which have thus been declared to require very special and slow study*. And (3) That, *of course, Catholic research and study will, or indeed should, continue outside of the Commission; such study never, of course, claiming to speak with the Church's authority*.[1]

[1] Part of a letter, undated but certainly written and sent immediately after the nomination of the commission, quoted by Michael de la Bedoyère, op. cit., pp. 137-8.

But Loisy's comment on the same news was very different:

Revise the Vulgate, the Septuagint, the Hebrew text. Oh, the good people! They will need help. . . . It is clear that we need not have thanked anybody for this. . . . If the complete incompatibility of Catholicism and criticism is taken for granted, the *modus vivendi* which has just been established is meaningless. However, it is wrong to accept this incompatibility, seeing that neither Catholicism nor criticism is an absolute in the sense in which one would like it understood, so it is possible for these two *relatives* to have friendly *relations* if they make allowances for one another.[1]

Blondel's reaction was different too: here he refers not to the announcement on the biblical Commission, but to von Hügel's hopes, though he shared them rather more than Loisy did:

When I think of our poor Church and our poor France, I continually have the nightmare of a man holding his bucket of water and being unable to throw it on the fire. In the Catholic Church there are those who pray, those who live, those who suffer, and fortunately this is what is essential; but there are those who think, those who speak, those who write, those who discuss and appear to reflect, and all this is more than misinterpretation, sensationalism, blundering, incompetence, and error. The disproportion between thought and life is frightening; and unfortunately only a few of the words and thoughts have any influence on the actions and attitudes.[2]

He also wrote:

It is necessary to plunge into the unexplored depths of dogma. Do they think they can dispose of a Hegel or a Bergson with a few stupid remarks or scornful outbursts? No, no. The human mind—sophisticated, satiated, starving—needs stronger meat, a more exalted doctrine. . . . No 'novelties', nothing heterodox or suspect; and yet, the unformulated, the unperceived, the invigorating, the unforeseen. Those who imagine that their halberds will be able to cope with modern weapons are mistaken. Extreme weakness in the extreme presumption of ignorance. . . . My plan is to lay down the conditions and reasons for the union of the natural and the supernatural in man. I propose to discover how and why it is necessary and possible to believe in Christ. . . . To examine the fundamental problem in relation to apologetics, as Locke, Hume, and Kant examined it in relation to rational speculation. Nothing merely transitory, ephemeral, or 'modern', no polemics or allusions to present conditions. Two rules. . . . (a) never to forget that the 'reactionaries' can

[1] See *Mémoires*, II, p. 87.
[2] Part of a letter to Henri Bremond of 12 March 1903 quoted in *Correspondence Blondel–Valensin*, I, p. 71.

and often do act in good faith and with good intentions, and are zealous and virtuous people: (b) never to stop applying to oneself the demands, warnings, and criticisms one makes of others, for anti-Pharisaism is always in danger of becoming a new Pharisaism. One must be wary of being right too often, of speaking too definitely and looking for exact meanings. . . . Appeal for a new type of co-operation, more modern than that which put twelve scribes at Saint Thomas's elbow, freer and more impartial. Collaboration between strangers, enemies, waverers, even the unintelligent, in an effort of joint goodwill.[1]

When the Catholic hierarchy made these two moves, the attitude of the two sides may thus be summed up: on the one hand, von Hügel's friends believed wholeheartedly in the possibility and necessity of collaboration between the two sides, on the other the Church refused to respect or consider their opinions; again, von Hügel's friends believed in the need for mutual help within a mystical unity, while the Church believed there was no possible alternative to its opinion; von Hügel's friends also overestimated the importance of private research.

Some time before, the Church had spoken out in a way that, from this distance, and bearing in mind the reactions of the Catholic clergy and laity, seems well worth considering. But von Hügel and his friends and correspondents seem not to have commented directly upon it. On 22 January 1899, Leo XIII sent Cardinal Gibbons, Archbishop of Baltimore, the apostolic letter *Testem benevolentiae*, in which, moderately but firmly, he condemned a movement that had appeared among the American clergy, later named Americanism.[2] It was not so much an organized movement, or a precise way of thinking, as an attitude taken by some of the higher clergy in America towards 'dissidents'. The

---

[1] Personal notes quoted in *Correspondence Blondel–Valensin*, I, pp. 70–1.

[2] On Americanism see A. Houtin, *L'américanisme*, Nourry, Paris, 1904, which uses documents sent to the author by the two principal exponents of the 'heresy' in France, Abbé Klein, propagandist of the movement, and Abbé Periès, its main adversary. On its work, see Minocchi's critical examination in *Studi religiosi*, July–August 1904, pp. 429–33. See also the curious judgement of Fr. John Gillis, in *Catholic World* of July 1949: 'The time has come—it may seem to have come and gone—to speak plainly about the supposedly heretical movement named "Americanism". It was the subject of violent controversy half a century ago, but since then it has been pretty much forgotten. The disturbance should never have arisen . . . There was no heresy and no schism [yet] the state of affairs in which priests must become miners, factory hands, day labourers, in order to obtain access to the people might not have happened if the Catholics of France had appropriated rather than repudiated American methods.'

Americanists maintained that, in order to take Catholic doctrine to those outside it, the Church should do more to adapt itself to an adult civilization; it should be less rigid than it had been in the past, and make some concessions to recent ideas: this with regard not merely to everyday life, but to doctrine itself, in which was found the *depositum fidei*. In short, dissidents should be helped into the Church by ignoring or playing down certain elements of doctrine; the action of the Holy Ghost was enough to guide them, and external direction was no longer needed, because natural rather than supernatural virtue was best suited to the present age. One of the Americanists went so far as to say that these should be no barriers to entry into the Church and those guided only by their own reason should find their path into it smoothed. Besides, in a century that was above all else active—materially, socially, intellectually—the passive virtues that had suited previous eras were no longer needed. Martyrs and hermits and monasteries were outdated, vows were opposed to the spirit of the age, monastic or 'religious' life, as it was usually understood, was a denial of human freedom, suited to the weak, unsuited to the present Church and the good of society. The methods so far used must therefore be radically changed, and must give way to those of a new apostolate, an apostolate of action.

Americanism did not take the form of heresy in America, where it began; nor did it in France, where it spread, in particular through the translation of a biography of Father Hecker by the Abbé Felix Klein, Fogazzaro's friend and correspondent, and through the same Klein's translation of the sermons of Monsignor Ireland. Yet some of its fundamental characteristics either anticipated or coincided remarkably with those of the European controversies at the time: its emphasis on the need to bring the apostolate up to date corresponds to the European emphasis on the need to reform apologetics, and is what might be called its pragmatic aspect, its active side. Then, too, the emphasis on the ethics of welfare instead of sacrificial ethics which American Catholics had inherited from Protestantism, corresponds to the need to find a religious answer, on an ethical basis, to the Catholic hierarchy's attitude, both in its high-handed interpretation of the doctrine of papal infallibility, and with regard to what was called the social question. And, finally, the need to recognize that the clergy's main strength lay in the support of the people, whose love and appreciation the clergy must win—not overlooking their material welfare—corresponds to the religion without miracles Renan had already foreseen, which, with dogma cut down to the single dogma of papal infallibility, had become a means of education and of political action.

6. The Break in the Ranks

Dogmas are facts, Ireland used to say; but Loisy dedicated to the Abbé Klein, 'father or at least patron of a ghostly heresy called Americanism, condemned by Leo XIII, a single authentic representative of which has never yet been found in the old world or the new', one of the seven letters which make up *Autour d'un petit livre*—the fifth, on the foundation and authority of the Church. It was an ironical dedication, and in *Choses passées* Loisy writes with amusement that, in mentioning his walks at Meudon with the Abbé, and their discussions, he might, being already 'rather suspect', unwittingly have caused harm: for those discussions certainly ranged beyond such topics as the weather, and traditional notions of religion.[1]

Loisy wished to be the only one who understood, both later, when he looked back on it and made judgements, and at the time of the conflict itself. In November 1902 the *Études évangeliques* and *L'Évangile et l'Église* were published by Picard; on 13 October, a few days before 'opening fire in the first battle', he wrote in his diary:

I have rarely been so anxious about the moral impact of my publications as I am for the two volumes about to be published. Both of them represent an attempt to adjust Catholic theory to historical facts, and Catholic practice to the realities of contemporary life. Is this attempt necessary and can it be of some use? Looked at from a certain point of view, it may appear superfluous and even harmful. The Catholicism that officially exists and speaks objects to this adaptation and refuses to accept it. Many ask themselves, not unreasonably, whether in trying to change it one is not helping to destroy it. It seems to be so closely bound up with a certain view of the world, of life, and of society, and one which is not suited to the present time, that to invite it to modify its attitudes seems equivalent to suggesting a kind of suicide which one cannot delude oneself one would achieve by persuasion. And on the other hand, there have been such great changes in the past and the need to change is so urgent that it would be criminal not to say anything in a situation like this. The Church should be destroyed as a great enemy of human progress if she is not susceptible of improvement. But she should be

[1] See *Choses passées*, p. 264.

supported, defended, and enlightened in every possible way if she is still the great moral reservoir of civilization. Those who choose the first course have more than just pretexts to support them. However, I believe that the alternative is the true one.[1]

And in the name of the second party, Loisy defended the Church against what was then a widely successful interpretation of Christianity: *The Essence of Christianity*, by the Protestant Adolf von Harnack. To Harnack the essence of Christianity lay neither in dogmatic intellectual attitudes, nor in ritual that was authoritarian, traditional, and social, but in an inner feeling, in a particular transformation of the soul, in faith in God as father, and, as the essence of the teaching of Christ, in the love of the Father and of men as brothers; whereas to Loisy what mattered in Christ's teaching as revealed in historical criticism was his declaration of the coming of God's Kingdom; this was an object of faith, something quite distinct from a moral conversion, and the history of the Church and of religious thought, which was not the transmission or alteration of an earlier *depositum*, was the organic and vital development of an original seed.[2]

But *L'Évangile et l'Église* was not at all what it seemed to be,

[1] See *Choses passées*, pp. 242–3.

[2] On Harnack and Loisy's confutation, both Lagrange's *Revue biblique* and *Civiltà cattolica* soon spoke out. In February 1903 *Civiltà cattolica* condemned the two works together: '. . . insult allied to lack of knowledge is so obvious that any scientific discussion is pointless. But unfortunately we must bear in mind the weak, who find the rationalists' sneers and contradictions reasonable; and (what is worse) not only the weak. Because learned Catholics have argued with Harnack as if he were a decent person, and disagreement with him were merely over trifles. These learned men overlook entirely the sort of adversary they are fighting, and even get to the childish point of temporizing with him.' In a note *Civiltà cattolica* added: 'One of these is Alfred Loisy in his book *L'Évangile et l'Église* (the others were Semeria and a writer in *Cultura sociale*, probably Murri). Lagrange had spoken out against Loisy in the April number of his review: 'It is strictly speaking true that M. Loisy's critical theories are as deadly to Christian faith as those of M. Harnack, and the victory he enjoys in the ecclesiastical sphere does not amount to anything solid; for who would consent to accept the yoke of the Church—and it is a yoke—if it had not been founded by Jesus Christ and if nothing proves that Jesus Christ is God?' But Murri, who had been condemned by *Civiltà cattolica*, also jointly condemned the two works: 'Let us go on to Harnack. This is an heretical book, that authoritatively expounds heretical theories, his own Essence of Christianity, and is therefore strictly forbidden, and with the gravest sanctions; indeed, even to mention it openly may seem like a threat to people's consciences. . . . We have heard many perspicacious and learned men say that Loisy's book in reply to Harnack may do more harm to unprepared Catholics than Harnack himself. We are of the same opinion.' (In *Battaglie d'oggi*, III, Rome, 1904, pp. 183–4.) In France the campaign against

at least it was not merely a defence of Catholicism against the criticism of a liberal Protestant; it had, as Loisy was to write some years later, two objects: to tell the Catholic clergy quite quietly about the problems of the origins of Christianity, and in doing so to show, in the face of Protestant criticism, how the Church could appear to have developed, inevitably, from the Gospel. Besides this, there were two especially subtle elements in Loisy's book: on the one hand, his criticisms of Harnack implied a criticism of the evangelical sources far more radical, in parts, than Harnack's own; on the other, Loisy's defence of the Roman Church against Harnack's opinions implied that he had abandoned some things which scholastic theologians believed in absolutely—on Christ's formal founding of the Church and its sacraments, on the immutability of dogma, and on the nature of ecclesiastical authority. Loisy was not, in fact, simply criticizing Harnack: discreetly, and, it seemed, prudently, he implied the need for an essential reform of biblical exegesis, the whole of theology, and even Catholicism in

Loisy's confutation was carried on mainly in the *Univers* by the Abbé Gayraud, and by Mgr. Batiffol in the *Bulletin* of Tolosa, the circulation of which was increased by the controversy from 800 to 5,000. On *L'Évangile et l'Église*, Rivière, in *Le Modernisme dans l'Église*, Paris, 1929, speaks of 'theologians qualified to speak in the name of science, and clearsighted enough to see how subtle doctrinal perversion is working, disguised as criticism' (p. 169), and adds: 'two interventions, highly important for the honour of the Catholic interpretation, occurred simultaneously and at the first opportunity', referring to the studies of L. de Grandmaison in *Études* (20 January 1903, vol. XCIV, pp. 145–74) and of P. Batiffol in the *Bulletin* of January 1903, pp. 3–15; but on Batiffol see what Houtin writes in *Ma vie laique* op. cit, p. 153: 'N [by this letter Houtin means to indicate Batiffol, and one must remember that Rivière's book was written to justify the work of Batiffol, who, according to Loisy, was the creator of modernism] who had become the rector of a Catholic Institute in the provinces and (like Loisy) was seeking favour with the episcopate, turned against him. He opened up with his heaviest guns, called his book a hoax, and was foolish enough to say that he was acquainted with the author's private thoughts, as though Loisy could not have replied that he was equally acquainted with the other's thoughts and that they were not very different. N. was the real cause of the prompt stop put to the "hoax"; perhaps without him the book would have taken in a number of bishops, which would have been a serious state of affairs for the Church.' 'The truth is that the learned French Catholic exegete was not always quite calm in his criticisms,' Baldassarre Labanca wrote in his *Gesú Cristo nella letteratura contemporanea*, Bocca, Turin, 1903, p. 402. '. . . There is no doubt that many true, just things are said in it. But anyone who reads it calmly cannot fail to see in many of its arguments the passionate Catholic against the free Protestant.' The passionate Catholic wrote in his *Choses passées*: 'I insinuated discreetly but firmly the need for a fundamental reform of biblical exegesis, of the whole of theology, and even of Catholicism in general' (p. 246).

general. He was not, of course, putting forward a philosophical system, or suggesting any theoretical conclusions, or any way in which things could be done: he was simply setting down the facts, from the point of view of an historian. Yet, in doing so, he hinted at the results these facts would necessarily and properly have, and, while avoiding a quarrel with the official Church, suggested the reforms he considered must be made in the interests of the Catholic Church itself. In a sense, Loisy was acting, here, as von Hügel planned to do: from within the Church, which was attacked by its traditional enemy, he was offering it a means of defence and renewal that could reinforce its intellectual discipline. This, he was to say himself, was an honest and loyal attempt which did not deserve the accusation (made by the Roman authorities) that it was based on total agnosticism, or on political opportunism.

But the authorities took only a few days to reach a decision: on 17 January 1903, Cardinal Richard, Archbishop of Paris, condemned the book and forbade the clergy and faithful of the diocese to read it,

On the grounds that:
1. It was published without the imprimatur required by the laws of the Church;
2. It is liable seriously to unsettle the belief of the faithful in the fundamental dogmas of Catholic teaching, notably those of the authority of the Scriptures and tradition, of the divinity of Jesus Christ, of infallible knowledge, of the redemption brought about by His death, of His resurrection, of the Eucharist, of the divine institution of the sovereign pontificate and episcopate.[1]

The censure was handled with exceptional intelligence, as Loisy himself was to admit; he himself had seen that the book was likely to disturb people and had regretted this in his diary, while in public —not just in his private meditations, that is—he had admitted that he had had a share in influencing the younger clergy. Shortly beforehand, on 27 October, he had himself written to Cardinal Mathieu on the subject:

There is now among the younger clergy a trend of thought which could be worrying because no one is guiding it and because it cannot be cut off short since it is a direct result of present circumstances. From the position in which I have been placed, by means it would not help to recall, I am simply giving a stimulus to the movement, and I cannot

[1] See *Mémoires*, II, p. 194.

moderate it. I was thrust into an exclusively scientific environment, I was more or less forced to immerse myself in pure criticism, and it is clear that if I pursue these studies, I shall be able to continue furthering biblical knowledge, but I shall find it impossible to work effectively towards reconciling this progress with equilibrium of faith and Catholic doctrine. With the best will in the world, I cannot prevent my course at the Sorbonne being anything except a technical initiation into a discipline which perhaps not all my listeners are able to cope with. Although everything possible has been done to prevent clergy from attending, my audience still contains a large number of ecclesiastics.[1]

The Archbishop of Paris's censure was followed by that of the Archbishop of Cambrai, and by the bishops of Autun, Angers, Bayeux, Neuilly, Nancy, and Perpignan. On 3 February Loisy made his first retraction to Cardinal Richard:

Monsignor . . .
I bow to the judgement made by Your Eminence in accordance with your episcopal right.
  It goes without saying that I condemn and detest all the errors which could have been inferred from my book by interpreting it from a point of view completely different from that which I felt obliged to take, and did in fact take, when I wrote it.[2]

This remarkable retraction, which from an ecclesiastical point of view was anything but satisfactory, in fact shows Loisy's intention far better than the condemnation itself does. As Loisy himself was later to admit, his partial retraction pointed out errors the condemnation had failed to mention: for all Cardinal Richard had complained of was the likelihood that the faithful would be perturbed by reading the book and in particular by its treatment of subjects fundamental to Christian faith: in a way this retraction stirred up further trouble. Loisy was unwilling to abandon the young priests and laymen who had begun to follow him, and urged them to escape theological tyranny, or get out of the Church; and in doing this he behaved as if he had a right to do so, or rather he recognized his own responsibility as a leader, just as he had done in his letter to Mathieu. On the other hand, he no longer confined his work within religious limits: while retracting obediently, as was his duty, he showed in his retraction where his real fault lay, and what was his work's true meaning. As an historical work, all it could be accused of was wrong information or faulty research,

[1] See ibid., II, p. 146.   [2] See ibid., II, p. 207.

or, at the most, errors of method: for this reason, Loisy explains in a second letter to Richard, 'certainly I reserve my personal opinion of all that has happened and is still happening with regard to this history book in which they are trying to find theological errors'.[1]

So once more Loisy defends his own autonomy and his own spheres of competence, as the only means by which to keep his freedom there: the historical method may discover a particular truth within another truth; the other may contain it, but it cannot subjugate it. This was Loisy's official defence in the case of a minor condemnation; although it scarcely applied yet, it showed clearly how he regarded his own position and his autonomy as an historian in the face of ecclesiastical authority. Yet it was still a formal reply that really had no connection with what he had in mind. He submitted, and retracted, in a sphere of competence he no longer recognized, because he hoped to safeguard the researches of friends working parallel with him. But he refused to clash with the authorities because the argument was taking place in a field which he not only failed to recognize as his own, but even failed to understand, or at least no longer considered right. Perhaps the official Church, at which his reforming zeal was directed, might have been helped; but the Church failed to realize that the intellectual movement to which Loisy, though still a faithful member of the Church, belonged, no longer accepted the Church's guidance or discipline, and was moving boldly in the opposite direction, dropping such things as theological quarrels, congregations and biblical commissions on its way, and with them the obedience and the demands imposed by the old laws of truth.

Thus Loisy failed von Hügel's hopes: from now on he was no longer one of those who might have renewed Catholicism from within; in a sense, after L'Évangile et l'Église he was no longer an active 'modernist', but someone to whom the 'modernists' kept turning as a point of reference. Von Hügel and others like him would turn to him personally, or to his thought, in order to nourish their own religious experience within the Church, and were strengthened by his thought in their struggle with the authorities. Loisy himself still had some sort of ecclesiastical life, which indeed was to be copied by others, but he could no longer be considered as intellectually loyal, or as having any of a Catholic's sense of responsibility towards the Church.

[1] See *Mémoires*, II, p. 209.

Possibly the first person who realized the change in Loisy was Blondel. Where the correspondence between Blondel, von Hügel, Loisy, Bremond, and other minor friends, which has only partly been published, deals with the publication of *L'Évangile et l'Église*, it shows one of the key moments in their movement of renewal.

I had read *L'Évangile et l'Église* with the keenest interest. . . . But, while admiring such a vivid, sensitive, and concrete sense of history, I confess that all the time I felt an uneasiness, the cause of which I can sum up in two statements: the untenable position of the historian who claims, in this subject, to take a purely historical standpoint; and an inadmissible tendency to apply to the person of Christ himself that unconscious or unexpected method of procedure and deduction which is often that of the Church. One feels that M. Loisy has at the back of his mind a christology which he does not define but which certain disconcerting insinuations (as also in his *Études évangéliques*) make us suspect. But is this a reason for immediately 'insinuating' that he is a Renan, or worse still?[1]

But the same day Blondel developed these two topics in a letter to Bremond, and a few days later told von Hügel of his disagreement. Blondel's friend Wehrlé, though, did not agree and asked Loisy himself to explain his christology, which Blondel had referred to. And it was Wehrlé who at last had to declare himself beaten, and who wrote to Blondel:

I was not scandalized when I first read it. Why? Because I freely admitted the dichotomy between scholar and priest, because I took orthodoxy for granted instead of looking for heresy, because I refused to see a defection in something intended to be a defence. Intelligent but unsophisticated readers have had the same impression as me. . . . And you have enlightened me on two precise points: the inherent defect in the method, which is the cause of the flaw in the book, but which exonerates the author; equivocal gifts which might incriminate M. Loisy's *real* christology and which could become, not only the pretext for impassioned calumny, but also the cause of, in a sense, a just condemnation.[2]

But to Wehrlé Loisy wrote:

You are infinitely better informed about my christology than I am . . . My only firm opinion on the subject is that there is a problem worth studying. . . . I am only a simple exegete of texts and higher philosophy is not my field: may the philosophers enlighten me![3]

[1] See *Correspondance Blondel–Valensin*, I, p. 111.
[2] Ibid.   [3] Ibid., I, pp. 111–12.

The same day, however, Wehrlé, who had been confidentially told by a superior of the seminary of the Institut catholique about Loisy's loss of faith, told his friend Blondel: 'Comme vous avez été clairvoyant! Quelle leçon vous m'avez donnée!' Blondel replied that he was 'douloureusement ému—plus que surpris', and saying that he could not write to Loisy after Cardinal Richard's condemnation, because he could 'ni le plaindre sans reserve ni le conseiller'.[1] But some days later Blondel himself took up the correspondence with Loisy again:

I am not asking him to give us a christology—he should not be obliged to on every occasion, but I fear that by his very method of posing certain problems he is systematically destroying the means of discharging a debt of which the historian has no more right than anyone else to relieve us. . . . Let us not judge M. Loisy. In all good faith he believes in his faith; let us respect his sincerity, his suffering, his commendable attempt to submit, all the more because his habits of thought and turn of mind make more heroic his duty to submit where he no doubt sees only incompetence, lack of intelligence, routine, and intrigue in front of him. And all that, and more, is there![2]

After more letters, however, Blondel became more intransigent:

The more I think about it, the more horrified I become by the inevitable results of 'historicism', which is in its way an unconscious and hence more exclusive ontology. What a long chapter I intend to write on the Prolegomena (not in a Kantian sense) to Exegesis, and the Methodology of biblical criticism! Between the scholastic and Kantian blocs . . . there is still room for something else.[3]

And after a direct exchange with Loisy (who wrote to him: 'Monsieur, Vous étiez né pour écrire des encycliques . . .')[4] Blondel, who in a way had taken over from Loisy, made clear what his own thoughts were, in opposition to Loisy's:

I have wasted, or at least spent, a lot of time over a very secret polemic with Loisy, and it is not over yet. But this exchange of views is helping me to define what I shall have to say on the serious question of the method of exegesis. On the whole, M. Loisy seems to me still to be the victim of that intellectualism which considers the historical view to represent a piece of reality, to represent reality itself, whereas beside

[1] *Correspondance Blondel–Valensin*, I, p. 122.
[2] Ibid., letters from Blondel to Wehrlé, 6 and 14 March 1903.
[3] Ibid., letter from Blondel to Mourret, 17 March 1903.
[4] Ibid., I, p. 113 letter from Loisy to Blondel, 22 February 1903.

reality it is an artificial substitute. At least in practice, he admits of no other method of coming to know Jesus authentically than by the regressive analysis of history; he does not have the slightest idea of the power of verification, investigation, and resurrection contained in moral experimentation, the secular effort of Christianity to feel and interpret the religious life of Christ.[1]

'Histoire et dogme' appeared in the *Quinzaine* early in 1904, and made it publicly clear that there was a split in the ranks. Blondel wrote his essay at the request of his friends Mourret, Wehrlé, Laberthonnière, and others; but von Hügel and in particular Giraud begged him not to intervene and thus facilitate Loisy's condemnation, which was obviously imminent but would be all the more easily made if supported by Blondel's authority. In any case, von Hügel disagreed with Blondel: his letters, and better still what he wrote in the same *Quinzaine* of Fonsegrive, made explicit Loisy's christology (which was implicit in *L'Évangile et l'Église*), without any philosophical support from Blondel. His unfortunate disagreement with von Hügel and many others, his reluctance to throw even an indirect light on what Loisy's friends and enemies were thinking, restrained Blondel, but did not stop him.

Trying to overcome Blondel's reluctance to criticize openly, Wehrlé wrote to him:

We are going through such a dangerous and complicated crisis that our responsibility for what we say or write is multiplied a hundredfold. We owe it to the superior interests of Truth in this world to sacrifice even the *enjoyment* of our most precious friendships to it. We need point no further than to the authority of God inside us and that of the Church outside us. If this double conformity—quite unique in its depth—is to be achieved at the price of the 'circumcision of the heart', we shall make our hearts bleed. But doing it we can only become more pleasing to God and more useful even to those we shall have contradicted.[2]

And some time later:

It is not merely my personal gratitude that I have expressed to you; in so far as I may be allowed to speak for the anonymous group of those suffering in the search for truth and who do not know you, in so far as I

---

[1] Ibid., I, p. 113, letter from Blondel to Mourret, 8 March 1903.
[2] Ibid., I, p. 113.

can speak for the Church, I thank you in the name of the souls caught in the turmoil, and in the name of the Church shaken by the tempest.[1]

After the publication of 'Histoire et dogme' a priest could write:

At one of the most painful epochs of our intellectual history they [Blondel and Loisy] have succeeded in . . . producing positive solutions. The Church has condemned Loisy, and she could not do otherwise. But . . . an impasse blocked up does not make a way out. Who averted a sterile and demoralizing delay? The authors of 'Histoire et dogme' and of *Réalisme chrétien*. We knew, we had been told, that the author of *L'Évangile et l'Église* was mistaken. At last *we saw why*.[2]

Yet, although Laberthonnière and Blondel had told some of the clergy why Loisy would be condemned, even before he was in fact condemned (*L'Évangile et l'Église* was put on the Index on 16 December 1903, together with *Religion d'Israël*, *Études évangeliques*, *Autour d'un petit livre*, and *Le quatrième Évangile*), von Hügel and Loisy, and some of the clergy with them, failed to recognize the 'new' orthodoxy in Blondel's philosophy, or the new meaning of exegesis which Blondel seemed to be using in his own case. Loisy, in particular, when writing to Blondel and to von Hügel, and later in his *Mémoires*, emphasizing his position as an historian—and it was as an historian that he wished above all to be considered—found nothing in Blondel's method but a visionary mysticism. Blondel, he wrote, refused to be satisfied with what appeared to the historian, wanted to put the Christ–God, conscious of his own divinity, at the point of departure of Christian history, as a necessary start to its evolution; now this, he maintained, was neither philosophy nor even metaphysics, it was Blondel's own immanentism, set, by an effort of will, or rather by a sort of vision, at the heart of history. To postulate the divinity of Jesus Christ as an indispensable explanation of what had happened to Christianity was arbitrary enough; to deduce the authenticity of the Gospels from this was pure fantasy. If faith demanded facts that were attested as being essentially false, so much the worse for faith: this was no method, but a reversal of reason in favour of a visionary mysticism. In order to say what he believed so boldly, Blondel must have a clear knowledge of what God was and find it perfectly natural for this God to have walked in Galilee and Jeru-

---

[1] *Correspondance Blondel–Valensin*, I, pp. 125–6, letter of 18 February 1903.
[2] Ibid., I, from Archambault's *Réalisme*, pp. 115, 127–8.

salem, working in the body of Jesus. Blondel was free to think so if he could, free to believe it if he wanted to, but for a philosopher it took great courage to do so, since it all meant nothing at all. For an historian, a philosopher, or a psychologist, the problem simply did not arise. Admittedly neither history nor any other branch of knowledge could exhaust the mystery of life, of religious and moral life, of the spirit of humanity, but only history and science could determine historical facts. To claim that experience could deal objectively with the virginal conception of Christ, with his psychological make-up, with the divine institution of the Church and so on, and to ignore the uncertainties and probabilities of history and of science and the scientific outlook as it evolved, was nonsense; such experience was, and always would be, visionary. Besides, religious experience, in the sense Blondel meant it, could not help making the absolute concepts of revelation—Christ's divinity, dogma, infallibility—inconceivable, unthinkable, and irretrievable, judged by the purely human experience of our time.

In short, Loisy concluded, Blondel appealed to the Church and its evidence, but the Church had already shown what it was like; what we must now do, therefore, was appeal to the evidence of the whole of humanity, past, present, and future.[1]

---

[1] The relationship between Loisy and Blondel will be made clearer by the complete publication—soon, one hopes—of the correspondence kept in the Blondel archives at Aix. What has already appeared (*Au cœur*) is enough to alter, at least to some extent, what one may have thought of it after reading Loisy's *Mémoires* and Blondel's official publications. Blondel's silence, well before the official, definitive, fatal break, had in fact been broken in a series of letters both with Loisy, and with friends of his and Loisy's, on the subject of *L'Évangile et l'Église* in particular; and before this the two men respected and trusted each other, although this is scarcely remembered and there seems hardly a sign of it in their public statements. Loisy had hoped to form an alliance with Blondel: this is clear in the letter he wrote Blondel in 1897, thanking him for sending his *Lettre*. 'I did not want [to thank you] before I had read what you had written and meantime I have sent you my own manifesto. We are innovators. Your philosophy can coexist with my exegesis. They have in common the attribute of having been disowned as heterodox and have escaped (we hope) the censure which some would have drawn on them. Your views on the union of theology and Aristotle have greatly impressed me. In fact it appears that scholasticism has been carrying two hostile brothers in its womb. What you say about philosophy, real philosophy, which is autonomous in its own sphere, cannot be denied, it seems to me. I too think that historical criticism, real historical criticism, is autonomous in its own sphere. But I am very much afraid that we are preaching in the wilderness, between the fanatical followers of science and the rationalizers of faith'; and he ends by inviting him to contribute to his

Thus Loisy moved away from von Hügel, who in spite of it remained his close, devoted friend, interpreting his thought and his intentions in a religious way, attributing spiritual anxieties to him, and defending him against Blondel; and in doing so chose his own way (which to his friends seemed lonely, and to himself seemed traditional and right), among the 'free spirits' of the age, where he naturally belonged. To these men, history and science, inspired by positivism and with no need of theology, had their own truth, for they themselves were truth.

On the opposite side was Blondel, the 'visionary', who gave his intellectual effort to the Church; the Church condemned the development of reason in Loisy, and made use of Blondel's revealing 'action'.

---

review. For the letters between Blondel and Loisy of special interest, see ibid., pp. 85–111, and see Blondel's last letter, which received no answer, in which he formulated the fundamental questions more clearly: 'There are no distinctions or abstractions which persist: you must give a definite answer to the question of whether you believe that Jesus had the feeling of really possessing his divinity. For the spontaneous reply you make to this question sets the tone even for your history and the principles which govern your criticism. . . . It is no longer a matter of theories, academic explanations, or formulae to be interpreted, like the word "consubstantial" or the expression "hypostatic union". It is a matter of elementary, simple, irreducible reality, on which I cannot help thinking the future of Catholicism and the truth and effectiveness of our faith depend. It is for this reason that you will forgive me for speaking frankly. Even if you were to pour scorn on me, I could not keep to myself my conviction that nothing in your work implies, in my opinion, such a conflict of faith against faith; that your work will retain its greatness without it and will acquire, in sacrificing it, irresistible force; that it is anything but "artificially constructed scaffolding"; there is a recurring experience, everlastingly renewed, directed, and illuminated: that, briefly, from the moment when you say that the Church, as a whole, is alone capable of giving birth to the authentic Christ, it becomes impossible, by means of whatever evasion or whatever reticence, to reach the point of saying that she has substituted one person for another.' (Ibid., p. 110.) The letter ends: 'But this time I am preaching to the converted and blaming my own chimeras.' It was 7 March 1903; but on 28 March he wrote to Wehrlé: 'De Bellevue, c'est fini.'

PART II

7. Minocchi

Loisy's *Mémoires* are a rich source of information about the movement for renewal and reform, in France in particular, but also in Catholic England and in Germany. In them can be seen what the clergy, sometimes supported by an active, wideawake laity, was doing in the field of exegesis and religious philosophy. In the *Mémoires* Loisy mentions and quotes letters from others, who, like himself, were pursuing their solitary researches, and, like him, were chafing under the authority of the Roman hierarchy and eagerly seeking some other solution to the question of religious discipline. Loisy often mentions Genocchi, Semeria, and Fracassini, but it does not appear that he ever drew upon their thought, or pursued a course of study parallel to theirs, or spoke the same critical language as Italian Catholic critics. It was simply that they were friends, who might associate themselves with him in a more liberal discipline, but had a common background and remained faithful to their religious vocation. Von Hügel was constantly reminding Loisy of them and of what they were thinking, as if he feared Loisy might become isolated and thus more vulnerable to the attacks of Rome; he always put forward his arguments for the truth in personalistic terms, and in these terms Loisy's isolation was, to say the least, unwise. Besides, von Hügel thought that Loisy himself wanted other critics to help him in a critical way, whereas in fact Loisy seemed to care nothing for this; and to von Hügel it seemed that his Italian friends, Semeria in particular, could alleviate Loisy's loneliness, and serve him as spiritual guides. Semeria had obviously used Loisy's exegesis in his own biblical research, had attended the Fribourg Congress with von Hügel, had contributed to Minocchi's *Studi religiosi* and was well known in Italy for the religious fervour of his preaching. In fact, it would seem that what von Hügel hoped for from his Italian friends was not so much intellectual stimulus for Loisy—at least in those years —as support for him at the Curia, and a sympathetic interpretation of his ideas there. Besides, every time these friends of von Hügel's spoke on philosophical, and particularly on exegetical, matters they seemed to be referring to Blondel and Loisy's ideas. It was not, of course, that they accepted things uncritically, but that they were seeking intellectual and critical pointers that above all suited their particular state of awareness at the time. It might be said that thanks to Loisy and Blondel's researches and example, Minocchi, Buonaiuti, Semeria, and many others looked about them at the conditions of religious life in Italy, made comparisons and considered how they might themselves do something on parallel lines, leading to a common idea of renewal; and also looked again at the possibility of continuing the Catholic reform that could include among its promoters the great figures of Gioberti, Rosmini, and Lambruschini.

And what about us? What have we done, as Catholics, as Italian priests? [Minocchi asked in the first number of his *Studi religiosi*, January–February 1901.] What defence have we set up against modern rationalism? Alas, since the days of the revolution we have said and done so much to restore our social ascendancy, and managed so little; so how can we flatter ourselves that we have done anything in the matter of religious knowledge, which has so far been so much out of touch with modern thought? . . . What then should we do, we who are intellectuals of a new age, which is not the age of the Fathers or Doctors of the Church? We must imitate the Fathers and the Doctors in the unity of their thought, but also in the variety of means they used to protect it. The centre of religious discussion is now no longer the field of theology or of philosophy, but the field of history; so let us enter it . . . Let us imitate the Fathers and the Doctors, and trusting in the Spirit that lives in our Christian conscience, look at these enemies of ours, and examine their science. Let us take these German, English, and French books on the studies, researches, and conclusions of the new religious learning. Let us concede probability to what is probable, let us demonstrate, and not merely say, that such-and-such a thing is false; let us all work and co-operate to create the new Catholic science, the new apologetic.[1]

Italian Catholics had, in fact, done something, as Minocchi himself says, with legitimate personal pride, both in his unpublished memoirs and in what he wrote announcing the closure of his review, and looking back over its seven years' publication. Minocchi had helped to spread ideas, and had enriched his review with contributions from men of learning, both Italian and foreign, who,

---

[1] S. Minocchi, 'Gli studi religiosi in Italia', in *Studi religiosi*, January–February, 1901, pp. 21–6.

perhaps for the first time, were invited to express their ideas and the results of their own and other people's research in a moderate and fairly safe context. And before *Studi religiosi* there had been other reviews that had, as he said himself, persuaded him to start his: don Romolo Murri's *Cultura sociale*, and, before this, Murri's other review, *Vita sociale*. There were also young priests who had been influenced by the school of Giovanni Battista De Rossi, the 'critical' archaeologist in whose teaching Minocchi saw the first, decisive use of the critical method that later became that of some of the modernists. Minocchi said that the reawakening, the appeal to history that consciously echoed what Foscolo had wished for, was protected, indeed promoted, very definitely by the Pope himself. This was, he wrote, 'the orthodox modernism of more or less all the modernists—real or presumed—in my day in Italy, and in France as well, except perhaps for Loisy'; and the founder of it was De Rossi, 'who in this opposed Renan, and whose pupil Loisy was at more or less the same time as Louis Duchesne and Batiffol were, quite openly, in Rome'.

De Rossi [Minocchi went on] started his 'great work' in the darkest hour of papal reaction to science and modern criticism, when Pius IX, already fully disappointed in his own liberalism, was preparing the *Syllabus*. The German protestants maintained that today, especially considering archaeology, excavations, inscriptions and historical discoveries of every kind, Christianity could and should be reconstructed, all the legends and lies with which tradition had for too long covered it should be scraped off, and then an old, true religion would emerge that was very different from the one arbitrarily postulated by the Church of Rome. Why, for instance, did they not excavate the catacombs? Why was the Church, why were the Popes, afraid of what might come out from a study of the monuments to those buried there? Pius IX was, in fact, afraid. But something must be done or at least attempted, since Ernest Renan had already begun to study the origins of Christianity, and with ideas so alien to the faith. De Rossi, who was well qualified for the task, a really learned man who respected, but did not idolize, traditions, set out to do this, spending years and years in the Catacombs, discovering and bringing to light a 'subterranean Rome'. And it was a triumph. De Rossi became famous everywhere, and his fame was all the more remarkable and admirable when you consider that while on the one hand his honesty and the sincerity of his intentions and of his work satisfied the protestants and rationalists, on the other he also managed to satisfy what was demanded by the most obscurantist Catholicism—that is, the Vatican's. In my time, when I was at the Collegio Capranica, and we were already discussing biblical and patristic criticism among ourselves, I heard everyone praising De Rossi as an incomparable teacher, and as one who set an example in research and methods that would give Catholic scientific studies that apologetic tone and air, respectful enough of the truth, without which scholars were always in danger of the Vatican's suspicion or anger . . . And who can say what impression was made on the soul [of Leo XIII], as on that of so many other cardinals, by De Rossi's hard and successful work, which showed (or seemed to show) modern man the ancient splendour of Church and Papacy more gloriously than ever? Having made philosophy secure, and having canonized thomism, that good Pope was nevertheless to admit that 'incrustations' of legend and story—as in archaeological monuments and documents—had been accumulated during the history of Catholicism, and damaged the true faith more than they helped it; and that even the ecclesiastical traditions of Holy Scripture were not free of such 'imperfections'. It seemed to him useful, indeed necessary, in the face of the intemperance of some of the cardinals, to eliminate this or that, and to promote historical and biblical studies. And thus little by little Leo XIII installed a programme of science for the clergy that was entirely new and modern, a programme of healthy apologetics for Catholicism which would be of advantage to the entire Roman Church. He thought, or tried to convince himself, that it was easy to move from words to deeds.[1]

In his memoirs Minocchi idealized the figure of Leo XIII and set it up against that of Pius X; indeed, he made him look like some hero in a popular print, fighting tyranny, the liberal compared with the illiberal pope; indeed, it was in this contrast between the two popes that he saw the representative characters of the modernistic controversy in the years 1880–1910. Minocchi also described the way he had himself been sent unwillingly into a seminary at the age of ten, by an uncle who urged and forced him into it. At twenty he was in Rome:

This centre of learning, indeed of the whole of Catholicism [he wrote], could not fail to attract me, to draw me to it, and to produce a profound, lasting impression on my spirit. The aesthetic and even mystical feeling, which made me feel it was really religious, found complete satisfaction in me in that Rome of great imperial traditions and fine art, among those wonderful ruins and splendid monuments that had lasted so many centuries; and I felt that religious studies, reasoning on them with

[1] See S. Minocchi, *Notes for the Memoirs*, manuscript, pp. 14–16.

thought, could not fail to illumine with heavenly light these august and venerable shades that, from the ancient catacombs to the grandiose Renaissance basilicas, bore witness so marvellously to the Catholic faith, ever wonderful and uniquely true.[1]

Rome, Catholic, Italian Rome,[2] was certainly fascinating to the young provincial seminarist, as it was to all the Italian modernists, who could never quite break free of it; to some, like Buonaiuti, it was the ideal towards which all their own difficulties and sufferings, and even their own errors and those of the reformers, were aiming, the point where secular and religious truth came together. But to Minocchi it meant above all the place in which he studied, in which his mind was formed, and with him, in those years at the end of the century, Buonaiuti, Murri, and Semeria.

So we studied in Rome [Minocchi continues in his memoirs] as we had not done in the provinces, especially in philosophy and even more so in theology. When we were out walking from one basilica to another, or at recreation time in the college, we often talked—as I imagine they

---

[1] S. Minocchi, ibid., pp. 23–4.

[2] On Rome in those years, see, for comparison, Carducci's *XX settembre*: 'Is Rome cosmopolitan? Indeed it is: as much so as the Syrian Rome of Heliogabalus. Look at it! A crowd of Protestants, Lutherans, Calvinists, Anglicans, thronging into the Holy Week services in St. Peter's as if going to the theatre; a mob of beggars who in three days send forty thousand appeals to a schismatic despot still smoking with Catholic blood; a middle class of landladies, pious gift-shop sellers, antique dealers, who sell everything, conscience, holiness, learning, fake relics of martyrs, fake relics of Scipio, and real women; a class of monsignori and abbés dressed up in capes of every sort and colour, who also buy and sell and laugh at everything; an aristocracy of hall porters; a society that from top to bottom, sacred and profane, in church and court, at home and school, is just as Settano and Belli describe it in their satires—that is, shamelessly sceptical, delicately immoral, calmly refusing to believe in or to feel whatever others may believe, admire, adore, or dream of as lofty, noble, virtuous, and human. Oh, what a city! Its government is by a caste wearing cassock and surplice, its finances are the mounting debts of three centuries and Jewish loans, its laws are the wavering whims of men in black skull-caps or red, its army the mercenaries of all Europe; this is the government that could be bribed by murderers, and that, in a city all springs and water, produced a filthy populace' (G. Carducci, *XX settembre, 1895*). According to *Civiltà cattolica*, to go to the opposite extreme, Rome stood up only, almost touristically, on the Pope's presence there. A well-documented essay on its economic decline says: 'Rome is a city whose council is burdened with debts, that has no capital behind it, no industry, and almost no commerce except what it uses up itself, run by an army of poorly paid public servants, with its richest, gayest and most important citizens fleeing it for half the year. Where, then, can it provide for itself except through people who come in from outside and spend money there? And who attracts them there in particular? The head of the Church, the Pope, who has his

did in other colleges—about our lessons: philosophy, theology, historical and biblical studies. Of course, we sang the praises of the pope above all, and afterwards of the 'gloriously reigning' Leo XIII, who, as the new age demanded, had reinstated learning, reintegrated the perennial philosophy, and reached perfection in the thought of St. Thomas Aquinas, on the basis of the unchangeable Catholic dogma and philosophy; who had encouraged historical studies by opening the Vatican archives, which were then secret, to scholars of every nation; who had been especially interested in studies on the Bible, even on what was called scientific criticism of the sacred texts, renewed as modern knowledge demanded, and so on. Our admiration knew no bounds, as tends to happen; we admired not only him but others, ecclesiastical or lay, who had set to work with the highest critical and apologetic intentions: among them we admired the Jesuits most, and rightly so; since year after year they taught thousands of us an exact science which they had learned through long practice and passed on to us for love of God.

Modernism had already begun, and worked secretly in the soul of each one of us. So that, in spite of all the good intentions of apologetics, we gradually found it hard to reconcile present-day scientific thought, even confined to the field of history and criticism, with what we were learning, or to achieve the age-old harmony between science and faith, when confined to the Procrustean bed of dogma, within the limitations

---

seat there' (series XVIII, vol. VII, 1251, July 1902, p. 275). The idea of Rome: a great historian like Federic Chabod can trace it throughout the dark ages and in particular in its steep fall towards the end of the nineteenth century, keeping admirably level-headed; and from private papers and public documents, newspapers, and encyclicals, wisely show how this idea was necessarily lost and found again, and how it can be considered almost a part of the historian's interpretation or even one of the great germinal ideas that influence history—not merely Italian history. A great historian can and should do this; but in order to do so he must do more than simply judge the facts or interpret the way they have gone. The Rome in which the poor modernist priests were seeking an ideal or Jesuits were seeking a controversy was a more dismal reality; not all Minocchi's or Bonaiuti's ingenuous passion could make it the cradle of a religious revolution. As for Carducci's 'cosmopolitan' Rome, we should remember what Sella said in a speech to the Chamber on 14 March 1881: 'One evening a distinguished man, Mommsen, asked me excitedly: "But what d'you mean to do in Rome? This is what worries us all. No one can be in Rome without cosmopolitan ideas." I told him: "Yes, we can't help having one cosmopolitan idea in Rome: the idea of science." ' This was taken up by scientists because it was recognized as 'a scientific feeling that now pervaded every side of social life, the inheritance of the great and the humble, which was owed to those responsible for the great discoveries, the great ideas, and the fertile practical activity of the whole of contemporary society' (see V. Volterra, *Il momento scientifico presente e la nuova società italiana per il progresso delle scienze*, inaugural lecture given at Parma, 25 September 1907, quoted in *Saggi scientifici*, Zanichelli, Bologna, 1920, pp. 99–100).

of the theological ideas of the Fathers and the philosophy of St. Thomas. If we could take into account the Anglican or Lutheran scientific work done on the Holy Scripture or on patristic studies, why were we forbidden to study the philosophers, even the most serious Catholic philosophers, like Rosmini? And why should we be forbidden to study 'positive theology'—as the Jesuits had called it in the sixteenth and seventeenth centuries—that is, the history of dogma? And why were patristic studies forbidden, in theological studies that were reduced to mere theories on medieval Thomistic foundations, so that a theologian like Cardinal Franzelin, who had even taught at the Collegio Romano, now seemed 'outstripped' and useless? And lastly, why was even the Bible forbidden from theology, and why were dogmatic demonstrations reduced to some main text, which was not without its obvious difficulties, conveniently ignored by the theologians?

The fairly obvious disagreement between the two branches of science, the abstract medieval and the realistic modern, made me pause; not so much out of curiosity, or rather because I had to spend my time in the cloister, but because I felt the importance and the value of that disagreement, in order to judge the truth of the Catholic faith to which, although against my will, I was now resigned to give myself. St. Paul's remark that faith must be 'reasonable', that is, conforming to reason and a consequence of it, became my watchword; and I wondered what reason and truth there could be in a theology wholly made up of abstract assertions and syllogisms built up—you might say—in isolation, without any historical support deduced from patrology or biblical science. When I went back into the world, I hoped I would not be ashamed of my faith, for which I had accepted to wear a garment I so much disliked; and I had already realized that the problem of my religion lay in making clear the relationship between theology and Holy Scripture.[1]

Minocchi was filled with these thoughts and doubts when a friend of his at the Collegio Lombardo, Giovanni Mercati, gave him the first numbers of Loisy's *Enseignement biblique*. 'This is a man who will do a great deal of good in the Church,' Mercati told him. 'He's very young; a pity he has such poor health.'[2] Minocchi was also given fresh heart to carry on his studies after the publica-

---

[1] See Minocchi, *Memoirs*, pp. 26–7.
[2] As regards Loisy's ill-health, Houtin writes (in his biography, p. 95): 'I was only gradually to diagnose the disease which was gnawing at him, but he had defined it himself twenty years previously in a marvellously precise way: he was, he said, suffering from "great fevers", *laborabat magnis febribus*, the fever for knowledge, the fever for work, the fever for glory.' (Thus Loisy had written in an exercise book of notes dated 24 April 1882.)

tion of *Providentissimus Deus*, which, like von Hügel and many others—but unlike the more vigilant, hostile Loisy—he thought a document of approval more than of criticism. 'I read it; I was pleased with it; I was almost enthusiastic about it, thinking over a new version of the Bible which I had it in mind to do.'

'I did not know,' he went on in his *Memoirs*, commenting on that renewed enthusiasm of his, which was quite out of proportion with the doubts of faith and the 'incurable' disagreement he had already mentioned,

or I did not then understand, being just out of the Gregoriana and extremely ingenuous, against whom the Encyclical was really aimed— that is, Loisy and the modernistic tendencies in France, much more than the protestants and rationalists of Renan's type. I did not know or did not then understand that this is just the method or system of the Catholic Church: to wish to promote scientific truth in the outside world, in harmony with the truth of the Christian faith, understood as the Pope understands it, but in reality to try to limit its scope and value, if science comes up against the practical interests of Catholicism. Above all I did not know or had not yet experienced, to my own harm and that of my conscience, the fact that between saying and doing, between the fine words and generic approvals of an Encyclical and the real execution later of the studies promoted and encouraged as easy and profitable, there lies, in practice, excommunication, or otherwise the need, the obligation to speak, not the bare, simple truth, but suitable subtleties and lies, often veiled in solemn and even hypocritical words.[1]

'In spite of this,' Minocchi goes on, contradicting himself a little—he cannot or will not, in his *Memoirs*, stick to the moral chronology of his doubts, and puts all the blame for his fatal ecclesiastical mistakes on his lack of a vocation to the religious life; never mentioning a lack of faith that he needed to achieve, not merely perfection, but even the orthodox catholicism of his researches:

I set out, full of hope, to translate the Psalms from their 'Hebrew truth' and to document them; and in order to publish my work had to tell a few lies. A few half-lies appeared in the Lamentations; and when I came to comment on the Song of Songs and had to give it the official mystical explanations, it was all a lie. So then I went on to translate the Proverbs. There, I found more lies to tell. I was tired of it, and stopped translating. They were small lies, admittedly, nothing so very shocking; they were

[1] See Minocchi's manuscript notes, pp. 45–53.

to do with the origin, age, author and meaning of some pages of the Old Testament, to which the Church had no real need to attribute any dogmatic and immutable truth. In time, and with knowledge and persuasive education, the clergy might be persuaded of this, and soon young priests we had influenced would adopt our ideas, which the old men might disapprove of and despise, but which had never been shown to be contrary to dogma. We must start teaching at once, not within the seminaries, which were closed to us through the fear and envy of those same ignorant old men, made presumptuous by their following within the Church; but through the press.[1]

Minocchi's first chance to influence young priests came with the editorship of the *Rivista bibliografica italiana*, 'an undistinguished little review, judging by the contents of its early numbers', but one that little by little turned into an accurate source of information that was 'Catholic, but secular in tone'. Books on religious questions were reviewed in it—English and German, Protestant and Anglican; there, Mercati made Harnack's work known in Italy, probably for the first time. But it was short-lived, from March 1896 to July 1899. Minocchi's second chance came after the Fribourg Congress, which he, like Semeria, Lagrange, and von Hügel, considered the great meeting of the youthful forces of the Catholic clergy and laity in the movement for reform protected and promoted by Leo XIII.

But at Fribourg I felt new courage. The smell of battle was there and everyone's hopes for a renewal of the Church revived. It was impressive to see the fourth Congress of Catholic Scholars, which later proved to be the most significant of them all, held in that stronghold of Roman loyalties; and the Congress became much more than a simple scientific gathering—it proved to be a kind of ecclesiastical council, strengthened by many eminent laymen, to set out a new programme of Christian apologetics. In order to be on the side of truth, it was not enough, today, to say one was a Catholic; what we wanted was to breathe some of that proved, scientific truth, within the Church, that alone could revive our age-old wavering faith. And if any authoritative protection were needed, in case of suspicion at Rome, there was the Dominican Order protecting and inspiring the university, and proposing, indeed almost imposing, its own programme of religious apologetics, as it had once had to do, and managed to do, with St. Thomas Aquinas. So the atmosphere was reassuring; indeed, it made people trust that some good results would come of it.

[1] Ibid.

There were a great many French, and Germans, English, Belgians, and even Americans: and there were Italians, outstanding among them, for his liveliness, quick wit, and easy eloquence, Semeria. Together with Wilpert and Kirsch, the priest Pierre Batiffol stood out for his knowledge of early Christianity, for his gentle manly charm and the decorous way in which he spoke and persuaded, in short for a certain episcopal behaviour *avant la lettre*, which stood him in good stead with people. But those who were most noticed as leading figures there were a Dominican friar and a layman: Fr. Lagrange, and Baron Friedrich von Hügel, an Austrian Catholic now a naturalized Englishman. These two were, at the right moment, to deal with the central problem which the Congress had already decided to tackle and to present to Rome well and truly settled, in order to gain its approval or at least a patient, if not kindly, agreement to further discussion; that is, how the discoveries of modern historical criticism, which were now quite definite and certain, could be accepted in conformity with the recent Encyclical on Biblical studies. Fr. Lagrange, an outstanding scholar who for the past five years had edited the prestigious *Revue biblique internationale*, was a man of faith and of well-proved ability, and no-one could doubt Baron von Hügel's intentions or good will. The effort to present the new method of studies on the Bible to clergy and laity could not, of course, mean a study of the New Testament. It was necessary to stick to the Old, and to deal with some problem that was important enough to make it clear, from the authorities' attitude to it, what their attitude would be to the discussion of other problems of the kind. And the subject suggested itself: the origins of the books of Moses, whether they were really his, written by him, or else composed some time later and gradually attributed to him, possibly centuries later. Tradition was opposed to this solution of the question; but, as a result of modern criticism, it was now necessary to give up this traditional attitude and to agree frankly with what had, for a century or more, been the views of the Church's enemies, rationalist or protestant.

And so it happened. It was a memorable afternoon when Lagrange and von Hügel presented their views in a report in one of the University lecture rooms. The room was not large, but packed with priests and laymen who applauded openly and enthusiastically. Some Jesuit was there, to speak up against it with the usual reservations; but he was silenced, and the two were praised more than ever. The Rubicon was crossed. Rome then had to reply. Catholic scholars, lay and clerical, given to natural science and history in relation to Christianity, rather than to philosophy, kept their faith firm and trusted fervently in the Church, though they wanted to breathe. From that point the Congress was over; and those who had promoted and organized it went round to those who had had the honour of taking an active part in it, collecting the manuscripts that later formed that magnificent series of ten or more volumes which remained to testify to the trust then placed in the scientific studies promoted by Leo XIII.[1]

The Fribourg Congress encouraged Minocchi to hope for success, and to see ahead of him the prospect of collaborating with others. He was reassured by the prudent, vigilant support of Rome and of some priests who, though they lived in Rome and had confidential work to do, did not hesitate to say in private that they believed in the need for reform.[2] After another short spell with the

[1] See Minocchi's manuscript notes, pp. 61–8. See, in another version of Minocchi's *Memoirs*: 'The feeling of freedom excited us all. Away with the Middle Ages! Away with empty, dry theology! Faith and dogma, if you will; but reanimated by history, by life, by the sacred flame of thought. And there was a hope in everyone, or so it seemed: the hope of overcoming, with Truth, the blind suspicions of Rome, the hope of breathing and living again, of not having to be ashamed of being Catholics. ... Thus modernism was born, in fact thus it "took wing" through Father Semeria, and "triumphed in arms" even in Italy.' Leon Ollé-Laprune had written a letter to the President of the Congress; at the Fourth Congress, too, the American Mgr. O'Connell praised Father Hecker's *Life*, then translated into French by the Abbé Felix Klein, the holy writ of Americanism. Blondel, though not much interested in the philosophical discussions that took place there, attended the Congress, reminded von Hügel of the Hexateuch, and met 'l'excellent P. Semeria, si vivant, si intéressant, et si bon' (letter from Blondel to von Hügel in 1897, quoted in *Au cœur*, p. 20). On the congress, see Loisy, for contrast: 'Clearly the Holy Father does not value the work of Catholic critics for its own sake and for its scientific worth,' interpreting both the Congress and the papal letter to the clergy of France as an act of open, or almost open, repudiation of their efforts. In this he differed from his friends and correspondents, who were very much displeased about his attitude, in particular von Hügel. (See *Choses passées*, 1920, where he quotes a text of those years.)

[2] Among these, Fr. Genocchi, who, after maintaining, with von Hügel and Lagrange at Fribourg, that the Mosaic books should be ascribed to an earlier age (from which came the disbanding of the Roman Biblical Society, set up by Parocchi), entertained at the casa dei Missionari in Rome, where von Hügel, Duchesne, Vigouroux, Spalding, O'Connell, Semeria, Ghignoni, don Brizio Casciola, and Fogazzaro used to meet. 'The philosophy of the Jesuits,' Minocchi wrote in his *Memoirs*, II, p. 13, 'Billot's theology, Thomism itself, were all abused there; and equally so were Fr. Cornely's "pseudo-critical" attitude and even more so the Abbé Vigouroux's views on the Bible. We discussed the neo-Catholic theology of Ollé-Laprune and of Blondel with interest, and in particular that of Laberthonnière. But above all we approved of Loisy's work, far more so than Lagrange's so far as biblical learning was concerned, and for its sincerity too. We laughed and sneered at the Roman court but no more than we did at the Jesuits. The recent pontifical letter [8 September 1899] to the French clergy in favour of the "pure text" of Thomism and the condemnation of what was called Americanism were likewise branded. ... But besides, it was clear and well known in the Vatican that Genocchi wished or urged or allowed *much that was true* to be said informally among Catholics. The only thing was it must not be

Rivista bibliografica, Minocchi founded *Studi religiosi,* and gathered round him scholars, both Italian and foreign, who believed that hope lay in the education of young priests, rather than in the persuasion or conversion of the old.

In this work I was encouraged [Minocchi wrote in his *Memoirs*] by the fact that meantime I had been in touch with students at the Pontificio Seminario Pio, and had been assured that such a review was eagerly awaited by the more intelligent of them. It would even be sure to reach the neighbouring Seminario Romano, with suitable precautions; this had so far been thought a stronghold of orthodoxy, but even there, young men who wanted a renewal of theology were to be found.[1]

Indeed they were: six or seven of them sent a secret letter to *Studi religiosi* when it first appeared, praising it and urging it to renew minds and spirits in a reform of the Church which—as they put it—was about to be lost in the lower depths of theology and speculation. Ernesto Buonaiuti was one of them, and in 1904 he began contributing to *Studi religiosi* with an article on Spencer and his work from the religious point of view, and an essay on neothomism at the university of Louvain.

When Minocchi took leave of his readers after seven years, he looked back over the work he had done and the history of his review, and was quite rightly able to claim that it had played its part in the cultural education of the Catholic clergy and laity. He mentioned the contributors and the subjects dealt with, year after year, in spite of all difficulties, and was able to say that he had collected all or nearly all those who were involved in religious research at the time (together with Semeria, Buonaiuti, Genocchi, Fracassini, von Hügel, Harnack, and Ghignoni) and all its problems too. In all this he had been faithful to the 'moderation which, though it may not win over its enemies, at least appeals to people of good faith', and had stopped short of a break with the authorities. When, in fact, they had at last spoken out definitely, he had submitted. He left others to argue over the rights of the case, and stood out not only and not so much for freedom of research as for that primary, unsubdued private freedom; that is, he was faithful to 'orthodox modernism', and, according to others,

---

written, or expressed in public. The Roman Church always behaved like this, Duchesne explained to us: indifferent to logical speculations and very careful of the way things were going and the religious feeling of the people.'
[1] See Minocchi, *Memoirs*, II, p. 14.

stood apart from the true modernism of the dissidents struck by *Pascendi*. Others, among them some of the contributors, could look back on those seven years of influence and renewal, and, unlike Minocchi, see, in the preparation which they meant and *Studi religiosi* so often illustrated, the reason for the break with authority: and in it, they found the strength to hold out. So it was with Buonaiuti and Murri.

8. Buonaiuti and Murri

Buonaiuti was too young to take part in the Fribourg Congress. He was born in 1881, and, after going to church schools, entered the seminario dell'Apollinare in Rome at the age of fifteen. In 1903 he was ordained. Unlike Minocchi, he was in no way forced into the priesthood; on the contrary, he had a definite religious vocation, and was conscious of it, from his earliest years. His need to understand the faith, to reason with Catholicism, was something he felt as precisely and as early in life. He read widely, especially in philosophy, but also in history and exegesis, and his immediate superiors viewed this with suspicion. In his autobiography Buonaiuti says he considered this reading was necessary to his faith: it provided rational and cultural comment on it. Reading, he says in his memoirs, 'only rekindled my enthusiasm and made me more and more interested in the affairs of that marvellous organism the Catholic Church, which I was approaching in order to become part of it, and in whose atmosphere . . . the warmth of spring seemed gradually to ripen.'

When he was nearly twenty, he read Kant and Blondel.

. . . I remember as if it were today the deep sense of pleasure with which, on the first night of the twentieth century, I spent the hours of darkness awake, deep in that masterly work, overflowing with the 'spirit of delicacy', in which Blondel tried to make out, bit by bit, the long road along which our need for Eternity and the Absolute, which cannot be overwhelmed or appeased in this world, climbs up to God, during our life.

Kant, on the other hand, left me hostile and unresponsive. It was probably my own physical and spiritual nature that made me incapable of appreciating speculative reflections that were not continuously and indissolubly linked to the reality of the perceptible world and to positive human and historical experience. But it was very much more the victorious, impassable impression I had received from my teacher Chiesa that made me thus. Instinctively, I was drawn to a vision of reality that everywhere and always meant perceiving an external world superior to and independent of any subjective capacity of thought, and I could not then and have never since managed to feel at ease in speculation that is a solitary analysis of our own mental condition, as if the world could not be considered except by it and through it. The apologetic of action, on the other hand, appeared to me the complement—in no way secondary or negligible—of the objective vision of reality that my constant study of St. Thomas's *Summa* only reinforced. I was to be a follower, all my life, of the traditional Mediterranean philosophy, codified by Aristotle in the classical world, and by St. Thomas in the Christian. I was, it is true, to do my best to clean up all those extraconceptual and extradialectical elements with which Thomistic thought is pervaded. I was to work perseveringly to make the experience of the Divine that which traditional Christianity really meant it to be, or rather, I was to try to restore to it features that were not strictly rational instead of those which metaphysical traditions have given it, and which are always an obstacle to what religious faith, in its original, definite form, can say and do. But all through life I was to feel, with growing vehemence, how absurd and harmful, how tragic and annihilating, were those forms of modern thought that, with foolish arrogance, have reduced reality to spirituality and spirituality to knowledge.[1]

Conjuring up the past and reconstructing what happened, telling the facts and making judgements upon them, Buonaiuti's autobiography gives a good impression of him as a young man. Minocchi's, though less inspired, had dealt with parallel experiences. A comparison between the two is at once significant. Minocchi, forced into considering matters that did not really interest him, considered that the whole problem turned on the opposition between two generations of churchmen, their contrasting attitudes in matters of faith and in particular in matters of scientific research. This was really all he put forward. In a way he took no part in the discussion but merely noted it and produced careful information for its use, in the donnish way of one whose personal dedication to the cause had no effect on the task carried out. Buonaiuti, who was slightly younger, saw in the opposition between the generations a struggle that was much wider and more meaningful than the usual disagreement between age-groups. From the beginning he realized there was a crisis: this, rather than a revival, was what he saw. And in this crisis not only the Church was involved, but the Mediterranean civilization whose wisest and most official exponent the Church itself was. To Minocchi, modern thought offered techniques of study and truths which the Church's teaching might employ; to Buonaiuti, this same modern thought and

[1] See Buonaiuti, *Pellegrino di Roma*, pp. 43-4.

these same truths meant an alternative to the Church's truth. Though it was always reappearing, it had so far been overwhelmed and reabsorbed in the wholeness of truth, but now it was violently seeking to assert itself independently of religious thought, and not merely against it.

Buonaiuti also considered the horizon of his life as a young priest, fearing for the Church he believed in. He realized, of course, that there was opposition between the generations and early chose which side he was on. But the point was not, or not merely, the struggle between progressives and reactionaries in the ecclesiastical hierarchy: it was a matter of the entire living structure of the Church. Like Tyrrell, who was also generous and religious, Buonaiuti had no use for hair-splitting and relative truths. Others, like Loisy, might be content with historical truths and exegetical discoveries, because the scholastic discipline meant nothing to them, and had had no part in forming their minds. But those who, like Tyrrell and Buonaiuti, had found the framework of scholasticism decisively important, felt that the only chance and hope of salvation lay in finding a way of reintegrating in it 'irrational', extraconceptual, and extradialectical elements, and of recognizing such elements, both in the real Thomistic thought itself and in the new course it had taken, when reinterpreted by Blondel. If the Church failed to recognize the danger of reaffirming her rationalism, absorbed from modern thought and mistakenly attributed to scholasticism, and if she took over the notional aspects, the special techniques, and the positivistic successes of this modern thought, then indeed she might be lost, though she had the chance—perhaps the last chance—of salvation within herself.

But the Church hardly seemed aware of this, as Buonaiuti, 'a young priest lost in the great world of Rome', came to see. Efforts were made to stop him studying, and Mgr. Benigni, who was to become one of the most pitiless organizers of the anti-modernist front, said with scornful sarcasm in the face of his hope and optimism: 'My dear friend, do you really think men are capable of any good in the world? History is one long, desperate retching, and the only thing humanity is fit for is the Inquisition.'[1]

And yet [Buonaiuti wrote] some obscure instinct made me feel that in this new age the priest, who represented the missionary tradition of the

[1] See Buonaiuti, *Pellegrino di Roma*, pp. 50-1.

Gospel, should fight with all his intellectual resources, in the field of religious knowledge and historical research. Even with my youthfully restricted view of things, I felt around me a disquieting sense of bewilderment, as all the old positions held by Catholic apologetics seemed to be tottering; so that those who stood for the new age saw a pressing need for a programme that would transform entirely all the old forms in which modern Catholicism was being mummified and sterilized. On the other hand, in the glow of Leo XIII's pontificate, which had striven above all to increase the clergy's influence and authority, I felt convinced that anyone who sought admission to the priesthood at the end of the nineteenth century must be very carefully prepared for it, culturally speaking, and must wish to serve his neighbour by educating him for, and guiding him towards, the new lines of thought and social conduct along which, it was clear, the future of the Gospel in the world now lay.[1]

---

[1] See Buonaiuti, ibid., pp. 46–7. See also *Una fede e una disciplina*, pp. 31–3: 'My vocation to the priesthood grew and was nourished from the dreams and hopes of the brightest years of Leo XIII's pontificate. It seemed then, between 1895 and 1900, that Catholic priests had the widest possibilities and the most promising plans before them. In cultural matters, as in social activities, it looked as if there were no peak we could not scale, no achievement in thought or organization too hard for us, that did not promise further development, and the blessing of Christian understanding and approval. An anxious, fearful man on the fringe of awareness, waiting to choose his way of life and to undertake work that would mean dedicating himself most fully to the highest, purest ends, would then have found, in the Catholic priesthood, the promise of a rich, healthy harvest.... My early days in the Catholic priesthood seemed full of hope for the future. I was very early called upon to teach Church history in the school in which I had done my theological training, and, young and fervent as I was, I felt that all my most deeply-felt wishes would be granted from then on, and that I could consecrate all my energies to the development of Italian catholic culture in the field which modern research had prepared on such a broad scale, and which the nature of culture demanded, that of historico-religious inquiry. But in my very passion to seek the historical development of Christian society in the analysis of the documentary evidence available lay the beginning of my own private ruin and anguish. The long seminary training in philosophy and theology had formed me in a certain mould of ideas, methods, and attitudes. From this I was suddenly thrust into a disconcertingly original discipline—that of the laws that governed historical studies; and this sudden change gave me new attitudes in my work, quite apart from those that were already a matter of faith and vocation, and, changed but not impoverished by the conflict, I dreamed more ardently than ever of proselytizing. I tried to do more than ever and with incautious enthusiasm sought to create forms of work that would allow the research into religious history, well known and well considered abroad and likely, in the future, to give our age its characteristic appearance, to become known among us in Italy. This was my undoing. Indeed, for the past fifteen years, my whole bitter existence might be said to have expiated my youthful dream of taking Italian Catholic culture to the level it had found in other countries, in matters of religious learning.'

Buonaiuti first considered these 'new lines of thought and social conduct' jointly in his memoirs; but then at once he tried to distinguish between them, in order to make clear what kind of renewal was needed, as distinct from the parallel movement for the political activity of Catholics, of which, from then onwards, Romolo Murri was the most active and best supported promoter.

Buonaiuti's first article, as a very young man, was in fact an open letter to Don Romolo Murri, which appeared in *Cultura sociale* in 1901, signed 'Novissimus'. In it Buonaiuti described the task of Christians, thus:

> In the uncertain, ambiguous dawn of the twentieth century, [the task] could only be one: that of putting all their spiritual energies into the difficult yet joyful task of recovering the real values of the spirit and of the Gospel, to use them, not as the flag of a party fighting against others, but as the soul of all social reforms that aimed at levelling up classes and bringing all souls together.[1]

Thus Buonaiuti already refused what was called political or social modernism, the third form of modernism, according to some historians, together with critical-exegetical modernism and literary modernism. Looking back from a distance of forty years, he did not alter the historical perspective, but simply remembered and set things down, as he had already done in the history of Catholic modernism in 1927.

The conflict with Murri was in fact an old one, and went back to Buonaiuti's early days. It was a clash of personalities that was to continue to the end of their lives, even after the crisis of modernism, and each was to take up a stand that bore out the reasons for their disagreement, right from the start. It was not a private quarrel (or at least it was not clarified or supported by personal invective), but went deeper than that; it corresponded to the cleft of opinion on the exponents and critics of modernism, and on its historians.

Indeed, a radical appraisal of the whole meaning of the modernistic movement, in Italy in particular, is involved when we consider Christian Democracy as an integral part, and as a practical projection, of a single movement of thought when the Church renewed its contact with the age it lived in; when we consider and understand the Roman authorities' attitude to the conflict between

---

[1] See *Pellegrino di Roma*, p. 60.

Catholic progressives and conservative theologians. The progressives—partly helped and partly hindered—tried to take a political part in the young Italian nation, pledging public support for 'the true values of the Spirit and the Gospel', which they may have wanted only as part of what was generally new and desirable. If, on the contrary, we refuse to recognize the relationship and see the fact that Catholics were taking part in public life as an aspect of nineteenth-century Italian history, something quite independent of the crisis of modernism in Italy and elsewhere and due to the break in the Catholic front that followed the forced ending of the Church's temporal power, we cannot fail to consider the meaning of modernism in a different way.

Some, like Murri, wanted Catholics to regain temporal power; wanted them to take over from those who denied the faith in the very field in which, entrenched in their new ideas of social justice and democracy, they seemed strongest. Others, like Buonaiuti, cared nothing for all this. And the two sides could not fail to be in conflict. For to those who thought as Murri did, the Church at the end of the nineteenth century and in the early years of the twentieth, after the decrees of the Vatican Council, was a solid, historically determined reality under the Pope's disciplinary and doctrinal authority, a living organism in the community of the faithful that must prove its truth with the means and the methods that history had provided, and in present-day conditions. Whereas those who thought as Buonaiuti did considered that the Church could not set up as a temporal power: when the whole principle of the world was totally alien to it, there was no question of making a choice between this or that in it, or supporting now this side, or now that. Murri felt that the whole idea of the world must be combated; Buonaiuti that only this idea could restore the Church's authority. So each side judged the ecclesiastical authorities in its own way, particularly with regard to their apparent awareness of what needed to be done at that particular time.

We stand with the Church and with Rome, and shall always do so [Murri wrote in an article entitled 'Forever with Rome and for Rome' in *Cultura sociale*, 1 November 1901]. But when the longing for change becomes so intense that the Church seems to follow too slowly, when any declaration fails to find approval, either in itself or because it goes too far—and truth that goes too far always contains some error—, when there is any conflict in which Rome can be clearly distinguished on the one hand, and those it opposes on the other, then we shall always be, without hesitation or discussion, on the side of Rome, [for] once the strong unity of faith and trust in the Church's authority is lost, nothing remains but each individual's subjective, personal standards and the authority of the State; the latter pagan by nature, the former uncertain by nature and so infinitely variable.[1]

But this being 'on the side of Rome' was something quite unlike Buonaiuti's yearning for Rome, and can be considered as being a party stand against a long-term prospect. Indeed, when he recalled his early years, Murri insisted, coherently, on his awareness of the world of history, just as Buonaiuti, equally coherently, insisted on his criticism of the Church's misuse of history, of the way the Catholic hierarchy apparently accepted the world of empirical values, which was radically opposed to the true essence of Christianity.

I understood that even to serve Catholicism [Murri wrote in the preface to one of his last books] and the truth I undisturbedly possessed, it was not enough to *believe* and *think*: it was also necessary to *see*: to realize the historical conditions in which Catholicism developed, and the close relationship between it and all the other historical factors, as it developed. When I suddenly came into contact with modern thought, its social movements and political doctrines, I realized with the liveliest interest that this was where we must carry the fight, this was where we must make a careful study of our opportunities and obstacles, of those who might support us and those who would definitely oppose us. In particular I realized that there was a growing historical force in the proletariat's new and legitimate awareness of its own humanity. Evil teachers were exploiting this force, which must be freed and led elsewhere. The materialistic denial could not plumb the depths of Christian truth and spirituality; but historical criticism made me realize that many militant Catholics had no understanding of history and supported what was politically old and shaky, a disintegrating world. . . . And so an entire broad plan began to come to me, one that would awaken Catholics, bring their culture up to date, and lead them to new social and political action.[2]

Murri was never puzzled, and in his doctrinal thinking was always scholastically orthodox ('scholastique ferme et inconvertis-

[1] See R. Murri, article quoted in *Politica di parte cattolica* (1898–1901), *Battaglie d'oggi*, Vol. I, pp. 18–19, Rome, 1903.

[2] See R. Murri, *Alla ricerca di te stesso. Saggio di una dottrina della personalità*, Bompiani, Milan, 1939, p. x.

sable', Loisy was to define him[1]). His revolution consisted in asking militant Catholics to seek the reasons for their weakness within themselves, as he put it, and to consider Catholics just as if they were a political party or group. This idea of a religious class was, as Buonaiuti realized at once, a dangerous heresy within the framework of official Catholicism.

But Buonaiuti was probably the only one to point out the 'political' danger, and to take up a stand on it straight away. In a letter signed 'Novissimus', followed by a second letter on the same subject a few days later and also published in Murri's own review, he inveighed against the error of unnaturally mixing faith and reason and therefore political and religious life, and he was one of the few who refused to see any connection between modernism and 'Christian Democracy'.[2] Not the only one, though: for Murri also saw no connection between the two movements and for this reason did not consider himself rebuked by *Pascendi*. But what the two men had in common was more their behaviour towards the authorities: both refused to obey. Buonaiuti took a stand against the doctrinal orthodoxy of the Church, for he believed there was an error inherent in it; Murri against the Church's disciplinary authority, for he believed in the political freedom of Catholics. For both, it was as if the Vatican Council's work for

[1] See Loisy, *Mémoires*, II, p. 561.

[2] See what Buonaiuti was to write supporting this idea in his *Modernismo cattolico* (Modena, 1943, but earlier in a French edition, Rieder, Paris, 1927): 'In examining the specific expressions of modernism, I have deliberately avoided dealing with what is called "Christian democracy". This had no really religious intention and implied no attitudes that were actually opposed to the spirit of orthodox Catholicism. This is proved by the fact that when the Popular Party produced its complete political and social programme in Italy, the authorities in the Church solemnly gave their approval. Besides, in a more general way, there were very few points of contact between the Christian democratic movement and the profound crisis of ideas that shook the established Christian churches. The Popular Party's lack of success, in fact, shows this plainly; it shot meteor-like across the horizon of Italian politics, and left no genuine Christian spirit behind it' (p. 133, in a note, Italian edition; p. 98, in a note, French edition). But see as a contrast, Murri, *Dalla Democrazia cristiana al Partito Popolare Italiano* (Battistelli, Florence, 1920) and, among the historians of modernism, Paul Sabatier, *Les Modernistes* (Fischbacker, Paris, 1909), for whom 'the originality of Murri and his associates in the Lega Democratica Nazionale lay in their pursuing simultaneously a double renewal, political renewal, and intellectual and religious renewal' (p. 69). Sabatier even maintained, not very credibly, that *Pascendi*'s lack of emphasis on political modernism was due to the fact that those who drew up the document, all being non-Italian theologians, were unwilling to allow an Italian, that is Murri, so much importance in the modernist heresy.

unity of discipline and doctrine, authority and orthodoxy, had never been.

Moreover, once they were aware of what they were doing, Buonaiuti and with him Loisy in his early days, von Hügel, and Tyrrell, planned to take action within the Church, to work on the Church itself; Murri planned to work on Catholics, both clerical and lay, but lay in particular. Buonaiuti and the others aimed to reform the Church, Murri aimed to form a great party of democratic Catholics, free from obedience to the religious authorities in matters of social organization and in the exercise of political power; and their dissimilar estimate of Leo XIII's pontificate also bore out the conflict between them.

Buonaiuti's conviction was shared, in an imaginative way, by von Hügel; and the contributors to Minocchi's *Studi religiosi*, who like him aimed to promote a religious culture among the Catholic clergy and laity, seemed sympathetic; but it found few real supporters. In particular, the laymen whose support could have meant an alliance of men capable of restoring hope in a 'spiritual' Catholicism, failed to agree with Buonaiuti. When these laymen, and many clergy as well, came to consider recent Italian history and culture, up to the Catholic renewal that followed the ending of temporal power, they kept finding, in Gioberti and Rosmini, examples of 'Catholic reform' condemned by the Church. These great men's thought could, of course, be reconsidered, and indeed the same 'modernist' reviews had articles on Gioberti and Rosmini; but this thought of theirs seemed not to have worked within the range of religious culture, within the very thought of the Church itself: Leo XIII's new use of scholastic terms appeared at the same time as the proposals dealt with in Rosmini's works were condemned again; an entire new Syllabus could be made from Gioberti's notes for his *Libertà cattolica*, and this new Syllabus could be shown for approval to Gioacchino Pecci himself, who had the idea of the original Syllabus and had handed it on to Pius IX, and who, as Leo XIII, might not have denied what he had done earlier; few knew anything of the solitary Lambruschini's solitary thoughts, and Gino Capponi himself seems to have destroyed the letters addressed to him because they were too compromising. So what hope was there of a national religious culture in opposition to the Church of Rome, what chance had Gioberti's idea of 'reforming positive religion and bringing it into line with science and civilization'? It was Rome that must reform Rome, Gioberti had written, those who needed reforming must reform themselves. But what had happened to the proposal, which he himself had admitted was a hard one?

'Catholicism will gradually transform itself and realize all possible hopes based on it,' Gioberti went on.

The more intelligible, rational and participating it becomes, the more it will become rationalism. But Catholic rationalism will always show its supernatural past and origins; it will no more sacrifice the past to the present than the present to the past; it will never allow change to defile and destroy what is unchanging. But the more it develops, and implements certain ideas that until now have been confused, the more it will become the kingdom of the Spirit, the Gospel according to St. John. But all this will be done in a spiritual, ideal and participating way; there will be no new apostolate, no new rite, no new revelation. The exterior form of worship will last for ever, like the hierarchy; and, as the Church is master of the sacraments and its orders, it will alter both hierarchy and forms of worship to suit the times. The hierarchy will become simpler and more liberal, the forms of worship more spiritual; and thus it will become protestantism, but a gradual, orthodox protestantism, without anything violent, aggressive, revolutionary or insubordinate about it, a protestantism that will destroy neither the apostolic continuity of the priesthood nor the essence of the liturgy. . . . A new age is to begin for Rome. An age of great ideas in theology, an age of civilization, of tolerance . . .[1]

This was inspired writing, certainly, but it was looking to the future, a future in which freedom would be found, and with it the kingdom of heaven. Reform was to come later, and Gioberti could prophesy the way it would be to those who, like himself, were waiting and longing for it, both for themselves and for the Church; but half a century after he wrote, the vision was still prophetic, the future still lay ahead, and its constant postponement could not fail to alter people's view of it.

It was to this reform in the future that Murri opposed the present: 'We have ceased to submit to Italian life, we are beginning to understand it and to overcome it; we no longer speak in protest and *prophecy*, but to express an active, overwhelming desire.'[2] And

[1] V. Gioberti, of *Della riforma cattolica*, in E. Buonaiuti, *Il modernismo cattolico*, pp. 129–30.
[2] R. Murri in *Cultura sociale*, 1889, reprinted in *Politica di parte cattolica*, p. 168. Murri often returned to the subject of Gioberti: 'Of the Primacy's

it is easy to see how many of the Italian Catholics, anxious to promote reform, hailed as something new and healthy his grasp of the reality of history and his demand for effective, pragmatic action. Here, at last, things were being done instead of merely planned. Young priests and Catholic laymen who wished to take part in public affairs gathered round Murri.[1] Ordained in 1892,

widespread tendency, for a few years after Gioberti's book, to involve the Church in Italian politics, and its fleeting success in doing so, I will say nothing here, for it did not influence the Italian clergy in any substantial way. Even Rosmini's and Gioberti's bold efforts at reform I will mention only briefly, for the Italian clergy fully opposed their ideas, which were partly extreme and therefore intemperate, and so, instead of helping the clergy to change, they indirectly held it back for some years and stirred up trouble that still continues. Rosmini and Gioberti both had fine intellects, but—and this was especially true of Rosmini—their fore-knowledge of the future was not matched by tolerance of and respect for the present, which could not, after all, suddenly be abolished.' Murri considered that Gioberti's work was made pointless and unproductive by his dispute with the Jesuits, which he thought was a great battle fought for the good of religion and of Italy; whereas, Murri considered, it was nothing of the kind, but did widespread damage. Even more harmful and dangerous were the philosophical and ideological ideas of the man who started it. 'The truth is,' Murri continued, 'that the dispute did enormous harm to cultural and political progress in Italy, because it ended by dividing Catholics and reformers more than ever, under-mined Pius IX's generous approaches completely, and produced the policy of pointless immobility on the one hand and headlong change on the other that has led to today's dissensions.' Murri, who by examining Gioberti's failure deduced what had to characterize his own actions, considered that a fault of moral Christianity, which a future historian was to point out, was a failure to analyse social vices and defects 'in seeking for ways in which to lead, not isolated souls, but whole generations of Christians, in seeking how to rise to a perfection ever higher than the entire human duty'. Murri, that is, was seeking a morality for whole peoples, for human groups, instead of a morality for individuals, or inde-pendent of public morality; a social ethic that was not necessarily the result of individual ethic: the object of the clergy's apostolate was now collective rather than individual, and in fact it foreshadowed the role of the party as the practical symbol of the ethic of the group. 'Let morality emerge from the restrictions that have hemmed it in for centuries, and show man how to do good, how to do all that is good. Recall the Catholic conscience to the study of its political, economic and social duties, as of all the rest ... Why not (in place of the confessor's morality) have the morality of the whole Church, raising individuals and whole peoples to spiritual and supernatural ends, taking over and perfecting all the great ethical standards of morality in the light of the Gospel? ... We should thus widen and raise the horizons of the Catholic moralist ... and make practical, positive plans for a social, economic, political and artistic morality that reformed not only the individual but social life itself' (*Battaglie d'oggi*, II, *La cultura del clero, Lettere a G.[iovanni] S.[emeria]*, Rome, 1901, but written in 1898 and appearing under the signature P. Averri in *Cultura sociale*, pp. 47, 49 and *passim*.

[1] Romolo Murri, born at Montesampietrangeli, in the province of Ascoli Piceno, in 1870, attended seminaries in Recanati and Ferno, and took his degree in philosophy in 1887 and in theology in 1892.

Murri had immediately started an academic review, *Vita nova*, the first number of which appeared in February 1895;[1] some years later he produced one of the most remarkable and important clerical reviews, *Cultura sociale*, which soon after the appearance of its first number on 1 January 1898 had 4,000 subscribers. Both *Vita nova* and *Cultura sociale*[2] differed from other Catholic periodicals at the turn of the century in the emphasis they placed on politics: in the very first number of *Vita nova* the review's programme shows the group's social bias: 'Owing to the particular conditions at the moment,' it said, 'we have decided to give special attention to the study of social questions.'[3]

The *Rivista internazionale di scienze sociali e discipline ausiliarie*, published in Genoa from 1893 under the editorship of Giuseppe Toniolo and Mgr. Salvatore Talamo, following the First Italian Catholic Congress of Social Studies held in Genoa the previous year, and started at the wish of Leo XIII, kept to research and toed the encyclicals' line. If it can be called the Catholic answer to *Critica sociale*, its answer consists in particular in opposing the political use of the social question. The conflict between the two positions was soon clear, besides, in the first draft of the Christian Democrats' programme, drawn up by Murri and G. B. Valente towards the end of 1899: fundamental points in this were preparation without direct participation ('preparazione nell'astensione'—against the other formula 'Né eletti, né elettori'), the idea of a Catholic party to compete in the new democratic age, and the postponement of a settlement of the Roman question. A few months were enough to spoil the chances of a common

[1] See, in the January 1896 number of *Vita nova*, the remarkable contrast between the editorial, entitled 'Il segretario del popolo' ('Public assistance officer') where expressions like 'The state studies inefficacious laws, collectivism incites hatred, takes advantage of suffering to make propaganda ... only the Church teaches and acts: only she can give an effective hand to restoring social evils, only she has shown that she is capable of improving them' are found, with the mellifluous poem: *Landscape*, dedicated to Luisa A., by Salvatore Minocchi.

[2] In the first number Murri praised 'those who have contributed to the present civil independence and internal political freedom in Italy', and maintained that he 'wished not only to accept, but actually to promote, those values traditionally considered outside the range of Catholics, and especially of priests, such as independence from foreign powers, civil liberty, constitutional life, popular franchise, progress in every form of culture and public activity'.

[3] In the same year, 1895, the first number appeared of *Ora presente*, a religious and literary journal started in Rome by Giulio Salvadori and Antonietta Giacomelli, and influenced mainly by the Christian anti-materialistic movement. Tommaso Gallarati Scotti's first religious essays appeared in it.

plan or even of collaboration: in January 1901 the encyclical *Graves de communi* admitted that the name 'Christian Democracy' was allowable, but in the sense of Christian good works in favour of people in general, 'without any political meaning' (Filippo Meda then wrote in *La scuola cattolica* in Milan that Christian Democracy had thus 'come of age and reached its full juridical capacity'[1]). In January of the following year the official instructions on the reform of the statutes and regulations of the Opera dei Congressi forbade the formation of a party and said 'Catholic democrats must always keep alive in the people a sense and a conviction of the intolerable conditions the Church found itself in after the invasion of its secular state'. In August of the same year, 1902, Don Romolo Murri in his speech at San Marino asked for 'freedom for the Catholic laity to break with the past, which the young Christian Democrats do not feel they want to inherit in its entirety, explicit condemnation of "clerical" social politics as conservative, and rejection of the bishops' right to political direction of the Catholic movement for renewal, which was now looking in new directions'.[2]

---

[1] In *La scuola cattolica*, January–February, 1909.

[2] The speech was published in Rome in *Domani d'Italia* on 31 August and in a pamphlet entitled *Freedom and Christianity. A speech given 24 August 1902 in the Republic of San Marino at the solemn meeting of the International Christian Democratic Congress*, Società I.C. di Cultura Editrice, Rome, 1902. On 23 September a bulletin was issued by the Vicariate: 'A speech made in the Republic of San Marino on 24 August has particularly saddened the fatherly heart of the Supreme Pontiff, whom many Bishops, worried about its ill effects, thought it their duty to inform. When this speech was carefully examined it was found to be shameful and worthy of censure. We also deplore the writings inspired by the author of the speech at San Marino, which we often see. Catholics should instead fully trust the Second Group of the Opera dei Congressi, since it is faithful to the Pope's teaching and in particular to the instructions and standards laid down by the Holy See on 22 January of this year.' Don Romolo Murri submitted on 27 September (see *Giornale d'Italia* of 27 September). The same number of *Civiltà cattolica* that quotes the bulletin declares: 'By the Most Reverend Father Superior of the Sacred Palace we are authorized publicly to declare that neither this number [of July–August 1902] nor any other of the Florentine journal *Studi religiosi* was ever approved in Rome by the ecclesiastical authority, either on its own initiative, or, still less, by the pontifical delegation, although this approval was requested' (contrary to what had been said by the Libreria Editrice Pustet, co-publisher of the journal) (*Civiltà cattolica*, series XVIII, vol. VIII, No. 1255, 26 September 1902, p. 76).

9. Fogazzaro

When we consider the various groups, and their particular attitudes, it becomes clear that those years, in Italy too, were characterized by a movement for reform that started within the Church itself. The reformers hoped to alter either the Church's doctrinal discipline or its disciplinary structure, and for a while it looked as though the hierarchy would support such changes; but, after a period of uncertainty, the reformers had to admit that it was impossible for them and the authorities to carry on freely together, whatever form their disagreements took. However, not all the reformers despaired at the same time or in the same way: while some took a radical stand, others continued to hope for a compromise. It is possible, too, to find obedience and intransigence in the one person: Murri, for instance, was convinced of the need to break with the Catholic hierarchy, so far as its efforts to direct the social and political activity of Catholics were concerned, but he was not upheld by a parallel conviction of the need to refute the Church's theological teaching; Buonaiuti considered that both Murri and the hierarchy interpreted the Christian message in a positivistic way; Minocchi believed in the need to raise the standard of culture in the clergy, but, apart from a personal hatred of scholasticism, had no plans for a radical reform of apologetics and foresaw no social activity for the newly educated clergy, as a result of their new education. And the fact that these attitudes—submissive or rebellious—existed side by side meant that there was not a single battle-array, and that, at least for several years, the reformers could collaborate with men whose own experience and spiritual gifts seemed to increase the hope of conciliation.

Of these, Antonio Fogazzaro is certainly the most revealing. If Italians, then, were interested in, or rather anxious about, the problems of contemporary religion (which they were traditionally indifferent to at the beginning of the century), this was due largely to his fame as a writer. The way he used religious feelings and sometimes ideas in his novels meant that a certain Catholic spirituality was established, hardly typical of the new way religious culture was tending, yet influential in spreading the new attitudes and in diminishing the atmosphere of anti-clerical indifference and irony, especially in certain sections of the liberal middle classes. Fogazzaro was as sincerely committed as he was ideologically confused, he was curious in matters of religion and culture and ingenuous in matters of theology; a man who was always sensitive yet had some critical acumen, which is often denied him, and some courage as well—far more than his Milanese friends, who in the name of prudence criticized some of the stands taken by their 'revered master'. All this meant he was rather more, rather better, than a decadent writer who turned out a single good novel and any number of lyrics dealing with faith and adultery. Certainly Fogazzaro, between bouts of tenderness, peppered letters to his mistresses with outbursts on faith and morals, spiritual reading, and religious doubts; but then his letters to Mgr. Bonomelli, his beloved confessor and confidant, contain ideas of redemption through love affairs, those to clerics have gobbets of novels in them, those to his family plans for political renewal. All this annoys us today, as it annoyed his correspondents. But Fogazzaro never made conscious use of his own ambiguity in thus combining opposites of feeling and experience, and never sought to press his advantage by exploiting the interest which such ambiguity might in itself have aroused. He was subject to religious upheavals, and, in the best tradition of European decadence, these upheavals generally occurred when the flesh was tempted; his religious poetry belonged to the same world as his literary poetry, his religious heroes had the tastes of secular lovers. But all this did not mean that he was not personally interested, often just as passionately, in religious disputes, or in ideas on the religious education of the laity or the political responsibility of Catholics. Admittedly his *Santo*, together with his tempted foreign ladies, is all too easy to caricature; but we should bear in mind the fact that it was put on the Index not for offending against good taste but because, at two removes from reality, through his medium-hero, Fogazzaro was proposing reform.

Fogazzaro was also responsible for the fact that some Catholic laymen in Italy conceived the idea of taking part in the life of the Church. Following his example, they even dared to intervene in matters of doctrine, and thus belonged to the ideal group of learned Catholics von Hügel hoped to see formed; a group he duped himself into thinking actually existed in his friends and correspondents, lay and clerical. Fogazzaro, indeed, seems to belong to this ideal group. He was ten years older than von Hügel and thus not a part of the generation of Buonaiuti and Murri, the most radical of the Italian reformers; and he was ahead of them in matters of faith in that he had already given a number of lectures in Italy and France on the possible religious interpretation of the theory of evolution. These lectures were not essays, studies, or the results of research; Fogazzaro believed that by speaking he would spread his ideas more widely, and he had a missionary zeal in doing so. The talks were widely discussed and drew the first fire of the Catholic press, in particular that of *Civiltà cattolica*, which reproached him less for individual ideas than for the fact he, a layman, 'had on his own authority proposed to teach the faithful what it should or should not believe or how it should in future conceive the creation, in order to get a worthier idea of the Creator'.[1] Fogazzaro had assumed the right to take part in the Church's doctrinal life, and had violated its discipline 'where it mattered most', as *Civiltà cattolica* put it. In reply Fogazzaro publicly invoked the freedom of lay believers to fight for their own faith.[2] Possibly those who attended his lectures—both hierarchy and laymen—were more interested in this right and the violation he was accused of than in the doctrine he put forward explicitly

[1] See *Civiltà cattolica* of 15 and 31 October 1893, which continues: 'There is no difference between setting up to teach religion and giving lectures, and preaching in church, except that those who preach do so in cotta and stole, and those who lecture do so in tails and white tie; but Catholic laymen should not usurp the function of the priesthood.'

[2] See Fogazzaro's letter to L. M. Billia, editor of the *Nuovo Risorgimento* and published by him under the title of *Pro Libertate*, vol. IV, No. 2 (printed in *Ascensioni Umane*, Milan, 1899, 4th ed., pp. 185–99): '. . . I should like to say to my critic in *Civiltà cattolica*: "Of necessity we mix more than you do with the enemies of Christ and of the Church. The proudest, most intelligent, and most famous of these today agree in proclaiming the ruin of our faith through a scientific hypothesis supported by the great majority of natural scientists. Many ignorant people throw this up at us. And yet we believe that if the hypothesis were proved tomorrow it would not move our faith in the least, in fact it would give even greater glory to God. Allow us to say this at our peril. Do not approve us publicly, but do not condemn us either, do not throw us unarmed under the feet of the enemy. We will never say that your silence implies approval. Silence is silence. If the hypothesis crumbles, all our work crumbles with it; if it is confirmed, you will not regret having ignored us." Besides, in my speech, I was careful to make it clear that I was not trying to teach a doctrine but only trying to defend a freedom I use against materialistic philosophy . . . All I meant to say was that what St. Augustine could do, I could do too.'

and fought for. But Fogazzaro was moved to share his ideas by a wish to free his personal faith, and through it that of others, from the influences of current theology, and to stand up to the efforts of science, and in particular of the theory of evolution, to undermine the basis of Christian revelation. This he had been led to do by the works of German and American scientists and religious, who found that the theory of evolution could be brought into line with the theory of creation as it was found in St. Augustine.[1]

Fogazzaro's attitudes and religious ideas are very tellingly expressed in a letter to Gaetano Negri, written in the same year as the lectures:

. . . Just because you value me a little, you will find it easy, dear Negri, to believe that I would have been happy if you had said: 'Fogazzaro is guilty of presumption in dealing with matters which are not his business and he is quite unfitted to tackle, his work has been useless, nothing but empty poetry; yet the ideas he has served so ill have a future.' Because if you really think me presumptuous, you're right—I think the same myself. What I mean is—I feel I am not up to the ideas I have put forward. Ardently persuaded of their truth, I have spoken and written in order that others may speak and write, in order that what is so excitedly discussed elsewhere may be discussed in Italy as well, and if my small tinder could light a great fire I would not care if afterwards I were thrown to the ground and trampled under foot as useless. I am not going to discuss your agnosticism now. As you must know the arguments *against* it I will say that I am very hopeful of Sirio's help, because you sometimes listen to him. Instead I would urge you to reconsider the basis of your view on the immobility of Catholicism, and see if a process of continual evolution is not taking place within Catholicism—not in its dogma, but in the understanding of its dogma. I would urge you to see whether even in Catholicism there is not a force that tends to preserve the ancient forms and a force that tends to produce new forms, if the very things you (= you all) write of Rosmini and others do not prove this; if Rosmini's work has really been destroyed by a partial condemnation; if absolute immobility is not just the tendency, just the plan of a *party* in the Church; if this party is not essentially represented in the

---

[1] In particular Joseph Le Conte, *Evolution and its relation to religious thought*, Appleton, New York, 1888 (to whom Fogazzaro wrote: 'votre livre a été pour moi de la lumière et du bonheur'); E. Payson Powell, *Our heredity from St. Augustine*, 1891; Minot Judson Savage, *Religion and Evolution*, 1876. On the subject of other efforts by Catholics to defend or accept the theory of evolution, and the withdrawal from circulation of two works by their authors since it was 'known that the Holy See was opposed to [their] diffusion', see 'Evoluzione e domma' in *Civiltà cattolica*, series XVIII, vol. VI, No. 1234, pp. 75–7.

Church itself by the Italian element in particular, and by the Latin element in general; if a living, vital Catholicism, infused with the modern spirit, is not heard and seen at work in Germany, in England and in America, a Catholicism Rome does not love, admittedly, but recognizes and respects.[1]

Fogazzaro's theological learning, which neither friends nor enemies ever recognized, was in fact nourished by his reading of English, German, American, and French writers, and by conversation with learned friends, clerics, and in particular those in von Hügel's circle: among these, Father Semeria, Felix Klein, von Hügel himself, Genocchi, and, more than the rest, Bonomelli. In short, Fogazzaro was already steeped in ideas of religious renewal within the limits of Italian Catholicism, based on the freer studies taking place outside Italy, and his letters to Crispolti, Bonomelli, and his young friend Tommaso Gallarati Scotti, give his views— always moderate and often intelligent—on the works of such authors as Sabatier, Houtin, Loisy, Laberthonnière, Blondel, and Tyrrell. He did not give his views on matters of dogma, on the Council's dispositions, or even on biblical criticism; what he dealt with was, in a sense, a critical culture with a basis of doctrine he imagined his correspondents already knew, a culture he thought might appear relevant to modern man, since the old arguments of apologetics could no longer convert unbelievers to the eternal truth. It was a culture of religious research, as opposed to the culture of religious affirmation. And, as Americanism had already shown in practice (Fogazzaro knew this through his friendship with the Abbé Klein), an integrating part of this research was the practical attitude taken, both in the matter of participation in political, literary, and artistic life, and in that of the personal

---

[1] See the letter to Gaetano Negri, dated Vicenza, 26 November 1893, quoted in T. Gallarati Scotti's *Life of Fogazzaro*, pp. 222–3. But see also what Negri wrote some years later, as if replying to Fogazzaro's hopes: '[The formation of a conservative party in Italy] is not possible because such a party can arise only on the basis of the Church. In fact a truly conservative party is necessarily a party that stands still. Well, in the modern world, which is whirling round dizzily, only the Church is strong enough to stand still, since the reasons for her stillness are not passing, relative considerations and interest, but a "motionless end of eternal wisdom" [Dante]. The Church will never give the new Italy this conservative, resisting force, and there is no point in dreaming that what is called conciliation may come about. It will not come about because, in order to reach it, the modern state, in exchange for what she took from her, would have to give the Church rights and privileges incompatible with the essential reasons of her own existence' (*Giornale d'Italia*, 8 December 1901).

relationship with God. This relationship with God had a pragmatistical origin and character that Fogazzaro translated into
terms of spiritual experience and inner conflict.

In his plan to further religious culture, then, Fogazzaro seems
to limit himself to declaring that the understanding of dogma
would develop: this seemed to him, or seems to us, as far as his
researches went, a simple formula that would take in his entire
experience in the programme of renewal. But what he meant by
understanding of dogma is not made clear either in his lectures or
in his letters, though he often refers to it. Very likely he was not
even very clear about it himself; in fact he seems to have guessed
a truth expressed by the formula, rather than understood the
value of dogma in any other sense thanks to the formula. There are
many references to his difficulties in his letters; here, explicitly,
is one in a letter to Giacosa:

. . . I am dissatisfied with myself as a rule because I am too much like
some of my own heroes, ever hesitating between good and evil, between
fervid activity and listless inertia. Answering that letter of yours . . . was
hard because I was afraid to concede too much; and to concede too much
in writing is much more important than to do so in conversation . . . Now
the very word *concede* is one I dislike. If we have a discussion on truth
and error, it is absurd to think of truth conceding anything; and if the
discussion is between truth and error partly mixed with truth, truth
doesn't concede anything, it merely takes over whatever is true on the
other side. To take it over truth must establish its ownership, and this
is not always easy to do in black and white. This is why I didn't answer
you. Note this as well. You know my ideas on Christian dogma. To me,
the dogmas remain unchanged in their superhuman reality, whereas the
understanding of them evolves in man, with his individual and social
evolution. Just now understanding of these dogmas is evolving very
actively. Much that I have read and many talks with learned priests
have actually pushed me beyond where I had stopped and I confess I
haven't yet found the next stopping-place. This makes me very reluctant
to argue in a way that involves taking a definite stand on certain facts.
Now if, when I got your letter, I had read a book by an English Jesuit
which I read later, I could have suggested to you two of its ideas: that
every formula of faith is necessarily inadequate, imperfect, symbolic;
and that the faithful should be anxious over only one thing: the practical
realization of their relationship with God, according to the idea they
have of him.

Dear friend, I read and discuss these things a great deal; not so much to benefit the book I should write, as to benefit my own spirit. Does it do me any good? Sometimes I feel it does, but later, when the spirit fights for ascendancy, I find myself almost as weak as before. As a rule I find mystical books much more helpful than theological books, and I feel the truth of something that Annie Besant said in speaking of Asiatic mysticism: it did not, she said, destroy the energies suited to function on other 'planes' of life, in fact it intensified them. I don't know about the Asians, but I do know that in rare moments of mystical fervour this is quite true for me.[1]

Fogazzaro read Tyrrell and quoted his fundamental ideas, but seemed not to notice the contradiction between them and what he had said before about the immutability of dogma. He had not actually mentioned truth, it is true, but *superhuman reality* (so that the contrast is weakened), but his attitude again becomes contradictory when he refers to the ascendancy of the spirit: all is finally settled and balanced in his remarks about mysticism. This letter shows the role Fogazzaro assigned himself and which in fact he assumed: that of the curious onlooker, the interested talker, unable to express logically what he must have had an inkling of, but able to use the learning of others in his own studies and to filter it through to his own writing. Fogazzaro was to use all he had heard, all the crises he had seen and soothed, in his own novels, particularly in *Il Santo*; and this was his reply to the problems he was faced with and had to some extent dealt with. Nor was it purely a literary exercise: as one might expect in the case of a man with the romantic concept of art and the artist's role, he merely—and he was aware, sadly and accurately, of his own limitations—made a character out of his ideas and put into him the truth he had understood intuitively. This meant he could shrug off the ideological responsibility for what he was saying, which he was incapable of shouldering in philosophical argument, and that a fictional character could express psychologically what in strictly conceptual terms was inexpressible. It all meant that this character acted out Fogazzaro's idea, lived it and died it, and by becoming a hero purified it of its particular imperfections, and made sure that his message had a vitality that did not depend on its strictly rational reliability.

The book Fogazzaro mentioned in his letter to Giacosa was

[1] See letter to Piero Giacosa, of 26 December 1902, in *Selected Letters*, pp. 495–6.

Il Santo, which was to appear at the end of 1905. In it Fogazzaro made use of all he had learnt from his correspondents and friends, in particular the 'learned priests' who were generously entertained at his house and discussed religious matters there agreeably and excitingly. Through them he kept in touch with developments in the movement for reform within the Catholic Church, and, like von Hügel, became a link between the priests who also were interested in forming a group of Catholic opinion that was informed about the latest scientific development, but for this no less faithful to the eternal truths and spirituality of the Church. Fogazzaro and his friends, Italian and foreign, felt that the opposition between science and faith, between Catholic truth and scientific thought, could be resolved by perennial, ever-recurrent truths, and that the Church could indeed approach the modern world—as at least some of Leo XIII's declarations had seemed to suggest was necessary. And Fogazzaro also believed that it would be fatal for the Church to refuse to face the problem, as at least some of the hierarchy (the 'Italian party' he mentioned in his letter to Negri) now seemed to be doing. Perhaps laymen could break down prejudice rather more easily than priests, for they were in more direct touch with the dangers of unbelief, and freer to discover what was new in scientific thought and in theology, and to speak out without any doctrinal responsibility. Besides which, Catholic laymen should work in the social field to defend the values compromised by advancing materialism, and with this in mind Fogazzaro welcomed the end of the Church's temporal power.

The authority and prestige of the Holy See have grown immensely since the fall of its Temporal Power [he wrote to Crispolti in 1897]. When you recognize that with the end of the old alliance between throne and altar a new vitality entered into Catholicism . . . that one can and should ask the Italian government to be truly and completely liberal in legislating for the Catholic Church, which heals old wounds, to respect the Catholic religion practically and completely—not in order to protect it too much, but to ensure that its manifold activities may develop peaceably; to show an example of reverence towards it, and to relieve people of the difficulty of fulfilling their religious duties; when you 'clerics' recognize all this, and enter into political life to obtain it all; when you accept the unity of the country as a fact, or at least not plan to restore the Temporal Power, and stop interfering: then how many will want to join you in your social work!

Your newspapers speak of us Catholics who are hostile to the Temporal Power as if there were just a handful of us. I think they are mistaken, that there are a great many of us and that when Italian Catholics have stopped quarrelling among themselves they will, so long as freedom of conscience is respected, appear in public life, and science, and literature, and the arts, with a brighter glow than the clerical party has achieved or looks likely to achieve.[1]

Yet gradually, as his ideas and those of his ecclesiastical friends on Catholic reform developed, Fogazzaro's optimism gave way to a more realistic uncertainty, which appears in the progressive changes in his hero:

Piero not only comes back to the faith, but does so in a way that throws doubts on his mental state, he says he has been called to give himself wholly to God [he wrote to Filippo Crispolti in February 1909]. In the last chapter, which is very short, having renounced everything of his own, he vanishes without a trace. It is clear that he means to prepare himself, through prayer and penance, for some special personal mission in the Church. Some will see him as hysterical, some as a future *saint* of reform.[2]

Crispolti had to some extent publicly advised him to give up his book—which had more than a narrative purpose; and it was to Crispolti that he wrote again a few days later:

I don't know if I can take your advice and give up Piero. You should know, however, that however much I feel the human side of our religion needs reforming, I am profoundly convinced of the stupidity of undertaking and carrying on a movement for reform against the Church's constituted authority; I mean opposing it in a way that Catholics are absolutely forbidden to do, or rather going beyond the degree of opposi tion allowed to some of the saints . . . [3]

To some calm, reasonable, positive people, Piero seems neurotic or crazy, ready for an asylum not as visitor but as patient. But Don Giuseppe Flores takes a different view of him. Even Don Giuseppe doesn't take an absolutely firm stand, though. He puts that off for the future, when the results of the conversion are seen [he wrote to his cousin Anna in the same period].[4]

---

[1] See letter to Filippo Crispolti of 29 October 1897, in *Selected Letters* pp. 381–2.
[2] See letter to Filippo Crispolti of 24 February 1901, ibid., p. 442.
[3] See letter to Filippo Crispolti of 28 March 1901, ibid.
[4] See letter to Anna Fogazzaro of 5 April 1901, ibid., p. 443.

Il Santo, then, avoids being judged because his mission is so remarkable, but enjoys the good opinion of a priest, the Don Giuseppe Flores whose words ('which are my own', he was to tell Gallarati Scotti[1] years later) were Fogazzaro's spiritual testament. This, Fogazzaro at first meant to publish in *Rinnovamento*; but it never appeared there and was published after his death by Gallarati Scotti. In the same way Fogazzaro used the opinions of the 'learned priests' he knew in his novel; there they expressed their hopes of reform, which they hoped to see in a way that was acceptable to calm, reasonable, positive people, and took no stand against the constituted authority of the Church. But later these views of theirs were expressed in an exceptional way, and through the strange mission of Fogazzaro's hero; while Fogazzaro himself, when both his book and the entire reformatory movement had been condemned, continued to sound like one of those priests, who had now become quite imaginary, exemplary characters.

Thus Fogazzaro moved from reform in general to the single, unrepeatable example of a saint; from religious inquiry to prophetic preaching in which the Church was reformed from an odd visual angle quite foreign to what was happening at the time, quite impossible to judge by standards of historical reason, political opportunity, or the current state of religious understanding. Yet this was the only way in which reform could be discussed in really religious terms, that is terms that transcended the existing structure of the Church's hierarchical condition, its existing profession of faith, even its concessions to modern thought. *Il Santo* is so much outside all this that there is no question of it dealing in a calm and rational way with the reformers' efforts to work within the historical conditions which the Church, like any other human institution, could not fail to be involved in. From a mystical, anti-historical plane, it demands a radical and a historical criticism of the national-institutional element in the Church.

The novel was in fact conceived during the final years of Leo XIII's pontificate, that is at a time when things looked well for the reformers, and concluded under Pius X. Thus the dialogue between Fogazzaro's hero and the Church's highest authority reflected the change in the relations between the reformers and the Roman hierarchy: instead of seeking reconciliation, the hierarchy

[1] See letter to T. Gallarati Scotti of 2 December 1907, ibid., p. 621. *La parola di don Giuseppe Flores* was published in T. Gallarati Scotti, *La Vita*, pp. 504–11.

had put forward the programme of 'restoring everything in Christ', and instead of tolerating dissidents, the Church was now condemning heretics.

Fogazzaro, indeed, was one of the first laymen to foretell what the new pontificate would be like:

I hoped for a Pope who would raise the intellectual level of the hierarchy and have a sense of the modern spirit [he wrote to his friend Antonietta Giacomelli in August 1903]; who would nominate Bonomelli or at least Scalabrini cardinal, who would favour men like Semeria, who would look kindly on Rosmini's followers. I care more about things like this than about the abolition of the 'non expedit', since that is a political act; and I expect none of them from Pius X.[1]

A pope, that is, who would carry on the work of Leo XIII, as Fogazzaro described it in an obituary notice in *La Stampa* of 22 July, 1903.[2] He was opposed to the dead pope's theocratic and national politics, but in his notice he stressed the element of intellectual reform in what he had done, which was understood and remembered by the modernists in particular. But it was soon clear that Pius X was not going to continue his predecessor's policy in prudently bringing traditional and advanced points of view closer together, in giving moderate concessions with a strategic skill that

[1] See letter to A. Giacomelli in T. Gallarati Scotti, *La Vita*, p. 382.

[2] Fogazzaro wrote: 'He moved away in slow majesty, he was lost in mystery. Never did he seem as great as in the last hours of his long, long life, in the protracted waiting for the end, calm and so busy that it reminded me of the attitude and the last words of Septimius Severus. It was not only those who believed in him who were worried about him, but those of other faiths and even those without faith at all, except perhaps for a few who were short-sighted and proud. . . . The name little prince no longer suited him. Emperors and kings could not try their strength against the sovereign greatness of the Vicar of Christ: in comparison with him they seemed rulers of dust before a ruler of the spirit. He was raised so high . . . by divine Providence, which is preparing to purify others, and to raise others to the Holy See ["with the usual mixture of error and truth", *Civiltà cattolica* remarked, quoting part of what he had said in their 10 August 1903 number]: in him the virtues of the Catholic priesthood were complete: he gave the highest service to religion, in a seat that could be seen by the whole world; for the faith that shines out in a pure life and in blameless spirituality has there its own supremely rational proofs.' For contrast, see Loisy: 'He [Leo XIII] had not the first idea of criticism' (*Mémoires*, I, p. 297), 'in the security afforded him by his ignorant infallibility . . . he knew very little about the things of the mind' (ibid., I, pp. 308–9); 'There has been far too much praise of Leo XIII's generosity of mind; he was never more than a great politician. In the intellectual field this Pope was no more than the very worthy predecessor of Pius X' (ibid., I, p. 578).

might appear that of an inspired parliamentarian. He quickly snapped the threads of a wide network of alliances, a network far-flung in order to enmesh what had long been lost, and put forward an alternative to what, though incomplete, could already be called alliances. And *Il Santo*, which might have contributed to the work of Leo XIII the vague yet generous spirituality of its author and of those who felt they were obeying the Pope's own proposals for reform, thus became the final, almost aberrant expression of a literary interpretation of liberal Catholicism.

10. The Pope Speaks: the First Encyclical

Among the Italian reformers, only Murri reacted favourably to the new Pope's first encyclical. He thought it perfectly clear that whichever cardinal succeeded Leo XIII, his work could not continue. Nor, personally, did he hope it would.

It is vital to get the action of Church and clergy into more direct contact with life, to find a way of penetrating it and to welcome new signs and suggestions of it in secondary and subordinate things which are means; and, for this reason, it is vital to break down that synthetic programme into its elements and to start again, point by point, from these,

he wrote in *Battaglie d'oggi.*[1] First, most important and fundamental, was the restoration of Christianity. And it was in the light of this that he not only justified but actually approved of the condemnation of Loisy, whose most important works were put on the Index on 16 December 1903. The other reformers, though, saw it as the first sign of the new Pope's intransigence, an intransigence that was to end by excluding from the Church, one by one, all the members of von Hügel's group.

We have heard it said by many [Murri wrote], and among them men who are both shrewd and learned, that Loisy's book in answer to Harnack [he was referring to *l'Évangile et l'Église*] might, in the case of unwary Catholics, do more harm than Harnack himself. We agree. But quite apart from the quality of his methods and the conclusions he reaches, Loisy claims to be a Catholic, and says that like the good priest he is he wants to write in defence of the Catholicism he loves. But in defending Catholicism he has involved himself in the field of modern studies, problems, and methods, since he is addressing the doubtful, and those who are suspicious of Catholicism simply because they think it seeks, and with good reason, to avoid examining criticism and science. Now, after the results he has obtained, after the uncertainty and bewilderment his two books have sown among so many Catholics, does one

[1] See Romolo Murri, *Battaglie d'oggi*, vol. III, *La vita cristiana al principio del secolo XX*, Rome, 1904, p. 189.

not spontaneously wonder whether, in the present state of Catholic culture, the harm and danger did not lie in the very fact that, in order to defend Catholic truth, he chose to use—with cold accuracy, too—the weapons of criticism and factual science, and to challenge things that had for so long been revered as being quite certain? Do you not find something strange and regrettable in this—which appears in the mere process of putting it down? The obvious proof of a remarkably abnormal culture among present-day Catholics?[1]

Vigorously, pugnaciously, and simplifying what he dealt with, Murri dubbed the culture born of a whole tradition, and the hope of the generation Buonaiuti called 'the generation of Exodus', 'abnormal'. Then he went further, to action which he thought would be guaranteed by Pius X's restoration of the integralism in doctrine. But the others, Fogazzaro, Buonaiuti, and their friends and correspondents, whether laymen or clerics, Italian or foreign, tried to consider the fact that Loisy's works had been put on the Index as something that was merely disciplinary, a matter of prudence, the inevitable result of an attitude that had been too openly polemical, almost arrogant, and not the condemnation of a movement of thought. They saw it as a warning, and not a definite stand on the part of the authorities, the final act in a struggle that had already raged round one individual, and was now won because Loisy had lost his influence in the Roman Curia, since new men were now influential there, with the coming of the new Pope. Minocchi, for instance, claimed that the Pope himself had spoken favourably of Loisy's book, calling it one of the few unwearisome books on theology; Fogazzaro accepted that one man be sacrificed to save the germ of truth his ideas contained, in the certainty that they had a future, which the present sacrifice might indeed promote. Von Hügel published essays interpreting Loisy's doctrines, certain that the Roman hierarchy had made an error of interpretation. In fact everyone saw that the measure must not be taken as definitive. In order to reinforce their conviction that it was not, people turned to Loisy himself, for they thought they could still make use of his authority, which if anything stood higher since his condemnation, to carry on the movement of reform. Now, if one can make definite moral judgements (on the steadfastness of his ideas, on his determination to speak out, whatever the cost to himself): at the time of his condemnation by Rome in December

[1] See Romolo Murri, *Battaglie d'oggi*, III, pp. 183–4.

1903 this attitude of his was certainly ambiguous. And this ambiguity tended to increase the unfavourable impression he made in the end on some, particularly those who, like Buonaiuti, had expected something more religiously exemplary of the critical method strictly applied to the examination of religious disciplines. The series of partial retractions, partial submissions, and private corrections of public behaviour which Loisy lists and often enlarges upon in his *Mémoires*, all show that he was more hesitant than he cared to admit. He had certainly never deluded himself as to the heterodoxy of his profession of faith, and the ambiguous way his work might be interpreted in the light of Catholic apologetics. But he had always declared he stood above any judgement made by the Catholic hierarchy. Whereas now he saw himself obliged to take up a position *vis-à-vis* an authority for which he personally felt no respect, but which he realized was respected and taken into account by those to whom his work was specifically addressed: his clerical friends and the laymen he himself had had so large a part in leading to a more intelligent Catholicism, and one that could better justify its own claims. To some extent, in fact, the way in which he reacted to Rome was imposed on him more by the reformers than by Rome itself—indeed, the authority of Rome now no longer existed for him. If he had refused to retract anything at all it would have meant that he rejected a discipline with which he knew the whole meaning of what he had done was in a sense bound up: freeing his friends from the ties of this discipline would have meant plunging them into the growing freedom of his own search for theological truth. And this would have meant hastening a decision, it would have meant going forward to anticipate a victory which to him was awkward and difficult, and to others might have seemed premature and impossible. Loisy wanted Rome to declare him a heretic, and to condemn him without hope of appeal; he was not going to miss this before the time was ripe, and let Rome get away with a mere warning. And yet the whole business repelled him.

Besides, Loisy was a priest, and however doubtful a priest may be about the sincerity of his own initial vocation (and Loisy was indeed all too doubtful of his), the habit of celebrating Mass and taking part in the sacraments, the conviction that he belongs, in fact if not in belief, to the small band of those trusted to guide the faithful, that he is a member of the priestly caste, cannot fail to modify radically his feeling of individual responsibility; and this is not wiped out simply by adopting other standards, which involve other responsibilities and other duties. The fact that Loisy had ceased to believe some time before was a matter of individual opinion, which did not relieve him of his duties as a priest: his lack of belief may account for his indifference to what the hierarchy might do, his sense of responsibility as a priest for the stand he took towards the hierarchy, and the traditional way he faced them.

'Catholique j'étais, catholique je reste; critique j'étais, critique je reste,' he wrote to *The Times*;[1] and to Cardinal Merry del Val, on 11 January 1904:

I respectfully acknowledge the judgement of the Sacred Congregations and I myself condemn whatever may be felt to be reprehensible in my writings.

Nevertheless I should add that my compliance with the verdict of the Sacred Congregations is of a purely disciplinary nature. I reserve the rights of conscience, and I do not imply that by bowing before the judgement of the Sacred Congregation of the Holy Office I shall reject or retract the opinions I have expressed in my capacity as an historian and critical exegete. It is not that I ascribe to these opinions a certitude which is not in accordance with their character; I have never ceased to perfect and correct them to the best of my ability during many years' work, and I am sure that they will continue to be perfected and corrected, by me or by others, in the future. But at the present state of my knowledge, and until more plentiful and more concrete information is available, they are the only form in which I can imagine to myself the history of the sacred books and of religion.[2]

But this was not thought enough, and on 24 January Loisy wrote again to Merry del Val:

I deeply regret that the Holy Father has not judged my obedience to the decrees of the Sacred Congregations of the Holy Office to be sufficient. I should have been neglecting the duty of sincerity if I had not explicitly reserved my opinions as an historian and critical exegete. It had not occurred to me that I could be asked to retract purely and simply a whole body of ideas which, as the substance of my books, touch on several fields of knowledge over which the Church does not exercise direct jurisdiction.

[1] See *Mémoires*, II, pp. 310-11. Letter of W. Sanders and Loisy's reply in *The Times* of 30 April 1904, but written in January.
[2] See ibid., II, p. 313.

Monsignor, I accept all the dogmas of the Church, and if in explaining their history in the books which have just been condemned I have without wishing it expressed opinions contrary to the faith, I have said, and I repeat, that I myself condemn whatever may be felt to be reprehensible in these books from the point of view of the faith.[1]

Lastly, on 28 February he wrote to Pius X:

Very Holy Father
I know Your Holiness's kindness and it is to your heart that I address myself today.
I wish to live and die in the communion of the Catholic Church. I do not wish to contribute to the destruction of the faith in my country.
It is not in my power to destroy in myself the result of my work.
As far as I am able, I submit to the judgement brought against my writings by the Congregation of the Holy Office.
As proof of my goodwill, and in order to set minds at rest, I am prepared to give up my teaching in Paris, and I shall likewise suspend the scientific publications I have in preparation.[2]

This was what Loisy said officially, and it was also the result of his collaboration with friends, in particular Mgr. Mignot and von Hügel, who intervened to suggest less intransigent expressions to him (for instance, the 'acceptance' of dogmas, in place of 'I believe'), and to keep the international public, which was excited at the idea of such a key figure being condemned—as he was certainly going to be, and soon—exactly informed about his thought. But while this was going on around him Loisy confided to his diary the thoughts he kept to himself—to that part of himself which he felt stood outside the current argument and was thus no business of those who were trying to help him: indeed, what he wrote in his diary dealt specifically with the kind of knowledge he had declared did not fall within the Church's discipline, in an official document addressed to the secretary of the very Pope who planned to unite the disparate elements in a restored christology.

I have given myself a lot of trouble for nothing in this world. I have taken my life and the Church seriously, which has led to my losing the one and displeasing the other. It is not a man's job to look for truth; for a priest it represents the greatest danger. I have not been a Catholic in the official sense of the word for a long time. I have thrown my intelligence and energy to the four winds of the ideal. This has brought me an empty existence, a career without achievement. I gather up my remains

[1] See ibid., II, p. 322.   [2] See ibid., II, p. 351.

to carry them to Marmousse, old before my time, suspected in the Church, abandoned by the world, soon to be forgotten. After great dreams, the anticipation of the grave.

Whatever the fate of Catholicism may be in time to come, I cannot change it. What the religion of the future will be, I do not know. Roman Catholicism as such is destined to perish, and it will deserve no regrets. It could continue if it transformed itself, but it does not wish to. It is not for me to wish in its place. Let us seek peace. Nothing would put me in a more ridiculous position now than if I were to launch into theological squabbles. I have no responsibilities whatsoever towards the Church, and I have the right to organize what remains of my life as I please.[1]

A month later, however, uncertainty appeared again in his diary:

10 May. This morning while saying the prayers in the missal I almost wished that it was for the last time. Do I still believe enough to call myself Catholic, and is what I believe Catholic? I am staying in the Church, not for reasons of faith, but for reasons of (moral) expediency. It would not need much, very little, for me to be unable to continue honestly in my calling as a priest. If this very little happened, I should not be surprised, I do not think that I should even be annoyed.

12 May. I suffer a great deal. There are times when I begin to long for something which would make me leave the Church. I do not believe that this will happen; I believe that I am condemned for ever to the galleys. . . .

I am still following a middle course, and one which will deprive me of whatever support I might have been able to obtain from the Right or the Left. I wish to remain a priest and a scholar, *res dissociabiles*. I ought not to rely on events to liberate me. Events do not liberate those who submit to them, but those who dominate them. I should have let the excommunication take place and do what I have done afterwards.

I remain in the Church so as not to unsettle certain people, but I am unsettling myself in the process. Is not helping to perpetuate an influence which is far from being wholly beneficial, contributing to man's unhappiness? Catholicism as it really is is not such an invaluable ingredient of moral progress that one can afford to turn a blind eye to its faults. It is a considerable obstacle in the path of intellectual progress and of the real morality of the contemporary world, which only asks to be allowed to exist. . . .

Liberal Catholicism, that is, the religion of humanity, without moral despotism or theological infallibility, could be the true religion, but it is not Catholicism. Pius X, the head of the Catholic Church, would excommunicate me most decidedly if he knew that I hold the creation

[1] See *Mémoires*, II, pp. 379–80, dated 9 April 1904

to be a purely metaphysical symbol, the virgin birth and the resurrection to be purely moral symbols, and the entire Catholic system to be a tyranny which acts in the name of God and Christ against God himself and against the Gospel. Carry on, my son![1]

Of course, in all their comments and requests Loisy's friends took account of his official attitudes: of his private thoughts they could know nothing. Besides, Loisy never confided them even to his closest friends, who, although he trusted them and told them how he felt, still believed that the beginning and end of the problem lay in his relations with the Church authorities. So, when his books were condemned these friends continued to support him in a mistaken way, from which Loisy himself wished to be freed, and still assigned him to a role for which he was no longer fitted. Loisy was at pains to develop a new concept of the religion of humanity, one which could include the particular, historical aspect which the spirit of truth had in time assumed according to Christian doctrine; whereas to his friends this particular, historical aspect still was or appeared to be the one to put forward in opposition to the anti-historical aspect of truth propounded by the Roman hierarchy.

At the time of the condemnation, Fogazzaro declared his respect for Loisy in terms similar to those used by Genocchi and von Hügel:

Sir. Your books have been condemned. I assume and hope that you will not refuse to make an act of outward submission. It is all that your ecclesiastical superiors have the right to expect from you. Some Italian Catholics who admire and love you wish to tell you through me that they are profoundly convinced that the day will come when by the force of circumstance your arguments will be accepted by this Catholicism of the future which will be *practical and mystical at the same time* and which we are working to prepare for, each in his own field. You would certainly not wish to see us attack the decree which has come down on you, since you value ideas and not personal satisfaction, which could diminish their success. The ideas you have so nobly served remain alive and will not die. They have faithful servants almost everywhere, and we are of that number. Although we do not think it would serve any purpose to make your name our battle cry, we shall keep a place for it high up among those names most dear to our Christian and Catholic spirit. I am glad to be able to tell you this in this bitter hour when

[1] See ibid., II, pp. 386–7.

after winning a battle in the fight against protestant rationalism you are beaten by your superiors in the Church you have defended.[1]

In the end, Loisy did not refuse to submit; but submission was not as easy as Fogazzaro seemed to suggest. Indeed, it cost him an inner struggle between warring factions—abstract and conceptual realities—that liberal Catholics knew nothing about; and their unintelligent agreement missed the reality of this inner struggle. The Loisy who appears in these private confessions could not fail to find, in the mildness of men like Fogazzaro, who claimed they wanted to avoid using his name for flag-wagging purposes, a confirmation of their radical failure to understand the revolutionary significance of his research, and its historically biased, but metaphysically definitive, outcome. These men's attitudes could suggest to Loisy only his own refusal to join them in an opposition determined by an occasional coincidence of opinion against a concept of truth not alternative to the one professed by the new Pope in his first official pronouncement. Loisy was dealing with Catholicism as it actually was, whereas his friends (and among them their Italian mouthpiece) considered this not as something leading to the future, but as something harking back to the good old days of Leo XIII, with their anti-historical groupings and alliances. And what, compared with this actual Catholicism, was the Catholicism Fogazzaro hoped for, 'practical and mystical at the same time'?

In any case, Loisy, who some years later was to call *Il Santo* 'more orthodox than me', felt no need to discuss the reasons for his condemnation with his Italian friends in general, and Fogazzaro in particular. The man he was addressing, and to whom, ideally, he offered his research, was Blondel, whose 'Histoire et dogme' was published in the *Quinzaine* early in 1904 but was dated 20 November 1903, 'no doubt in order to avoid appearing to support the Holy Office';[2] and it was in reply to Blondel that von Hügel defended Loisy in his 'Du Christ éternel et de nos Christologies successives', also published in the *Quinzaine* in June of the same year.[3] The Italians, Fogazzaro among them, were more

---

[1] See Fogazzaro's letter to Loisy, quoted in T. Gallarati Scotti, *La Vita*, p. 391.

[2] See *Mémoires*, II, p. 392.

[3] See *La Quinzaine*, 1 June 1904, pp. 285–312. For editorial reasons, von Hügel wrote to Loisy, who quoted his letter in his *Mémoires*, II, p. 408: 'a most useful preamble has been suppressed, in which the solidarity of biblical criticism and of the historical method in general was established, and in which it was equally well demonstrated that the small part played by philosophy in this

interested in the personalities involved than in their views. When a learned man like Loisy was condemned it made news, quite apart from his opinions. For some years the Italian public had been well informed about the Curia by a new Roman newspaper, the *Giornale d'Italia*; and if a scandal were to break, as the *Giornale d'Italia* foresaw it would, since Loisy's condemnation was quite certain, then knowing what the argument was about added no special spice to it. Italian laymen were not yet educated to the point of being able to discuss the problems, apart from their basic aspects. In any case, everyone was anxious to discover, from the Pope's actions, what attitude he would take towards the politics of Catholics. Compared with the confirmation or abolition of 'non expedit' the fact that a few books by a French exegete were put on the Index, or that he was to be excommunicated, was of very minor interest; and very few, and these mostly clerics, sought to find any possible connection between a disciplinary provision such as this, and an act with such serious political implications as the other. Some people, indeed, and among them Murri, felt that if dissidents were condemned for doctrinal faults, priests who wished to work in the social field would no longer be suspected of conniving with them, and it might mean that a tradition begun under Leo XIII, in spite of the moderate condemnation of Americanism, might be revived: the proclamation of infallibility had freed Catholicism from theological disputes, and it could now concentrate on social matters, all the more freely if it refused to keep considering its historical and doctrinal basis every time the chance came and some new revelation was advanced; that is, if it refused to consider any religious question that sought to throw light on the essence of Christianity. For these men, Loisy was on

---

method did not call at all for the intervention of such a specialist philosopher as Blondel was in his theory'. In the August number of the same review, Abbé Wehrlé took Blondel's part against Loisy; in the 16 September number, von Hügel replied. But on the controversy see also the correspondence of Blondel, von Hügel, and Wehrlé quoted in *Au cœur*, in particular pp. 114–38 for the preparation and pp. 139–51 for the formation of von Hügel's christology. The controversy deserves special attention, for it was at the heart of modernism. The correspondence of those involved, which has been only partially published, should be published in full. It would appear that, as far as can be seen so far, the Italian modernists took no part in it and seem not to have realized what the opposing sides meant; although, even without the 'epistolary encyclicals' that passed between Blondel, von Hügel, Loisy, and Wehrlé, this meaning could be found in official documents.

a par with Harnack, as he was with Blondel, Laberthonnière, and Sabatier; all of them were restoring things that were already known, discovering truths already stated, either in the course of centuries through multiform Christian tradition, or else recently, in the last Council: men must heed what the Pope said, not an imaginary pope, freely interpreted according to what one wanted to find, but an actual pope now reigning.

Pius X had in fact spoken: on 4 October, a month after his election, he had set out his programme in the encyclical *E supremi apostolatus*: to restore all things in Christ; that is, to lead men back to dependence on God, the way to Christ being the Church; to recall human society, which was drawing away from the wisdom of Christ, back to the Church's discipline. In its turn the Church would submit it to Christ and Christ to God. 'By God we mean, not God as the materialists imagine him, unfeeling and indifferent to human affairs, but the true, living God, One in nature, Three in persons, creator of the world, wise arranger of all things, just legislator who punishes the evil and rewards the good.'

The Pope expressed his programme in extremely clear language, with nothing prudently rhetorical or roundabout in it, and something of a medieval flavour. What was first needed to put his plan into action was a clergy filled with zeal, ardour, and charity, whose only thought was for God and the care of souls, and who would not be led away 'by the insidious suggestions of a new, mistaken science that is not infused with Christ, and, with disguised and cunning arguments, seeks to let in the errors of rationalism and semi-rationalism'. In order to defend the truth and refute the calumnies of the enemies of the faith, young priests must arm themselves with useful doctrinal knowledge: 'And yet,' the Encyclical continued, 'We cannot conceal the fact, indeed We will declare it openly, that We prefer and always will prefer those who, while learned in ecclesiastical and literary matters, seek to care for souls through the exercise of the functions proper to a priest who is zealous for the honour of God.' With a zealous clergy, a zealous laity must work hard to restore humanity in Christ: 'not using its own judgement and ideas, but always directed and ordered by the Bishops; for no one, apart from you, whom the Holy Spirit has appointed to rule the Church of God, is to teach, order, or preside over the Church'. And Pius X also dealt with the laity's part in charitable works:

Our predecessors have long since approved and blessed those Catholics who have banded together in societies of various kinds, but always religious in their aim. We, too, have no hesitation in awarding Our praise to this great idea, and We earnestly desire to see it propagated and flourishing in town and country. But We wish that all such associations aim first and chiefly at the constant maintenance of Christian life among those who belong to them. For truly it is of little avail to discuss questions with nice subtlety, or to discourse eloquently of rights and duties, when all this is unconnected with practice. The times we live in demand action—but action which consists entirely in observing with fidelity and zeal the divine laws and precepts of the Church, in the frank and open profession of religion, in the exercise of every kind of charitable work, without regard to self-interest or worldly advantage. Such luminous examples given by the great army of soldiers of Christ will be of much greater avail in moving and drawing men than words and sublime dissertations; and it will easily come about that when human respect has been driven out, and prejudices and doubting laid aside, large numbers will be won to Christ, becoming in their turn promoters of this knowledge and love, which are the road to true and solid happiness.[1]

The Pope's plan was perfectly clear: in the renewal which he foresaw, what counted was not the culture of clergy and laity, but their profession of faith. The reformers could not fail to see that their hopes of renewal were dashed; and most disappointed of all were those who had thought the most important thing about Leo XIII's pontificate was his encouraging attitude towards learning and research, and above all the institution of the Biblical Commission. With remarkable explicitness, the new Pope contradicted all his predecessor's ideas on religious learning: Leo XIII had thought it important, Pius X saw only its danger. The new Pope spoke of faith, and called men to religious zeal; the reformers took faith and religious zeal for granted and were looking critically at them: their problems already went well beyond the rationalism merely mentioned, with its vaguely defined companion, semi-rationalism, as errors. Rationalism and semi-rationalism were things they had come to consider as an internal danger to the Church, not as a collective name for the world's knowledge, now set up in the crudest way against the wisdom of Christ. The Pope was giving a religious sermon, developed in terms of traditional apologetics, as if the religious crisis they had undergone, to emerge

[1] *E supremi apostolatus*, 4 October 1904.

later in support of the Church, had simply never taken place. The reformers had approached the world in an effort to understand it, had steeped themselves in its learning in order to oppose it. They may have gone rather too far in their inquiries and let themselves be convinced that doctrines and problems which Christian wisdom had long since left behind were still important; but the fact remained that the world had advanced and had come of age independently of the Church, and that, without the Church, or without referring to it, had built up a history that the Church of Rome had in the end to submit to in practice, though it might deny it in theory. If the new Pope ignored all this, if, in order to renew all things in Christ, things must be considered in their original state, their historical development, and the effect on the intelligence and sensibility even of Catholics, ignored, then what could Pius X's impressive programme mean, what was it destined for?

Fogazzaro knew nothing about exegesis, yet he may have been right when he wrote to Loisy about the Catholicism that was 'practical and mystical at the same time'. He was mistaken in approaching Loisy, but possibly right in his estimate of the new character of Roman Catholicism. For the new Pope's programme, as seen in his first encyclical, was indeed 'practical and mystical at the same time'. And even with regard to the laity, Pius X's newly affirmed refusal to allow it to take part in the Church's doctrinal life, and the way he stressed the laity's need to obey the bishops, might indeed be interpreted, since its work was considered at all, as a sign of the new 'working unity', the meaning and purpose of which were derived from the very fact of giving up pondering on its basic ideas. Catholic action, in short, might be the new truth. This, perhaps, was the meaning of truth as the new Pope saw it: working in charity and for happiness, yet in obedience.

The Pope had spoken and put out a clearly expressed programme, had put Loisy's works on the Index and declined half-hearted support; but the reformers seemed to take no notice, in fact made no attempt to interpret what he had said. Just as they had already found their way round the dogmatic pronouncements of the Vatican Council—not only those concerned with papal infallibility, but those found in *De Ecclesia* as well—so now they simply went ahead, and carried on with their researches, which had been interrupted merely to hear an authoritative voice speaking on matters that seemed to be none of their business. They certainly did not consider what the Pope said as a programme inspired by the hope of unity, or likely to lead to it.

Under Leo XIII, they had chosen what suited them in what he said: *Providentissimus Deus* and *Aeterni Patris*; while they ignored the 'social' encyclicals. To the doctrines he expressed they applied the exegetical standards they were picking up in the course of their scientific research. Now, when the new Pope spoke, they seemed to find nothing that concerned them. The reason for this was that They did not consider the Church's doctrine as a single entity, and what counted for them were the distinctions and spheres of competence that modern thought had elaborated as it developed. Besides, they maintained that renewal must take place within the Church, and through reform, not, as the Pope seemed to say, from above, through the supreme authority and some mystical declaration. 'Submission to God', a chain that passed from human nature to the Church, from the Church to Christ, and from Christ to God, seemed to them merely to repeat old formulas, and not to amount to a programme of religious renewal. Their first object, which they never abandoned, was to convert first the Church and then, thanks to the Church, the world. But if the Church failed to agree and clung fast to ideas that meant nothing to modern man, then the whole programme would be in vain, and merely anti-historical. Yet they too were anti-historical, in particular because they refused to take into account the Church's position and its present character. The Church they referred to was an ideal Church, the Pope an ideal Pope, Catholicism an ideal Catholicism; sometimes Church, Pope, and Catholicism from the past, sometimes those of the future. As happens in heretical movements, they harked back to the Church's pure origins, now corrupted by history, but at the same time they longed for a future that would purify the corrupt present: in their case, the prophetic weapon was criticism.

For this very reason—because they were looking both backwards and forwards—they could not avail themselves of the Church as it appeared in what the Pope said and in the accusations levelled against them by some in the ecclesiastical hierarchy; they could not even avail themselves of the culture of the laity, which in Italy had nearly always been, if not alien, at least indifferent, to religious problems. In fact when Buonaiuti, Minocchi, Murri, and other Italian friends tried to find critical developments parallel to their researches, which could show them definite results, and confirm their own conclusions, they found only isolated cases of men already spurned for apostasy or rejected as heretics by the clergy. Minocchi, in particular, mentioned his disappointment in the work of one of his colleagues, who after being a priest had become a freethinker: Ausonio Franchi's *Oltre la critica*. This was certainly not what Minocchi, who in any case was not strictly critical, was looking for as an example of clarity and freedom. Nor were professional philosophers any more helpful when, as sometimes happened, they considered problems of faith: a man like Labriola, for instance, who had taught Murri and Semeria, might have seemed worth noting, in dealing with the problems of the Catholic clergy and laity, with the materialistic concept of history, and with the possibility of interpreting their problems in a new way—in a religious concept of classes, or parties. But only Murri, with his special experience as a political priest, made any use of all this. And the general climate of opinion, Serao's novels, D'Annunzio's poems, Crispi's speeches, Pascoli's poetry, Carducci's *Chiesa di Polenta* (and his Hymn to Satan), gave outsiders precious little part in the development of Italian religious thought, which in actual fact and their own estimation had always, despite them, been a matter that concerned the clergy. Nor could what such men were doing help to further what was being done in recurrent efforts to solve the Roman question in terms other than those put forward by Church and State.

The Roman question: possibly this was what the new Pope was really talking about in his religious message. Perhaps he meant to set up the religious side of it in a new atmosphere, at the same time offering both sides a chance to reconsider their own positions and refusing to agree to the liberal settlement of the argument. If the matter were considered traditionally, no agreement was possible, but by considering what Catholics were doing in another way, as 'Catholic Action', no longer that of a party or a class, but of a complete, united body, organized and disciplined in obedience to its immediate superiors in the Church, 'Catholic politics' might be seen as an entity in which Rome's newly authoritarian role would appear to stabilize what both clergy and laity were thinking. During Leo XIII's pontificate, the idea of a 'cultural' renewal had been advanced; now, once more, the accent was on social matters. In Italy, the disputes between Blondel, Loisy, Laberthonnière, and the rest seemed of secondary importance: the field was open for the solution of problems in the relationship between Church and State and between Rome and 'lay thinking' in the political field; and relations between all these were probably eased by the current impossibility of doctrinal argument.

Thus were the reformers isolated, with no support from philosophers working parallel to themselves; they were also forced to take an active part in the problem of Catholics in the sphere of Italian history, that is, in spite of themselves, to consider Italian history decisive; or else they had to confine themselves to ideological discussion among isolated individuals, clerics and Catholic laymen already in practice considered heterodox, since the most important and most significant man among them, Loisy, had been condemned. The Church, they considered, was independent of, and higher than, any national history, if renewed as they hoped it would be, and if its metaphysical purpose were taken into account; but now they were brought sharply back to Italian matters and their field of endeavour was narrowed down to these. And although the Pope had expressed himself in a mystical way in his first public utterance, in fact everything turned on the relationship between one authority and another; and the argument raged round the extent to which freedom should be restricted by jurisdiction. So it appears that thought which had previously been directed to ends that were by no means temporal would now naturally turn to the question of temporal power, and Catholic Action seemed to them the best way in which to express Christian and Catholic truth, pragmatistically. What a few men were thinking could be made to matter only if it were turned into action; and so some of the reformers, abandoning their proper bent, were influenced by those (lay or clerical) who believed that basic truth could be turned into fact: that is, they looked forward to the religious pragmatism this involved. Le Roy was one of these, and a better example than the rest.

In giving way to a pragmatistic conception of truth, the Italian modernists again made contact with a movement of thought that already had some exponents in Italy. In its origins and in its current development it was not opposed to religion and metaphysics, since it did not consider religion in the way Pius X's 'rationalists or semi-rationalists' considered it, nor as the present-day theologians did, either. Indeed, it claimed to set up a 'pragmatistic' interpretation of what these very theologians had recently been saying. It was, or might appear to be, a way of renewing an alliance that had been faintly apparent at the end of the nineteenth century, and of once more giving the Church itself the benefit of a particular research; through Le Roy, the Italian modernists could again make contact with Blondel's ideas, which Rome had never actually denied; and the instructions found in Pius X's first encyclical could actually be justified in the 'primacy of action' which both Le Roy and Blondel called for, using remarkably similar terms.

11. Le Roy and Pragmatism

Apart from any question of restored hopes, the publication of Edouard Le Roy's essay in the *Quinzaine* of 16 April 1905, about a year after Blondel's 'Histoire et dogme' had appeared in the same review, marks the change from the first to the second phase of the movement of renewal, and clearly indicates its various exponents. Loisy, von Hügel, and their Italian friends who were to edit the *Rinnovamento* belonged to its first phase, together with Minocchi; Tyrrell, Buonaiuti, and *Nova et vetera* promoted the second. The first phase was one of textual criticism, with Loisy as its main exponent; and it was followed by a philosophical, pragmatistic phase, which in Italy found its liveliest voice in those who were grouped round Buonaiuti and the review *Nova et vetera*. These, too, were the men who went furthest from the original ideas of renewal and reform, in a revolutionary spurt that gave way to the Catholic, idealistic restoration.

When Le Roy asked 'What is a dogma?' and answered that 'the current intellectualistic concept of dogma makes insoluble the objections which the very idea of dogma raises . . . [while] a doctrine based on the primacy of action allows us to solve the difficult, burning problem, without giving up anything on the way, neither the conceptual rights, nor dogmatic exigencies',[1] he was, of course, not saying anything new: he was merely expressing himself more clearly on the fundamental problem (what was called the problem of the development of dogma or of the intelligence of dogma or, more generally, the problem of the development of doctrine), and was bringing together the ideas of thinkers, from Newman to Tyrrell—in particular Newman in his *Essay on the development of Christian doctrine* and Tyrrell in his *Lex orandi* and *Lex credendi*—who had contributed to Catholicism from a spiritual and cultural store that had matured outside Catholicism, indeed at first opposed to it. Le Roy expressed Newman's and Tyrrell's parallel achievements clearly and uncompromisingly, in a style that suited the disciplines he had been studying. He also enjoyed the prestige of coming forward as a layman, an independent thinker and no less responsible for this, and of

---

[1] Quoted in E. Buonaiuti, *Storia del Cristianesimo*, Milan, n.d. (but 1943), Vol. III, p. 634.

giving his theme, which he maintained was fundamental, all the effort and experience of a lay thinker accustomed to using the freedom of scientists in formulating their theories. His question, and the pragmatistic answer he suggested, led modernists to take their philosophical discussion once more into the field of ideas that then seemed most suited to the new generation, especially in France; and at the same time their clear affinity with the work of Bergson and James made Le Roy and the solitary Blondel feel they were an active part of a movement of thought, the exponents of which were not merely scholastic dissidents. So once more they could feel that, on behalf of the Catholic clergy and the laity, they were making contact with lay thought, and that they alone could bring to the Church the 'world's' parallel contribution in the field of learning—work that was pursued just as seriously as that within the Church. To pragmatism was also brought the kind of criticism and experience that had so far found no place in the movement for reform: that of the scientists.[1] So for a while it

[1] See in particular F. Enriques, 'Pragmatism', 1910, in *Natura, ragione e storia. Antologia di scritti filosofici*, edited by L. Lombardo Radice, Turin, 1958, pp. 198–218; but for the relations between pragmatism and modernism, see E. Garin, in *Cronache di filosofia italiana*, Bari, 1955 (and the bibliography in it); U. Spirito, 'Il pragmatismo' in *Filosofia contemporanea*, Florence, 1921 (in particular pp. 180–90 on Le Roy); but above all R. Berthelot, *Un romantisme utilitaire*, two volumes, Paris, 1911 and 1913; see also D. Frigessi in *La cultura italiana del '900 attraverso le riviste*, vol. I: 'Leonardo', 'Hermes', 'Il Regno', Turin, 1960. Others have spoken up recently about the relationship between pragmatists and modernists: in particular see the letters of and to Giovanni Amendola, in Eva Amendola's *Vita con Giovanni Amendola*, Milan–Florence, n.d. (but end of 1960), among which are some very interesting letters from James ('I think that pragmatism can be made—is not Papini tending to make it?—a sort of *surrogate* of religion, or if not that it can combine with religious faith so as to be a surrogate for dogma' (Letter of 3 October 1906, p. 109)), from Vailati (in particular one to G. Boine, in 1908, pp. 271–3), and from Boine. The Amendola–Papini–Prezzolini correspondence has been published in part; apart from that in the *Vita*, in G. Prezzolini's *Tempo della Voce*, Florence–Milan, 1960, but already earlier and better in *Nuova Antologia*, a. XCIII, vol. CDLXXII, No. 1855 (January–April 1958) and No. 1889 (May 1958). Other letters and other accounts will soon be published but it seems unlikely that anything substantially different from what we already know about the relations, the personalities, and the ideals of the two groups will emerge from them. For Italian pragmatists and Italian modernists agreed on the need to found a philosophical movement—which in fact never happened—against scholasticism on the one hand and idealism and positivism on the other; and this, rather than any recognition of what they actually agreed upon theoretically, was what really seemed to bring them together. Indeed, both sides contributed something that was gradually emerging—apart from the 'logicians', Vailati and Calderoni—outside their own speculations, however much these might appear to express a fairly well-directed system of

looked as if laymen and religious, philosophers and scientists, were all working together, and that, though they might not take much heed of the Church, they were not directing their inquiries against it. This was particularly so if one bears in mind, not the doctrinal course it was taking, but the practical results that might come from their researches. Besides which, as the more alert reformers already saw pretty clearly, pragmatism was not a definite corpus of rules for the mind, nor was it even a 'doctrine' in the strict sense of the word; it was a doctrinal course, a way of undertaking studies that might unite in itself, and give new life to, the divergent elements in so many fields, and direct them towards a single end. The most famous lay exponent of pragmatism, William James, promoted this 'experimental' character of pragmatism, and some time later he declared in his work that he continued to be, and wished to remain, in the field of research, without reaching or wishing to reach any definite systemization. In this he went against what many had expected, including Italians, among them Amendola.

But one pragmatistical idea appealed at once to the reformers, for in it they recognized what they themselves felt most deeply: the idea that religion, which the pragmatists were increasingly dealing with, was no longer linked with a solid machinery of doctrine, like that of Catholicism, or with a particular hierarchical, priestly structure. To the pragmatists, religion meant every aspiration directed to an ideal that was above self-interest and selfishness and animal passion. In a way religion had been replaced by an infinitely variable 'religious experience'. (This was not said in so many words, but rather more taken for granted.) Now, this idea corresponded to the refusal of a 'concept' of religion backed by theology and equally demanded by the Italian Hegelians.[1]

To James, indeed, 'the word religion cannot mean any single principle or essence, but is rather a collective name'[2] for individual

---

philosophy. It was a temporary alliance promoted not by those really involved in the two sets of ideas—which had not yet crystallized into a movement or a doctrine—but by their followers.

[1] Gentile, reviewing James when *Varieties of religious experience* was published in Italy, translated by Calderoni and Ferrari, Turin, 1904, in fact showed the absence of any logical system and saw it as a definition of religious principle implied rather than explicitly stated. See Gentile, *Religione e prammatismo per W. James*, 1904, reprinted in *Il Modernismo e i rapporti tra religione e filosofia*, Bari, 1909, pp. 158–83.

[2] Quoted in Gentile, op. cit., p. 164.

experiences with their roots in feeling. What was essential and primary was the individual's inner experience, the heart's feeling for the divine; not the dogmas of individual churches, nor the speculations of philosophers and theologians, nor ecclesiastical institutions. What came first was the way in which some privileged initiates experienced the divine; all intellectual decisions, all the speculations of philosophers and the dogmas of theologians, all ecclesiastical institutions and the rites they put forward and imposed, were based on the imitation and repetition of these states of awareness. Besides, James felt, it was in itself useful to consider the moral and social results of the religious condition, of religious awareness in general and the state of religious perfection (sanctity) in particular, from the point of view of the problem of truth, from the moment when the pragmatistic idea of truth demands something further than the satisfaction of logic. Finally, religious experience brought us into more direct contact with concrete reality than did scientific experience, and 'every theory that opposes the abstract concepts of the science of nature to the immediate intuition of the concrete dynamism of psychic life'.

So James came close to Bergson again, and the letters the two philosophers exchanged show the relationship between their ideas. They also show how their studies were running parallel to those of the modernists.

You have, it seems to me, succeeded in extracting the quintessence of religious experience [Bergson wrote to James in January 1903]. No doubt we already felt that this emotion is both a joy *sui generis* and the consciousness of a union with a superior power; but it was the nature of this joy and of this union which appeared to be capable neither of analysis nor of expression, and which nevertheless you have been able to analyse and express—thanks to a quite novel procedure, which consists in giving the reader in sequence a series of *impressions d'ensemble* which intersect and at the same time fuse with one another in his mind. ... The more I think about the question, the more I am convinced that life is from one end to the other a phenomenon of attention. The brain is that which directs this attention; it marks, delimits and measures the psychological construction which is necessary for action; in short it is neither the duplicate nor the instrument of conscious life, but its most advanced point, the part which inserts itself in events—something like the prow of the ship which is narrowed to cleave the ocean. But, as you so justly say, this conception of the relation of brain to mind requires us to maintain the distinction of soul and body at the same time that we transcend the old dualism, and consequently we must often depart from the lines of our customary thinking.[1]

Some years later, after reading *Pragmatism*, Bergson again agreed with James:

It is the programme, admirably traced, of the philosophy of the future . . . when you say that 'for rationalism reality is ready-made and complete from all eternity, while for pragmatism it is still in the making', you provide the very formula for the metaphysics to which I am convinced we shall come, to which we should have come long ago if we had not remained under the spell of Platonic idealism. Shall I go so far as to affirm with you that 'truth is mutable'? I believe in the mutability of reality rather than of truth.[2]

[1] Quoted in Ralph Barton Perry, *The thought and character of William James*, Boston, Little, Brown & Company, 1935, II, pp. 607–8.

[2] Letter from Bergson to James, 27 June 1907, ibid., II (1959), pp. 260–1 and see ibid., II, pp. 308, 323, 324, the reply to E. Chapui's inquiry. See also the letter from James to Bergson in 1907, quoted in F. O. Matthiessen, *The James Family*, New York, 1948, pp. 546–7: '. . . To me at present, the vital achievement of the book is that it inflicts an irrecoverable death-wound upon intellectualism. It can never resuscitate! But it will die hard, for all the inertia of the past is in it and the spirit of professionalism and pedantry as well as the aesthetic-intellectual delight of dealing with categories logically distinct yet logically connected, will rally for a desperate defence. The *élan vital*, all contentless and vague as you are obliged to leave it, will be an easy substitute to make fun of. But the beast has its death-wound now, and the manner in which you have inflicted it (interval *versus* temps d'arrêt, etc.) is masterly in the extreme . . . You will be receiving my own little "pragmatism" book simultaneously with this letter. How jejune and inconsiderable it seems in comparison with your great system! But it is so congruent with parts of your system, fits so well into interstices thereof, that you will easily understand why I am so enthusiastic. I feel that at bottom we are fighting the same fight, you a commander, I in the ranks.' On the relationship between Bergson and James, see G. Lukacs in *The destruction of reason*: 'It is easy to see how, in the conditions in which pragmatism functioned in other countries—conditions of highly developed and bitter class warfare—its purely implicit elements soon became explicit. This appears plainly in Bergson. It does not, of course, mean that pragmatism influenced Bergson directly, but is more a matter of parallel tendencies—which, indeed, the esteem which Bergson and James felt for each other emphasises, in a subjective way. Both men repudiated objective reality and its irrational recognisability, both reduced science to something merely technically useful, both appealed to an intuitive apprehension of true reality, declared to be essentially irrational . . . Bergson on the one hand developed modern agnosticism in a bolder and more decisive way than James, by reducing it to a clear arrangement of myths; but on the other hand, at least during the period of his decisive international influence, his philosophy was aimed far more at criticising the conceptions of the natural sciences, at destroying their right to express objective truths, and at substituting (philosophically speaking) biological myths for the natural sciences, than at the problems of

Now it was this very philosophy of the future expressed in the formula of reality 'still in the making', as against reality already formed and complete for all eternity, that Italian modernist readers of Le Roy and James, guided by Tyrrell, thought they could help to shape, or at least to make known, in Italy. A twofold aspect of this philosophy concerned them in particular: the crisis of reason which it implied, and the possibility, which it hoped for rather than propounded, of a new metaphysic. To them, the most important thing in the reform of the intellect lay in the fact that their knowledge, being based on reason, was unsatisfactory, and their most serious criticism of Roman theology was that it confirmed this limitation: the criterion of truth, which the pragmatists were reforming, corresponded to their need to free the individual man's religious experience from the reasoned revelation he was offered by current dogmatic theology, and at the same time they could be assured that religious speculation would continue in the new philosophy, since it contained elements of Newman's proposed doctrine of development. At the same time, there was hope of a new synthesis (this was contrary to the ideas of laymen a few years before); and indeed their work needed a synthesis, as it had until then been developing in disparate fields, only loosely connected. Besides, they could see that in the philosophy of the future something that was wholly foreign to religious reflection, and yet had been partly absorbed by some of them, by Loisy in particular, could be overcome: historicistic rationalism, if the relative character of truth (in which only the first term was changeable, according to the time and the conceptual ways of understanding) could be replaced by the changeable and active character of truth itself, its making of itself.

Tyrrell, intellectually the most vigilant of the reformers, had no need to wait for the publication of Le Roy's essay in order to plan a new philosophy or realize what it would demand. Unlike the others, he was little influenced by new books and by what von Hügel and others told him of what was going on, culturally speaking, on the continent. A solitary thinker, his ideas were gradually evolving through the reading and re-reading of a few basic books which he considered fundamental, in particular the works of Newman: he read the *Grammar of Assent* and the *Essay on Develop-*

---

social life. . . . Bergson's intuition turned towards the outside world in order to destroy the objectiveness and truth of scientific knowledge.'

ment and the *Apologia* three times.[1] Every time he re-read these books he took another step ahead in radicalism, until, thanks to Newman, he went 'beyond' Newman; he was, as it were, consciously distorting the ideas of his master, and that 'distortion' was his major theoretical contribution and led him to the pragmatists, whom he saw not as masters but as members of the brotherhood.[2]

. . . A continuation of the processes that operated in the past is no longer enough: something like a theological revolution is needed. And here I feel that Newman is no longer in a position to help us. It is not the articles of the Creed that need to be readapted, but the word *Credo* itself. . . .

If we differ substantially, it is that, while I agree with you that Newman's prophetic insight foresaw *in the vague* the intellectual revolution which is now upon us and with which e.g. Loisy is, I think vainly, trying to cope; he did not and could not have anticipated and prepared for the precise problem which is now presented to us.

Apart from the purely *ad hominen* and anti-Anglican values of the 'Essay on Development', it was a great service to show clearly, as he did, that the Church had practically and implicitly (and to some extent explicitly) acknowledged that same principle of development which is the dominating category of modern science and philosophy; and that she had in the same measure repudiated the rigid *semper eadem* conservatism of the Eastern Churches and of the high Anglicans; and was, so far, more liberal, more progressive than they.

But then . . . the Church, as J. H. N. would be the first to acknowledge, has no intention of being dominated by this development category; she adopts it only as an *ancilla theologiae*.[3]

But even Tyrrell did not feel that if the dogmatic framework of Catholicism were destroyed it would mean, as he wrote in his

---

[1] See letter from Tyrrell to R. Gout, 26 May 1906, quoted in *Autobiography* II, p. 209.

[2] See Tyrrell, 'Notre attitude en face du pragmatisme' in *Annales de la philosophie chrétienne*, October 1905, then in *Through Scylla and Carybdis*, London, 1907, pp. 191–9: 'Largely as we may agree with the general tendency of that philosophy, we cannot view it as more than a rough draft, needing careful revision and correction. Still, we do it an injustice if we suppose that its war against the Hegelian "Absolute" is a wholesale abandonment of metaphysics, or an opening of the door to pure relativity . . . Far from abandoning metaphysics, to deduce it from life and conduct, rather than from notions and concepts, is to place it for the first time on a firm basis, and to give it that interest which attaches to every study that bears, however remotely, on life and action.'

[3] See letter to W. Ward on 11 December 1903, quoted in *Autobiography*, II, p. 215.

famous 'Letter to a Professor of Anthropology' towards the end of 1903,[1] the end of Catholicism, or that it would involve leaving the Church; one must leave the Church

> if faith mean mental assent to a system of conceptions of the understanding; if Catholicism be primarily a theology or at most a system of practical observances regulated by that theology. [Not] if Catholicism be primarily a life, and the Church a spiritual organism in whose life we participate, and if theology be but an attempt of that life to formulate and understand itself . . .

The point of departure for his apologetics was the immediate psychological experience; whereas religious experience, which in its original forms was confused with revelation itself, was based, as in James, on and in the subconscious. The Church was a collective unconscious which became a collective consciousness through history, though in an obscure way, in the community of the faithful: theologians and Church leaders must interpret it in its growing degree of self-awareness, and in order to bring this about individuals were needed whose contribution would range from simple religious feeling to prophetic inspiration.

The way Tyrrell behaved, and with him those who declared to the end that they wished and needed to stay in the Church, in spite of the Church's opposition, was due to the fact that they knew they belonged to the small number of men needed to shape the collective awareness, and that at the same time they were convinced that Pius X's theologians were not its interpreters. They did not reach this conclusion through the ideas of the pragmatists, but found in these ideas a number of elements in common with their own, and the convictions they already held confirmed.

Loisy did not agree with the others. He felt that Le Roy's essay in the *Quinzaine* might cause serious upheavals in the 'theological world', but altered nothing, suggested no new regroupings. Loisy had no need to justify his studies philosophically because

---

[1] See Tyrrell, 'Confidential letter to a Professor of Anthropology'. On the fate of the letter, 'whose privacy was originally its chief justification', see George Tyrrell, *A Much-Abused Letter*, London, 1906, where, retranslating from the *Corriere della Sera* of 1 January 1906 to show some important inexactitudes, he says that the extracts are 'a rather curious patchwork of passages from different pages of the letter fastened together by a few sentences of which I cannot claim the authorship. Still, I do not quarrel with the result' (p. 5), whereas to the *Corriere della Sera*, the document 'sounds like a chapter of *Il Santo* and will no doubt interest the numerous readers of Fogazzaro' (p. 6).

he hated all philosophy,[1] and so, in particular, the new philosophy of the future. Other modernists seemed to be seeking the philosophical basis of their (religious) crisis and turned to Blondel, James, and Le Roy for doctrinal help, in order to put their own religious experience in a new way, and to justify their particular studies theoretically, in a new synthesis. But Loisy found this pointless:

His [Le Roy's] criticism of the official concept of dogma in the Catholic Church is irrefutable. But it is the traditional and orthodox concept he is refuting. His teaching fully acknowledges the right to think and carry out scientific research. It is less easy to see why the dogmas, in relation to the moral attitude they prescribe—or which according to M. Le Roy's interpretation they are thought to prescribe—should be upheld although they are not systematically thought out or demonstrable, and are furthermore subject to any new interpretation which will take into account their practical nature. It would seem to be a wasted effort, since it implies the contradiction of preserving the absolute character both of Christian revelation and of the authority of the Church.[2]

[1] On Loisy's non-philosophy, see Sartiaux, op. cit.: 'Loisy knows neither Plato, nor Aristotle, neither Descartes, nor Pascal, nor Spinoza, neither Leibniz nor Kant; of Voltaire he read the *Essai sur les Mœurs* for the first time only in 1920; he has no interest in, and no knowledge of, literature, art or archaeology; as for scientific philosophy, all he has read is Bergson's *Évolution créatrice* and a few pages of Poincaré's *La science et l'hypothèse*, which he opened one day when he had influenza "pour faire diversion à ses préoccupations de l'heure" ' (p. 193 and in a note). But see also what Loisy himself wrote in his *Mémoires*, II, p. 381: 'M. Parodi is right in remarking that my idea of reason is not the same as the one he shares with many modern rationalists; but I do not think that the difference is quite where he sees it; I have a dynamic and more or less relative conception of reason and knowledge, whereas the conception these philosophers have of them, whether they deny it or not, is more static and absolute than it should be'; and elsewhere, commenting on von Hügel's last letter: 'It is my opinion . . . that man's moral actions should be based on less ethereal foundations and that practical psychology, moral and social experience, a completely natural attitude to life can provide them with a better basis than any metaphysics. It is absolutely essential to find a positive foundation for morality in the immediate and concrete necessities of life, or morality will disappear without the metaphysicians being able to avert its destruction.' Among these metaphysicians he would include his old friend: 'Metaphysics had become second nature to von Hügel and, up to a certain point, it contributed to his nervous disability: contributed to and nourished it; debilitating nourishment.' (*Mémoires*, III, pp. 559 and 463.)

[2] *Mémoires*, II, p. 447. In order to see exactly what Loisy thought beforehand about Le Roy's work, see the letter he wrote him when 'Dogme et critique' was published (1907) with answers to the critics as well as the famous essay itself: 'Dear Sir, The idea I had of your book is slightly different from the reality. . . . I shall not conceal from you that I find the critical part of your work far more satisfying than the constructive part. Theological symbolism exists only for those who, intellectually accustomed to the old dogmas, still cannot accept their literal

This meant there was no need to stay in the Church, since it was impossible to interpret things differently within it; it also meant that he levelled no particular charges against the Church for the way in which it had expelled him. Loisy did not feel he should break with the Church, but if the Church broke the link that bound him to it, so much the better. He would then, if it were suitable, tell the public what had gone before his condemnation, and how it had proceeded, but would not discuss the subject fully. When he

---

meaning. But the moral significance of most of the Christian dogmas, those valid for us and our contemporaries, is so far removed from their original significance and their theological content, that I wonder whether there is any use in planning a metaphysical construction to act as a bridge between the old symbols and the present rules of action. Action is the only thing we can be sure of. The new explanation will collapse tomorrow if there is any risk of it being accepted today.

'Your doctrine of the resurrection is a beautiful poem: yet is it anything but a poem? Your general philosophy of knowledge is most interesting: yet is it anything but a brilliant essay, or perhaps a system on which moral beliefs should not be made to depend too much? May we be preserved from the scourges of *historicism* and *externalism*! And let us beware that we do not restore, baptizing in the philosophy of action, a metaphysic less logically deduced and more obscure than the old one.

'We have all condemned *spiritualism*. Occasionally I wonder whether what we are doing does not resemble it a little too much, and whether the religious pedagogy which is destined to prevail will not be infinitely more simple in its aim, its method, and its organization than our dreams of an intelligent and living Catholicism. Official Catholicism is not sparing of its warnings to us these days. Let us force ourselves to listen to them carefully.' (*Mémoires*, II, p. 521.)

Some days later, on 1 June, when the book was put on the Index, he wrote to him: 'I am taking advantage of the fact that one can still write to you without committing an offence to tell you how much I sympathize with you in what you are feeling. I am not talking of the blow you have been dealt, which is only beating the air . . . I see that that great Catholic philosopher finds this the right moment to announce haughtily that he does not think like you. In the same way, three years ago, he realized that he did not think like me. I do not know whether many people were likely to confuse his opinions with ours. Perhaps there is some truth—in all senses of the word—in his thinking himself to be the mouthpiece ordained by Providence for such pure and delicate philosophical revelation.'

Loisy was referring to the open letter addressed by Blondel to Fr. Bricout, who published it in the *Revue du clergé* (1907, vol. L, pp. 45–6). In a private letter to Valensin on 24 May, Blondel wrote: 'The intellectual difficulties and doctrinal struggles are becoming more and more serious. And there is, I think, a terrible danger in wanting to oppose, *en bloc*, "modernists" to "traditionalists". But it must be conceded that books like Le Roy's are such as to justify all the fears and restraints. . . . So I am not sorry that M. Bricourt has published, in the *Revue du clergé*, a letter—albeit a badly worded one—in which I have completely dissociated myself [from Le Roy]' (quoted in *Correspondance Blondel–Valensin*, I, p. 319). But Blondel had already expressed privately to Le Roy his fundamental disagreement with the double point of view of the 'theological applications' and of the principles and the philosophical method that inspired 'Dogme et critique'. See Blondel's letter to Le Roy, ibid., of 5 May 1907.

was condemned he would comment on it as on any historical event, discuss it as a contemporary matter connected with other contemporary matters. He would, in fact, deal with it as he would deal with any given text—dispassionately, without polemics or personal explanations. The lack of passion he would affect seemed to Loisy more important than what he was actually going to say.

Italian modernists, on the contrary, felt that the 'philosophy of the future' confirmed their own aspirations and encouraged them to continue their studies. Buonaiuti, in particular, found in pragmatism a new methodology, a logic without precedents, a philosophical attitude with which there was nothing comparable:

... so pragmatism does not lead to a determined philosophical doctrine, and at the same time it can lead to them all, if need be: if, at a particular moment, the pantheistic conception seems to stimulate life more intensely, it will appear pragmatistically as the truest conception of the universe; if, at another time, the deistic conception seems to incite men to action more profoundly in the face of the universe, then this will spontaneously be declared the truer. Pragmatism, in fact, no longer analyses pure ideas and their likely connection with reality, but attitudes of the spirit, and treats abstract formulas and systems in terms of these and of their normal useful development. This is our fundamental position, which has arisen from looking at our cognitive efforts. Our knowledge, all our knowledge, human and divine, comes from our inexhaustible will to live, to affirm and expand ourselves, to bring the force of our action to bear on the world, to make brute force obey us, to show how we dominate the non-ego as we go, to multiply infinitely what supports and advances our activity.[1]

Even for Buonaiuti, the most wide-awake and curious of the priests, however, it was not a case of adhering unconditionally to the new philosophy. It was more a matter of interpreting it in a way that seemed to enfold, though somewhat confusedly, all the reformers' requirements.

[1] See P. Baldini (Buonaiuti's pseudonym) 'La religiosità secondo il pragmatismo', in *Rinnovamento*, a. II (1908), No. 1, p. 49. But see also in *Studi religosi* (1905, pp. 413 ff.): 'Pragmatists up to the interpretation of pragmatism, we are convinced that every philosophical current answers to a determined social force.' It is curious to see, as a sign of the contradictions in Buonaiuti, what he wrote so polemically in 1926, in answer to Giuseppe Gangale: 'You call me "a mere importer of shoddy Anglo-Saxon goods from the firm of James and Co.": May I ask you to give a single example to show that this elegant label of yours ... is a polemical point that deserves respect, rather than an impertinence only slightly less vulgar than the others.' (In *Coscientia*, Rome, 24 July, 1926.)

12. The Pope Speaks: the Second and Third Encyclicals

In 1905, when Le Roy's essay, the manifesto of religious pragmatism, appeared, Buonaiuti launched his own personal review, the *Rivista storico-critica delle scienze teologiche*. Minocchi, who had welcomed the younger man's contributions to *Studi religiosi*, felt that the orthodox modernism inspired by Leo XIII was now split, and he expressed his regret in public. He felt that Buonaiuti's programme, which aimed, or so it seemed to Minocchi, to take a middle road between *Studi religiosi* and *Civiltà cattolica*, had already been followed by Mgr. Benigni's *Miscellanea di storia ecclesiastica*, and that, apart from being a disturbing influence, it had very little use.

What appeared clearly in those years was the fact that Buonaiuti hoped to fulfil a role he felt was quite natural to him—that of leader of the movement for reform, or at least that of educator of the clergy. This was a role that Minocchi had partly fulfilled, but he had done more to inform the clergy than to take any definite stand. In his review, Minocchi had given authoritative expression to what was best in the philosophical, exegetical, and historical studies of the foremost Catholic scholars, both Italian and foreign, and had been prudent enough to allow criticisms—often highly radical—to appear between the lines. All this had been part of the cultural education of the clergy for which Minocchi had hoped and worked; but it did not go as far as the reformers had now reached: they now proposed to make a break, and first to proclaim, then to set in motion, the movement for reform. In *Studi religiosi* Buonaiuti had declared that he meant to discover what was newest and most revolutionary in religious, and particularly philosophical, studies, and on the subject of the philosophy of action he had been remarkably persuasive, if not very accurately informed. But when he began his own review he seemed to suffer from the same critical limitations as Loisy had in his own review and as the first numbers of *Studi religiosi* had shown. This was why, on seeing the remarkably prudent first numbers of the new review, Minocchi felt there was little use in it, and was able to confuse it, with involuntary irony, with Benigni's *Miscellanea*,[1] in which the term 'modernism', which was from then on used by polemical writers, first appeared. But there may have been another reason why Minocchi could see no reason for Buonaiuti to launch a new journal of scientific and religious discussion. Minocchi lived a long way from Rome, where *Civiltà cattolica* was published and Buonaiuti's 'enemies' lived and worked. Buonaiuti, the 'pilgrim of Rome', had undergone all his religious experience, had carried on his confused and passionate warfare, entirely in the climate of Roman Catholicism. Tyrrell, the convert, saw Rome as his final goal, Loisy saw it as a distant, unintelligent threat, von Hügel, the cultured cosmopolitan traveller, as a place where all necessary information was to be found, since the most important figures in the Church were there. And to the Roman Buonaiuti it was, and would remain forever, the chair of Peter, the living image of Catholicism, which now, through some he considered unworthy, opposed everything he put forward, and in spite of all his efforts or those of others to face up to the seriousness of the present crisis, maintained that the truths expressed in the traditional formulas were quite certain. *Civiltà cattolica*, Rome's most influential journal, devoted a great deal of space to a detailed refutation of Loisy's errors; it examined his essays one by one, pouncing on deviations from orthodoxy with the harshness such an adversary deserved (officially at least he was a recent adversary, but the writer in *Civiltà cattolica* considered him an age-old enemy, since it was clear, from his criticism, that there was no hope of his repentance and that he was definitely committed to the rationalist position). But at the same time it casually and arrogantly denied that the present crisis in Catholicism meant anything at all.

Catholics [it wrote, in the number in which the refutation of Loisy[2] appeared] who for nineteen centuries have been establishing and refuting what the enemies of Christianity have said, need feel no obligation

---

[1] It is extraordinary, to say the least, that a well-informed observer should include Buonaiuti's journal on the anti-modernistic side: see J. M. Vidal, 'Le mouvement intellectuel et religieux en Italie durant l'année 1908', in *Revue du clergé français*, Vol. LVII (1909), p. 68. Rivière himself (op. cit., p. xviii) was to include it among the Catholic journals.

[2] See *Civiltà cattolica*, 1904, Vol. II, No. 1292, 'Razionalismo e Ragione', pp. 148–58.

to answer the rationalists when they write against the truths revealed in the Old and New Testament. They already have the truth;
and so there is no need for them to pursue the doubts and denials of
those who neither have the truth nor seek it, but fight it or else fashion
it however they please, since they have no sure and infallible authority
in matters of religion.

Indeed, the anonymous writer continued:

all the common people need to keep them faithful, and to defend them
from the errors that Protestant rationalists are cunningly propagating
from their so-called churches and chapels, and in pamphlets crammed
with false doctrines and tales, is the voice of their parish priest and the
explanations given in the catechism.

Pitilessly, intransigently, he went on:

... and the truth is that these matters of true religion are not merely
speculative, academic discussions in which the various opinions do no
harm to the soul's future; on the contrary, since they are of a supernatural kind, their error is fatal, for the man who does not believe, *qui
vero non crediderit*, is condemned by God to eternal suffering and the
depths of misery.

Of course, Buonaiuti was no unbeliever; but neither did he
think the voice of the parish priest was enough to keep people
faithful. He was one of the young, uncertain priests who felt his
uncertainty would not be ended by 'the study of Christian philosophy and the more frequent use of dialectic', which, according to
Civiltà cattolica, would disperse the fog of rationalism entirely.
Indeed, the very fact that this Christian philosophy and dialectic
no longer seemed to have validity and purpose was at the root of
the crisis itself. And because of the theological conviction that
despair followed upon the loss of faith, Buonaiuti felt he must
look elsewhere, without worrying if he became involved with men
in branches of learning where sin did not interfere, and with others
who sought, not for a truth that was already known, but for one
they hoped to find by pursuing the very studies that in fact were
the only thing *Civiltà cattolica* appeared to oppose.

Admittedly, *Civiltà cattolica* occasionally referred to a crisis.
But when it did so it mentioned single cases of some religious
who longed for what was new, longed to get away from philosophy
as it had always been. Instead of facing the fact that there was a
change taking place in the way the truths of the faith were con-

sidered, *Civiltà cattolica* clearly had a policy of creating a movement of 'innovators', whose characteristics it described, though against their will; and thus, by showing them up as an isolated group, diminishing their influence. From the end of 1904, whether it stressed what the Pope had said, or devoted essays to Loisy, Harnack, and other 'new men and old errors', that is to practically any of the new thinkers, *Civiltà cattolica* was in fact giving them a definite 'image': it was from then that the modernists began to take on a particular appearance, which gradually grew more precise, not so much from what they actually had in common, as from the criticisms of them made by the Jesuits of *Civiltà cattolica*. Thus, while the innovators were very gradually coming together, helping one another in the search for new truths they could share, there was a deliberate effort, in direct opposition to the spirit of their work, to isolate them, to make them appear a sect already working against the Church. Pius X's words pointed the way in his second and third Encyclicals, *Ad diem illum*, of 2 February, and *Iucunda sane accidit* of 12 March, 1904, dealing with the '*novarum rerum molitores*', and stressing much more strongly than usual the decline of religious feeling, which all the encyclicals had bewailed, including those of the 'liberal' Leo XIII. Pius X had no particular diplomatic tact: his writing was religious, and it is surprising to see how, once again, those who were attacked seemed not to realize it. In *Ad diem illum*, especially, put out for the fiftieth anniversary of the dogma of the Immaculate Conception, Pius X, in purely religious language, and using terms of 'popular' piety without any particular shrewdness, dealt with the key topic of original sin, which was clearly disagreeable to the innovators:

What truly is the point of departure of the enemies of religion for the sowing of the great and serious errors by which the faith of so many is shaken? They begin by denying that man has fallen by sin and been cast down from his former position. Hence they regard as mere fables original sin and the evils that were its consequence. Humanity vitiated in its source vitiated in its turn the whole race of man; and thus was evil introduced amongst men and the necessity for a Redeemer involved. All this rejected, it is easy to understand that no place is left for Christ, for the Church, for grace or for anything that is above and beyond nature; in one word the whole edifice of faith is shaken from top to bottom. But let people believe and confess that the Virgin Mary has been from the first moment of her conception preserved from all stain; and it is straightway necessary that they should admit both original sin and the rehabilitation of the human race by Jesus Christ, the Gospel, and the Church and the law of suffering. By virtue of this Rationalism and Materialism is torn up by the roots and destroyed, and there remains to Christian wisdom the glory of having to guard and protect the truth. It is moreover a vice common to the enemies of the faith of our time especially that they repudiate and proclaim the necessity of repudiating all respect and obedience for the authority of the Church, and even of any human power, [whereas the dogma of the Immaculate Conception] imposes [the obligation] of recognizing in the Church a power before which not only has the will to bow, but the intelligence to subject itself. It is from a subjection of the reason of this sort that Christian people sing thus the praise of the Mother of God: 'Thou art all fair, O Mary, and the stain of original sin is not in thee' [Mass of the Immaculate Conception]. And thus once again is justified what the Church attributes to this august Virgin, that she has exterminated all the heresies in the world.[1]

All heresies because the Virgin, being without original sin, the origin of all heresy, was against all its consequences. Among them, modernism.

It is hard not to imagine Loisy smiling. He seems to have been particularly surprised by the words of the third encyclical, *Iucunda sane accidit*, a few days earlier, where Pius X said:

For take away the supernatural order and the story of the origin of the Church must be built on quite another foundation, and hence the innovators handle as they list the monuments of history, forcing them to say what they wish them to say, and not what the authors of those monuments meant.

Many are captivated by the great show of erudition which is held out before them, and by the apparently convincing force of the proofs adduced, so that they either lose the faith or feel that it is greatly shaken in them. There are many, too, firm in the faith, who accuse critical science of being destructive, while in itself it is innocent and a sure element of investigation when rightly applied. . . . But these errors will never be effectively refuted, unless by bringing about a change of front, that is to say, unless those in error be forced to leave the field of criticism in which they consider themselves firmly entrenched, for the

---

[1] *Ad diem illum*. 2 February 1904. The text is that given by *The Tablet*, 20 February 1904.

legitimate field of philosophy through the abandonment of which they have fallen into their errors.[1]

The very philosophy that Loisy refuted, in fact, but for which Buonaiuti was seeking a new basis. Indeed, he thought he might have found one in the still uncertain method of pragmatism, and suggested in Le Roy's 'pragmatistical' turning-point.[2]

The Roman hierarchy, in fact, refused to take account of the 'total revolution', or rather were putting off taking account of it until they had sharpened up the weapons with which to oppose it. All the same, one feels they were in fact making ready, and that the unanimity they kept stressing was wishful thinking. For occasionally even Catholics were obviously influenced 'by the insidious Kantism', and it is hard to believe that the Thomist revival had implanted the philosophy of Aristotle and Aquinas very firmly when, in spite of the serious blow it had given the philosophy of Kant, it had not managed to extinguish it. Experience had shown, too, that many young men were not deeply influenced by the philosophy they had been brought up on, since so many of them were an easy prey to the dazzling new opinions, and despised the

[1] *Iucunda sane accidit*, 12 March 1904. The text is that given by *The Tablet*, 2 April 1904.

[2] Nearly every number of *Civiltà cattolica* urged the importance of philosophy, and argued hotly in favour of more time being given to the teaching of philosophy in the seminaries; it mentioned with satisfaction that if the current timetables used in lay and religious schools were compared, it was found that philosophy was more respected and studied more fervently in the religious schools. *Civiltà cattolica* mentioned Le Roy's essay and scornfully included it among the hidden influences of the current errors, which were as harmful to the progress of philosophy as they were to the progress of faith, and regretted the undeserved esteem in which it was held. 'This is an unfortunate sign of superficiality,' it continued, 'indeed of a complete lack of theological training and of seriousness in treating the most delicate questions. And it is unfortunate to find this not so much in the distinguished layman (a mathematician, not a theologian) who wrote the essay, as in the clergy, both regular and secular, who greeted it with bold enthusiasm, as the dawn of a new theology of our time' (10 November 1905, Vol. IV, No. 1330, pp. 464–70: 'Aristotele e Kant. Saggio di parallelo fra i filosofi'). Two years later, however, when the essay was published in book form, the same journal treated it less mockingly and was better informed about it; admitting that Le Roy at least deserved credit for having mentioned 'what is undeniable, such as, that the time of partial heresies is over, and denial affects not this dogma or that, but the very idea of dogma' (July 1907, Vol. II, No. 1368, pp. 641–59, *Dogma e critica*). The definition 'compendium of all heresies' was being prepared: the *Osservatore romano* maintained that Le Roy went even further than Loisy in boldness (May 1907 number), and *Civiltà cattolica* said in a note: 'We know, and are pleased to announce, that Blondel has denied agreeing with the doctrines or proposals of Le Roy' (p. 659).

simplicity and austerity of the Aristotelian philosophy of Aquinas as medieval. Even Catholics, in fact, were now divided in what was a 'war of two worlds'.[1]

It was to reinforce this, which intellectually had not yet found an exact answer to the innovators' questions—though the attempt to isolate them seemed to have had marked success already—that the Church reminded Catholics very clearly of the need for discipline and a spirit of total obedience. At the same time the Pope, in the most elementary language, recalled them to the realities of the faith and the primary meaning of its dogmas.

---

[1] See *Civiltà cattolica*, 1905, Vol. IV, No. 1330 (November 1905), p. 464 ff.

13. Murri and 'Political Modernism'

1905 is considered the year of 'political modernism'. In this year Catholics were divided into two groups, modernistic and clerical. *Civiltà cattolica*'s leading article: 'The new year: Italy at the cross-roads', which appeared at the end of 1904, gave an idea of the future programme: 'social action in the constitutional field of the modern state', 'the only way in which the interests of the people and their religious conscience can be defended against the tyranny of the anti-Christian parties'. In other words, the paper's tone had changed a great deal: it now admitted that Italian Catholics had become a party, or at least had acquired a collective image of their own.

So long as Catholics kept to their Achilles' tent, an air of mystery surrounded it, but, as an element essential to the general order of national politics was missing, there was always something hypothetical in them; in fact, an unknown element, since no one knew if and how Catholics would emerge from their 'non-expedit' tent and what effect their participation in political and parliamentary life would produce. . . . either we are wrong . . . or else it seems not unduly optimistic or presumptuous to say that . . . in the last decade public opinion in general, both in Italy and outside it, is substantially more favourable towards the political action of militant Italian Catholics; so that, without denying or hiding any of their principles, they are now recognized as capable of taking an equal part with the other parties in political action and for that reason in the government of the country.[1]

Italy, *Civiltà cattolica* maintained, was now in a quiet period, since the weariness of the parties to the quarrel had successfully spiked all their guns; and in face of the danger of anti-clerical socialism, it now appeared as it really was—religious and conserva-tive. With its fundamental good sense in the practical things of life, it had seen at last that the only popular reaction that could arrest, weaken, and ward off the ever-growing invasion of socialist propaganda was to be found in the Catholic movement. 'If the papacy would only follow what so many of its bishops have

[1] See *Civiltà cattolica*, 1905, Vol. I (December 1904).

suggested,' Nitti had written in *Il socialismo cattolico*, far back in 1891, 'if only it had the courage to proclaim peace between capital and labour, recognizing the rights of the latter over the former and seeking to promote agreement, it would find itself at the head of a movement that no one could halt and that might realize the old Catholic dream in the Church.' Was Nitti's prophecy to be realized?[1] Yes, what Nitti had foreseen was being fulfilled perfectly 'before [their] very eyes', *Civiltà cattolica* wrote, while ignoring the label 'Catholic Socialism', which, it said, was 'by now out of date' and 'other expressions [they found] inadmissible'.[2]

The prophecy was not, in fact, to be fulfilled in the way Nitti had meant; only in the sense that the Catholic movement was the only one capable of standing up to socialism. The Catholic movement *Civiltà cattolica* was writing about had no programme, and promoted no reforms as radical as, or more radical than, those of popular socialism. All this it had abandoned: *Rerum novarum* was forgotten; like the name 'Catholic socialism', it was now out of date. The *Opera dei congressi* had been dissolved; the priests who promoted a 'political' movement within it were now considered enemies of the clergy; obedience to the Pope, who was promoting a religious restoration in Christ, had been restored.

The Catholic group whose strength had been recognized, or rather the alliance between the conservative aristocracy and the Catholic hierarchy against any form of renewal, was described in the encyclical *Il fermo proposito*, the fifth in Pius X's pontificate, on 11 June 1905. It was addressed to the bishops of Italy, and its purpose was to set up and develop Catholic Action, a lay association for the propagation of the Catholic religion in the non-Catholic world. In it, having made it clear that the restoration of all things in Christ referred 'not only to what belongs to the Church's divine mission to lead souls to God, but also to what . . . Christian civilization as a whole, and its individual elements,

[1] See F. S. Nitti, *Il socialismo cattolico*, Turin–Rome, 1891, p. 356: 'The Catholic socialists', Nitti wrote, 'are not, like the Catholic liberals of the school of Lamennais and Lacordaire, solitary thinkers. They have large numbers at their disposal, they are at the head of widespread discontent and their criticisms and aspirations are based on a real, profound evil, and on a real need. Unlike the democratic socialists, they wish to reform society in the name of God, but this does not mean that their reform is any less radical and less profound, and their influence over the workers is no less intense and dangerous.'

[2] See *Civiltà cattolica*, 1905, Vol. I, 'Il centro sociale e l'unità dei cattolici italiani'.

derives spontaneously from that divine mission', the Pope continued:

You see . . . how helpful to the Church are those choice bands of Catholics who bring together all their living forces, in order to combat anti-Christian civilizations with every just and legal means they can: in order to repair in every way the serious disorders that are derived from it, to put Jesus Christ back into the family, the school and society; to re-establish the principle of human authority as representing the authority of God; to have the interests of the people especially at heart and in particular the interests of workers and peasants, not only instilling in them the religious principle, which is the sole source of consolation in the sorrows of life, but seeking to dry their tears, lighten their sufferings, and improve their economic condition by making suitable provision for them; which means seeing that the laws are just, and that unjust laws are corrected or suppressed and finally to defend and uphold in a truly Catholic way the rights of God in all things and the no less sacred rights of the Church.

The combination of all these tasks, undertaken and promoted mostly by the Catholic laity and varying according to the needs of each nation and the particular circumstances of each country, is what is usually called in a special and indeed noble way *Catholic Action* or else the *Action of Catholics*.[1]

This new form of 'guelphism', however, met opposition from some of the clergy, headed by Murri. Ten years later, Eligio Cacciaguerra, who belonged to this group, praised Murri extravagantly and described the atmosphere of international opposition which Murri succeeded in arousing among Catholics, both clerics and laymen.[2] This opposition lay in saying that it was permissible for Catholics to form themselves into a political group, foreign—even if not hostile—to ecclesiastical discipline; not the last link

---

[1] *Il fermo proposito*, 11 June 1905.

[2] See *L'Azione*, Cesena, 8 September 1912: 'I was twenty when we went to Rome for the first meeting, which was held one evening on the Aventine. It was another *secessio plebis in montem sacrum*. There was Sonnenschein, an extremely likeable German priest with an Italian spirit, who spoke every language, there was Marco Sangnier [founder of the movement of Sillon, later condemned] . . . there was Vercesi . . . and there was Murri. This was the first time I saw him. Small, lively, with a feminine face and a sweet voice, but with vibrant gestures. There was something Napoleonic about him. And there were many others, laymen and priests. . . . It was the time of crisis in Italian Christian Democracy. There was the threat of our secession . . . Professor Toniolo was trembling with religious fear. And we thought we would raise a revolution in the Church and in Italy' (quoted in L. Bedeschi, *I cattolici disubbidienti*, Naples–Rome, 1959, p. 84 in a note).

in a hierarchical chain, but the free expression of the political and social wishes of some, if not all, Catholics. That this meant opposition was clear to the movement's promoters. The Pope had been quite explicit, and what the hierarchy had written, to clarify and illustrate what he said, was just as explicit. Yet Murri and his followers seemed to be saying that they had a right to interpret things in their own way. This was quite illogical, for the distinction they made between obedience in theological and moral matters and obedience in political matters presupposed a 'political' field which the Pope had repeatedly denied existed: these elusive politics, he had stressed, must be brought back to the real, theologically inspired, and direct social action. As he refused to compromise in his efforts to achieve unity, the Pope refused to recognize that any political action was open to Catholics. The only way Murri's attitude can be justified is by supposing that he and his followers misinterpreted what the Pope had said. When the 'nonexpedit' was in practice abolished, they may have believed—as some people actually did—that Catholics now had a chance of political action outside the conservative and liberal parties. Either all Catholics had a right to political action, and could join whatever political party they liked; or else they had no rights at all, and all 'political' Catholics should be disowned by the hierarchy.

So Murri was not so much asserting a right as drawing attention to a practical contradiction, which meant that other contradictions, such as accepting the political action of Catholics in other parties, were equally permissible. Besides, Murri had another quite definite object: to avoid at all costs—even if it meant the loss of his early popularity—having Catholics identified with the conservatives and the liberals; that is, to avoid the traditional alliances always implicit whenever the clergy had anything to do with the ruling classes, or the ecclesiastical hierarchy with conservative politicians. Why should the clergy not be allowed to align themselves, politically, with the working-class movement, and fight side by side with the socialists? Why should Catholic laymen not be in the forefront of the social revolution? Why should priests not sever their connection with those who always stood for tradition against whatever was new, and now opposed the very evident social movement with the rights of the rich and the fear of revolution? These men might now identify themselves with the national good, but had they really guarded and defended it over the past hundred years? This did not mean that it was necessary to repudiate the Pope's directives—indeed, Murri always claimed to be the only true interpreter of what the Pope really meant.[1] Nor did it mean joining the movements for intellectual reform which were taking place throughout the Catholic world. A revolution in matters of political choice certainly did not presuppose adhesion to a movement for the reform of doctrine; the wish to make social changes in no way implied a wish for theological changes; the doctrinal truths that regulated a man's religious life would allow him to act in the political field without being overwhelmed or destroyed by a different morality and theology. In principle, Murri declined to take part in the 'great movement' of the reformers. Like Minocchi, he stood, in a way, for a system of alliances, a religious democracy that allowed the various voices to be heard and to contribute to the natural, necessary, and religious progress of truth. He belonged to the age of Leo XIII, whom he admired for having looked calmly

[1] In February 1906 *Cultura sociale* could still write: 'Only *Cultura sociale* (we may say without immodesty, since it is obvious and no credit to ourselves) . . . intends to be the interpreter and the intellectual instrument of Pius X's programme: *instaurare omnia in Christo.*' Four months later it ceased publication, 'not unaware' as Murri put it in his farewell article of 1 June 1906, 'that for some time the higher ecclesiastical authorities have disapproved of this journal's ideas and political attitudes'. Fifteen years later, Murri reaffirmed his own orthodoxy: 'No one has so far managed to say exactly where lay the error in what was called "Murrismo"; it denied that we owed the Pope absolute obedience in social and political matters, and in this it agreed with the whole of Catholic doctrine and tradition, and could find support in the very words of St. Thomas Aquinas. If there was any heresy in this, it was in the Vatican. Its greatest error, for which Pius X refused to allow it to remain within the Church, was the political autonomy of Catholics, which twelve years later, with the Partito Popolare Italiano [Italian Popular Party], became officially true' (in *Dalla Democrazia cristiana al Partito Popolare Italiano*, p. 24). It must be borne in mind that these were 'personal differences' between Murri and Pius X. When Pius X was patriarch of Venice, in a letter addressed to Count Paganuzzi, President of the Opera dei Congressi, he criticized an article by Murri entitled 'Il crollo di Venezia' (27 August 1902). Angrily, Murri wrote to him: 'I have seen your letter in the newspaper . . . which, apart from interfering in a journalistic argument that is the business only of Catholics in action, makes grave accusations about an article of mine and goes on to judge the spirit and intentions of a priest whom Your Excellency does not know and whose writings you have probably not even read. . . . But, as a Christian and as a priest, I must protect my dignity and my character . . . and I appeal to Your Excellency's episcopal spirit and character for just reparation and hope that Your Excellency will examine the facts and what I have written more carefully. If you do so, you will certainly find that your very serious accusations are unjust and will withdraw them, leaving my superiors to watch over my *spirit*, and the Lord, *who judges*.' Presumably Pius X continued not to read what Murri wrote; and vice versa.

at the modern world, for adapting the age-old principles of Christian wisdom to it, and for being esteemed by all great men; in short, for being reasonably progressive.

And it was Leo XIII's *Rerum novarum* that first showed awareness of a problem that had since grown ever more serious, until now it was beginning to overshadow the intellectual and moral interests of the whole nation.

But, in raising the disciplinary aspect of all this, Pius X fatally linked the reformers of doctrine with the autonomous Christian Democrats: 'There can be no Catholic action in the true sense without immediate dependence on the bishops,' he wrote to Cardinal Svampa of Bologna, on 1 March 1905, in a letter that was later made public, and continued:

The so-called autonomous Christian Democrats, through their wish for an ill-understood freedom, show that they have shaken off all discipline; they seek new and dangerous goals the Church cannot approve; they affect an authoritative manner in order to assert themselves, in order to judge and criticize everything; and they have actually reached the point of saying they are ready to submit to infallibility, but not to obedience. If any argument were needed to prove that, by logically developing their principles, they have become openly rebellious to the Church's authority, it could be found in what they say at their meetings, when they declare themselves independent, by what they publish in their journals and newspapers to champion what they are doing and to justify their conduct; and finally by the fact that their reply to the solemn prohibitions of venerable prelates is either that these prohibitions have nothing to do with them, either collectively or personally, or that the Pope and bishops have a right to judge matters of faith and morals but no right to direct social action; so that they consider themselves free to carry on with their work.[1]

Rome also wished to connect the political rebellion with the heretical movement that was developing; and because of personal relationships between individual members of both groups, the two were in fact drawn more closely together. These personal relationships did not of course mean any identity of views, on doctrine or anything else. In the early days of 'modernism in action' the reformers themselves had seen how they differed among themselves, and those differences later grew more marked. No one,

---

[1] Letter from Pius X to Cardinal Svampa, quoted in *Civiltà cattolica*, 1905, Vol. I, No. 1314 (11 March 1905), pp. 744–6.

for instance, thought Murri, with his violent, clearly defined scholasticism, was a follower of Loisy or a colleague of Blondel. But *Civiltà cattolica* tried to conceal these differences, and the reformers themselves preferred not to disrupt their own unity. This was not because they expected a single doctrinal system to emerge from their work, or a single intellectual result that would correspond to some political or social activity; but because they could see the ever-increasing hostility of Rome, and thought it best not to encourage this by revealing their own uncertainties. In spite of this, though, the innovators did not think themselves in danger, for they failed to realize the significance of the opposition they were arousing. Just as they failed to realize that they belonged to a movement that was gradually leading them into radical opposition, so they failed to realize that others, whom they often attacked but did not always recognize individually, were forming an equally radical opposition to them. These others were implacable in ferreting out the innovators wherever they were to be found; they always accused them of a single outlook, a single desire to shake off all restraint and to refuse obedience to the Pope; and this at the very moment when the obedience of Catholics seemed the one thing necessary to save the country—and through it humanity—from the grave danger of atheistic socialism.

On the other hand, when an offer of collaboration was made to these dangerous other forces, it seems not to have been welcomed. Turati sarcastically refused the alliance Murri suggested,[1] and *Civiltà cattolica* published the two letters 'to serve as an example of human error'. Turati's reply, it said, 'in a form that [was] ostensibly courteous but in fact contemptuous' gave 'a humiliating lesson to both the man and the priest'.[2]

Murri's problem, as the third priest guiding the reforming movement (the others were Loisy and Buonaiuti; Minocchi was then losing his effectiveness as a cultural leader and being over-

---

[1] The letter from Murri to Turati appeared in *Critica sociale* in October 1905. Turati replied: 'Regular fornications, no; even to think it possible is mortal sin. . . . We are eldest children of the devil, or rather of free-thinking, and carry our father on our backs wherever we go. In heaven and on earth; here and there; in our thoughts and at work. . . . He is a devil; and therefore dangerous to let loose. The conservatives are more logical. And no fear of electoral failure will make us give up this satanic primogeniture.' Turati ended with a personal attack: 'for us to agree you might have to take off the clothes you wear,' he wrote.

[2] See *Civiltà cattolica*, 1905, Vol. IV, No. 1329 (October 1905), pp. 355–8.

reverential to the Pope, referring to one of his audiences in ambiguously respectful terms[1]), was that of directing the Catholic laity. Or rather, quite apart from his personal ambitions and his character, which was polemical rather than intelligent, and as dynamic as it was illogical, Murri was doing in the political field what he had done before—defending his work and the legitimacy of what he was doing against the traditional attitude of the hierarchy to the laity. Because, no matter how much other priests superior to him in the hierarchy might dislike or disapprove of him, Murri was still a priest, and as such he guaranteed Christian Democrats in fact and in conscience not merely support from a religious authority, but—which was more important—the charismatic inspiration that any activity needs: in this case, it was political activity.

[1] See the report in *Giornale d'Italia*, of 12 March 1905: 'It suddenly struck me irresistibly, that I was visiting a good parish priest in his study. . . . All Don Giuseppe Sarto's apostolic simplicity requires as Pope are the four or five rooms of a presbytery; but three hundred million Catholics want to see him in the Vatican. . . . Pius X is not a scientist, nor need Peter's successor be a man of science. But Pius X knows as much as he needs to know about the inquiries of religious science; and as "a poor priest"—which was what he liked to call himself to me—he has read and studied the Bible, and in it has found support for his faith in the revelation of God and the divinity of Jesus Christ. . . . Of historical criticism applied to the Bible, reason's sharp weapon which was brandished against the Christian faith in the last century, Pius X is rather mistrustful; his solemn warning showed how worried he was about its possible results today, although it is now well known and received by the Catholic clergy. But this does not mean that he is against every form of criticism: he accepted my work kindly, and showed that he was glad to see the historical learning, which in the hands of unbelievers is used to oppose the faith, was to be found among the clergy too, respecting and supporting the faith. Removed from the limitations of time and space, the quarter of an hour I spent with Pius X took on the importance of a great historical moment in the life of the Papacy. The eternal struggle between reason and mystery; the eternal seeking, the hard painful study needed to establish harmony between science and faith.'

14. *Il Santo* and its Followers

On 5 November of the same year, 1905, Baldini and Castoldi of Milan published Antonio Fogazzaro's *Il Santo*. Assuming the right to intervene in ecclesiastical matters, as he had done when he lectured so controversially on evolution, Fogazzaro, a layman, now put forward his own ideas of reform. *Civiltà cattolica* itself, which had become the mouthpiece of the ecclesiastical hierarchy when it first refused to listen, immediately repudiated the reformers' proposals once again:

For our part, we sincerely regret that such a gifted writer, instead of writing something filled with the goodness some people had led us to hope, should have betrayed our expectations. Fogazzaro's thesis is mistaken. It is not the Church that needs reforming, but rather society, which fails to listen to the Church, denies God, disregards his laws, and plunges into the most corrupt materialism and the most dreadful anarchy. It is not the Church that should adapt itself to society, but society that should submit to the Church, the infallible fount of the truth men must receive and learn from her. Really, if one may say so, it is bitterly ironical to publish a book accusing the Church of being greedy and masterful when human laws disregard its sacred rights, when its religious are robbed and scattered, and when sectarian hatred triumphs over its ruins. Whereas from abroad we have splendid works inquiring how men may be brought from the pride of disbelief to the humility of faith, the author of *Il Santo* has suggested to his Italian admirers nothing less than the reform of divine Christianity through utopian ideas of a Christian humanism that consists of unrestrained investigation, mystical rationalism, Pharisaical scandals, personal independence and scorn of tradition, all wrapped up in a visionary's burst of asceticism. Society certainly needs no such saints to be saved, nor do they deserve a book to do them honour![1]

Nearly a year later, after describing Fogazzaro as 'without exaggeration, the prince of Italian Catholic reformism' and *Il Santo* as a 'classic example of anti-clerical reformist prejudice', and 'the most important work of international Catholic reformism', *Civiltà*

---

[1] See *Civiltà cattolica*, 1905, Vol. IV, No. 1331 (2 December), anonymous review, pp. 595–607; the extract quoted, on p. 607.

cattolica exactly defined the book's basic design. Setting aside its literary merits and faults (even though the review had been rather over-enthusiastic about its qualities on other occasions), the writer said that the fundamental issues of *Il Santo* could be reduced to three: the need for a reform of the Church (a radical reform promoted by the Catholic laity organized in a great religious order of Knights of the Holy Spirit, independent of the hierarchy because defending religious freedom against it); the definition of most of the higher clergy, helped by aged zealots and four evil spirits—those of lies, oppression, greed, and a refusal to change—as the greatest hindrance to this reform, and its proudest enemy; and the means by which this radical reform could definitely be imposed on the degenerate hierarchy: a personal mysticism based on a theory of universal evolution.[1]

But *Civiltà cattolica* did not condemn *Il Santo* purely from a theological point of view, or indulge in haughty irony merely at the expense of its many doctrinal muddles and mistakes; it suggested that careful readers might find some of its suggestions akin to some of those of some of the reformers, Murri in particular.

The most fatal result of progressive Catholicism as shown by Fogazzaro in his novel [*Civiltà cattolica* wrote] is, we consider, the fact that it hinders militant Catholics from organizing the people socially in a constitutional way, which is the most urgent and important task the Church in Italy has in the future. To some, this may seem strange; to us it seems perfectly certain that the way in which the young Christian Democrats have mixed the theoretical movement of reformatory Catholicism with the practical, popular movement for economic and social organization against socialism, has sterilized, hindered, and divided the second; just as it is impossible for the first to penetrate into the Church. As far as organizing the common people's economic interests goes, the catechism provided what religion was needed; but the leaders and agitators of Christian Democracy have tried to add the reform of the whole of theology! Thus has the democratic movement of action been hampered by the aristocratic movement of thought, and followed when it led; which shows why Fogazzaro and his *Santo*, though alien and opposed to Christian democracy, have been so well received by the autonomous Christian Democrats. Alas, there will be no true reform, and no true Catholic organization in Italy, so long as Fogazzaro's *Santo* is the ideal of Catholic reformers.[2]

[1] See *Civiltà cattolica*, 1906, Vol. IV, No. 1354 (7 November), 'Anti-clerical prejudice in Italy', pp. 401–33, *passim* and in particular pp. 401–3.
[2] See ibid., p. 427.

The truth was that it was not only, and not especially, the young Christian Democrats or their leaders or agitators who confused the democratic movement of action with the aristocratic movement of thought; nor did any of them, leaders or rank and file, lay much stress on the democratic character of either movement. 'Democracy' plays a fairly small part in the history of modernism, even if one seeks to view it on as broad a basis as possible without isolating its various aspects, and if one accepts that a number of cultural streams all flowed together into it. It would be a mistake to see what happened as a struggle between the higher and lower clergy, between the laity, seen as standing on the sidelines, or in a subordinate position, in the exercise of doctrinal power, and the clergy, seen as the ruling classes; between the owners of truth—and therefore of power—which means the Roman hierarchy, and their servants, lay or clerical. The history of modernism is doctrinal above all, the history of an attempt at Catholic reform made within the Church, and within its cultural orbit. Whether Catholics should take part in public affairs, their very 'democracy' and the fact of their forming themselves into a political party—all this in a way has nothing to do with modernism: it runs parallel with modernism, and contemporaneously, and there may well have been connections between the two; but what made them be considered as one were the prohibitions, lack of intelligence and intolerance on both sides (perhaps more on that of the Roman hierarchy), which for years kept stressing that the two movements had common origins. As for the reformers, they never showed the slightest political awareness; least of all Murri, who almost absurdly, before, during, and after his condemnation, believed that the Church would have for a time to exercise a political power that ought, in fact, to have been exercised by the laity:

... if, in the early stages of Christian civilization, we find the Church and its people taking a leading part in all fields of civil activity, dealing not only with individual consciences but with public affairs and public order, from the humblest financial tasks to the highest in social and international legislation; or if the Church has at times engaged in titanic struggles against the secular power or against a whole complex of civil and social institutions; this happened on account of the fundamental double historical law in the Church's life, by which the Church, as the highest promoter of civilized living, takes on functions which the State or individuals neglect and which she and the faithful think necessary to the progress of civilization. In this case the Church does all in her power to protect and promote the cause of civilization, where it is in danger through the aggression of enemy leaders or the spontaneous and violent dissolution of civil institutions. In the Church's history these functions have been of every kind: economic, political, scientific; even, when it defended civilization against the Turks, military.[1]

This was written at the end of the century, but Murri remained loyal to it: loyal to the Church as substitute for the State and to the concept of culture as a tool of the apostolate, a valuable tool which the clergy—he complained to his friend Semeria—seemed to lack, in those days. But, to return to *Civiltà cattolica* (and Murri never had any doubt that there was in fact one *civiltà*, and one only—the Catholic one; unlike many of the reformers, who thought there was an error in the very name of the enemy review), the distinction it made between the two movements, though it was as arbitrary as the structure it assigned *Il Santo*, had an element of truth in it. The young Christian Democrats, their leaders, and Murri might not think so, but *Il Santo's* followers were wholly convinced that reform was not only independent of any success democracy might have, but must come about through the rational and mystical efforts of a few chosen souls:

Dear friend, I myself suffer sadly from irritation in the face of religious disagreement [Fogazzaro wrote to his young friend Gallarati Scotti at the time he was writing his novel]. It is a human weakness and the reason why religious wars were always the most savage. I hope reading Tyrrell and seeing Father Bremond have done me much good as far as this is concerned. They help me to respect other people's ways of seeing God, however different from ours, provided they are sincere. Those of us who think as we do find ourselves disagreeing the whole time with other believers, and need great gentleness if we are to win even a few over to us.[2]

To win over even a few was what *Il Santo*, enormously successful in publishing terms though it was, seemed to hope for. But it seemed to be trying to win these few over one at a time, to convince people that truth was in a state of crisis. Fogazzaro, who had hoped

---

[1] See R. Murri, *Battaglie d'oggi*, Vol. II: *Lettere a G. S. La cultura del clero*, 1901, p. 96 (but already published, under the signature P. Averri, in *Cultura sociale*, 1898).

[2] Letter from A. Fogazzaro to T. Gallarati Scotti, 12 February 1903, in *Selected Letters*, p. 504.

for a saintly Pope, found himself with a Pope canonized shortly after his death, who had refused him an audience. ('As far as the next Pope is concerned, I don't dare to hope in Gibbon,' he wrote to Giacosa a few days after the death of Leo XIII, whose obituary he had written in *La Stampa*; although he did not believe that the new Pope could 'open up any new road [for them]'.[1]) But this did nothing to damp his confidence as a reformer; whatever reaction his words might arouse, he hoped to carry out something more sublime, 'God's invisible work', as Maude Dominica Petre, Tyrrell's friend and follower, defined it.[2] For this reason—the fact that Fogazzaro clearly considered the choice of *pars Dei* as one of the reformer's tasks—the criticisms of him as the major exponent of Catholic reformism, at least in so far as they are based on an interpretation of *Il Santo*, are not fully justified. Nor was the way in which *Civiltà cattolica* set down what it considered the book's main issues. This seems to be forcing the book's concepts into a particular form; whereas in fact they were more fluid, and possibly more suspect. *Civiltà cattolica* seems, indeed, to be seeking to impose a pattern on the reformatory movement itself, even if it meant protesting too much in self-defence. Of course, Fogazzaro was famous enough to justify some of the bitterness and irony at least: he was a typical literary figure, a gentleman and an intellectual who, though claiming religious doubts, had set himself up as the inspired spokesman of like-minded Italians and Frenchmen, and had gained religious approval for the doubts and difficulties he had sown, and even for the way he accused the clergy, and the Italian clergy in particular, of being spiritually retrograde, incapable of accepting what was new, rough and rude; but not for his new way of seeing God, more perfect than 'other people's ways of seeing God'; and both he and his hero sought out the

[1] Letter from Fogazzaro to Piero Giacosa of 22 July 1903, ibid., p. 512; and see the letter already quoted to A. Giacomelli: 'I hoped for a Pope who would raise the intellectual level of the ecclesiastical hierarchy and have a feeling for the modern spirit; who would nominate Cardinal Bonomelli or at least Scalabrini, who would favour men like Semeria, who would be well disposed towards the Rosminians. These things concern me more than the abolition of the *non expedit*, as that is a political act; and I expect none of them from Pius X,' quoted by T. Gallarati Scotti, *La vita*, p. 382.

[2] See M. D. Petre, review of *Il Santo* in *The Commonwealth*, June 1906. According to Gallarati Scotti, Fogazzaro gave his hero some of Tyrrell's characteristics. Tyrrell wrote to Fogazzaro: 'Your *Santo* will do much better than a *Blessed* would' (see letter from Fogazzaro to Filippo Crispolti of 19 January 1906 in *Selected Letters*, p. 576).

uncertain, rather than fought on a religious front, as they would have wished to do.

The elect of this aristocracy of the uncertain gathered round Fogazzaro, who had no great plans for victory and was certainly no revolutionary strategist. However ambitious his religious propaganda might be, he knew very well that he was no historian or prophet, but a creator of characters, a teller of tales; and the fact that he had written about a prophet was a happy chance, or a providential coincidence. In his efforts to form a group—if only on a cultural level—he always behaved towards his friends as a disinterested inspirer who urged them to be prudent: 'Think it over, and over, and over again!' he wrote to the young Gallarati Scotti, and urged him to be the first to drop his 'haughty, warlike ardour'. This was just on the subject of organizing 'Fogazzaro lectures'.[1] There was certainly a case for prudence, but Fogazzaro somehow made it sound as if he were talking of burglary.

Il Santo had many lay admirers, but laymen were among its severest critics, too. They were irritated by the contradictions in Fogazzaro: 'feeble, unbalanced, mad', was Vittorio Osimo's description of his hero in *Critica sociale*.[2]

What real hope is there that reform can come from within? [wrote Graf]. And why so firmly reject heresy and schism? If the future of the faith lies in the great Church and not in the small, why wish the great Church to bow down to the small? . . . First comes the cry of 'Freedom, freedom!' Then, straight after it, 'Bow down!' So what happens? At the first warning from the Vatican, the reformers at Giovanni Selva's scatter like a flock of sparrows. . . . How can we fight for the truth if at the first threat we throw down our arms? How can we forge ahead with what is new, if we have such respect for what is old?—by this I mean what is old and no longer viable?[3]

These very criticisms, with their moral accusations of its hero, show how seriously laymen took *Il Santo*. Whether for or against it, they were quite certain that here was a plan of reform which they must either support, or openly refute.

Fogazzaro's behaviour when his book was put on the Index, as it soon was, on 5 April 1906, was a good example of what Graf

[1] Letter from Fogazzaro to F. T. Gallarati Scotti of 1 January 1906, in *Selected Letters*, p. 576.
[2] See Vittorio Osimo, in *Critica sociale* of 16 June 1906.
[3] See A. Graf, *Per una fede*, Milan, 1906, pp. 100-3.

meant when he spoke of the contrast between freedom and sub-mission ('How can we fight for the truth if at the first threat we throw down our arms?'). To those who asked him what he would do, Fogazzaro replied in an open letter to Crispolti, published in *l'Avvenire d'Italia* on 21 April, but written some days earlier:

My dear friend,
You certainly have a right to know how I will behave with regard to the decree of the Congregation of the Index, which has condemned *Il Santo*. From the first I decided to obey the decree, as it is my duty as a Catholic to do, or rather not to dispute it, not to work against it by authorizing further translations and reprints apart from those which were contracted before the decree, and are impossible to break. Now you know my decision; I want everyone to know it, so I ask you to publish this letter in a newspaper chosen by you.[1]

But this did not scatter the reforming sparrows. Fogazzaro's 'practical obedience' was no business of theirs, just as the major reformist (and his hero) did not alter what they were doing. Material was then being collected for a publication that would 'make Christianity habitable', as Loisy was to put it: *Rinnova-mento* was first mentioned in Sabatier's correspondence, in August 1906. Besides, only the laity seemed to want things put down in black and white: the 'religious' reformers clearly realized that in religious terms, in the most elementary psychology of the faith, practical submission, inner freedom, obedience and refusal, made up the traditional structure of behaviour: the uneasy soul would not grow any more weary on account of a new sin, or a new refusal, or obedience to something else, nor—and this was especi-ally obvious—could it be permanently decided where the enemy was to be found, once the reformer realized that he contained within himself the enemy's arguments: 'in interiore hominis'—the Church's Latin exonerated them from taking a definite stand. Besides, first Loisy, then Fogazzaro and Laberthonnière (whose essays were put on the Index in the same decree as *Il Santo*[2]), then Tyrrell, one by one came up against the Church's dis-

---

[1] See Cardinal Svampa's favourable comment on Fogazzaro's letter in Gallar-ati Scotti's *La vita*, p. 450, and see ibid., pp. 450 ff., the approval of Cardinal Agliardi of Capecelatro 'a great gentleman with a Christian spirit', 'an old shepherd of souls', 'a gentleman of the old school' (as Gallarati Scotti calls him in his *Life*, p. 444) and of Cardinal Mathieu.
[2] See letter from Blondel to Laberthonnière at the time of the condemnation: 'Very dear and good friend, let us adore together the ever-loving will of God. I

ciplinary measures: and their behaviour was remarkably similar, if only in the way they justified their own freedom to the authorities, in their refusal to take account of a condemnation which they interpreted as being literally definitive but in spirit merely a matter of prudence, or foreign to the spirit of (to what was 'spiritual' in) the true Church. The small church stood firm, since those in it refused to realize they were in error, and in particular since no one would admit a moral value in it:

For though I should be very sorry to *deserve* suspension or even excommunication, yet I have no personal fear of a censure that is undeserved except so far as it involves pain and scandal to others and brings discredit on authorities, and ought therefore to be avoided by all *reasonable* and *honourable* means [Tyrrell wrote to the General of the Society of Jesus on 31 December 1905, that is, about the time *Il Santo* appeared]. Not to speak of Our Lord and His Apostles, who were excommunicated by lawful ecclesiastical authorities for refusing to be silent, I know, as St. Augustine testifies, that no man (not even your St. Ignatius) has ever served the Church largely without incurring the displeasure and censure of the officials, whose successors have built up his sepulchre and appropriated the credit of his work. But apart from such mystical considerations, theology tells me that when excommunication is undeserved it is spiritually a gain and not a loss. Temporally it has become fairly harmless since advancing civilization and Christianity have wrested the weapons of persecution, with the exception of the *gladius linguae*, from the servants of the Gospel of Peace.

To me personally it would be, physically, mentally, and morally, an immense relief to stand apart from a world of espionage, delation, and intrigue, and to feel that I had suffered the worst it could do to me, and might live in peace and tranquillity. Not that I would ever cease to labour strenuously for the true understanding of Catholicism and for its defence against the perversions of obscurantists.[1]

And some months later, he wrote to Cardinal Ferrata:[2]

Driven, then, from my rightful place at the Altar, I remain a priest as far as you will let me, in my conduct and the observance of my state . . . I still believe and will go on believing in and defending the Roman Church

hear that you have been crushed and feel for you from the bottom of my heart. . . . I believe this hour of mourning and despondency to be a pledge of the future fruitfulness of your work. I am conscious of your great courage and supernatural strength in the face of this ordeal, as, ignoring any personal considerations, you turn away from the obvious evils to contemplate only the passion of our Divine Lord and to conform to His spirit.'

[1] Quoted in *Autobiography*, pp. 483–8.
[2] Quoted in ibid., pp. 537–9, letter of 27 July 1906.

and thinking that she possesses a great truth unawares—a heavenly treasure in the poorest and shabbiest of earthly vessels. It was not to satisfy Your Eminences nor Your Paternities, but to satisfy my own conscience that I have laboured these twenty-five years in the service primarily of religious truth, incidentally of Catholicism. I believe sincerely in that revelation which constitutes the proper object of Catholic and Christian Faith. I accept the Church and her saints as my guides in Faith and Morals. If, however, you ask me about theology and ethics, that is, about the science of Faith and the science of Morals; about the efforts of uninspired and ordinary men like myself to translate revelation into the language of philosophy, living or obsolete; I confess that I regard such matters, not indeed with indifference or as unimportant, but as pertaining to the jurisdiction of science and natural reason. It is enough that I hold the *faith* of Simon Peter, no less and no more. As to his theological science—if he had any—I am no more tied to his categories and methods than are your Eminences.

These letters throw more light on their author's 'profession of faith' than a great many essays.

In this way [Murri had written[1]] I think I am going the way of all those who, in every age, have frankly and freely spoken out to show Catholics their wrongs and duties; the way of St. Peter Damian and of Dante, of St. Catherine of Siena and of Savonarola, who sometimes behaved violently, since his age made him so.

The examples were varied; apostles on the one hand, political saints on the other. But this did not alter the certainty that they were a legitimate part of the reformatory movement that had appeared perennially in the Church's history, and they could be compared only with the saints and heroes of thought and action who had always been opposed by 'obscurantist' powers in all countries, for the same reason. Whether violent 'as [the] age made [them]', like Murri and Tyrrell, or prudent, like Fogazzaro, these rebels never doubted that they were bringing light. As for Tyrrell's personal wish to get out of a world governed by spying, secret accusations and intrigues, this seemed especially justified by the fact that in May 1905 the first cyclostyled number of *Corrispondenza romana* appeared. This was an informative publication of Mgr. Benigni's, concerned with the violent repression of modernism. Some months earlier Tyrrell had celebrated his last Mass; in November 1905 it was Loisy's turn.

---

[1] Letter to Professor Toniolo on 1 July 1903, quoted in *Battaglie d'oggi*, IV, pp. 238–9.

15. After the Condemnation

So they were condemned: the novelist, the theologian, and, earlier and greater than these, the exegete. The 'politician', who was to be suspended *a divinis* in April of the following year, was forbidden to join or take part in the Lega democratica nazionale by the Pope's encyclical of 28 July 1906, *Pieni l'animo*. And yet it was in 1906 that the reformers in a way decided to start fighting. In particular, it was in 1906 that the need was realized for a journal that would express reformatory Catholicism in Italy. Those who were to be actively involved with it were those who belonged to the 'small church of the elect'.

The movement now had two clear aspects, the inner and the outer; the first expressing itself through sympathy, the second through criticism and denunciation. In *Civiltà cattolica*, after being singled out and criticized, Loisy was solemnly declared heretic, and his 'Italian followers' were included in the denunciation, Buonaiuti first of all, Minocchi and Semeria between the lines. Buonaiuti, in fact, was the first to be violently attacked by *Civiltà cattolica*; and Fr. Rosa, who attacked him, continued his criticisms with unabated bitterness until the end: indeed, he became a 'personal enemy' in the controversy that raged on both sides, sometimes vulgarly and privately. There had been signs of this controversy already, as we have seen; but in January 1906 the fight was brought out into the open. It was as if all the digs and allusions, the heavy irony and impatience that had appeared before, had been preliminary skirmishes: now the battle was admitted, and in public, either because the times were ripe for it or because Rome decided on a less prudent policy. Why had Rome waited so long, though? Had von Hügel's intervention deferred the suspicion of heresy, though it had not been able to avert it? Or had the heretics laid themselves especially open to attack in those months around the end of 1905? Whichever way it was, Fr. Rosa considered that the time had come to see clearly and to condemn:

There is a movement that might almost be called international, a branch of the times, if you wish, but teeming from the trunk upwards with old errors; a movement towards a complete, disordered innovation of doctrine, methods, and action, so strangely widespread that it seems almost to suggest a kind of universal alliance, natural and tacit, since ideas, suggestions, and sometimes even sentences and metaphors in books, periodicals, and newspapers in Germany, France, England, the United States, and finally in Italy, where everything is put to the service of the cause, are almost identical. It is clear that they are united by certain common ideas, aspirations, and tendencies; and the same wind seems to blow through the varied pages of pamphlets, periodicals, and journals, pages shrill with modernity, but not always equally serene, reflective, and knowledgeable.[1]

The terms Fr. Rosa used meant little, if they were in fact meant to describe the innovators' ideas: 'a movement towards something', 'profound renewal from within', 'a new accommodation of faith and dogma to modern thought', 'a theological adaptation of the philosophy of Kant and Hegel'. But what else could he say? Instead of making precise accusations, he took refuge in rhetorical questions.

Have these people made a profound study of ancient knowledge, or of the maxims of philosophy and theology they so cordially despise? And if they are ecclesiastics [that they were, and that he was dealing with Buonaiuti, the same article made clear after a few pages; the question within a question is part of the rhetoric], have they ever noticed certain rules suggested to those who studied sacred matters by his Holiness Leo XIII and recommended again by his Holiness Pius X? Do they really know these scholastic authors they despise?[2]

'Some things make one doubtful about it,' concluded Fr. Rosa, who certainly had no doubt about it, and rightly so. But in fact the best thing he could do was throw doubt on the reformers' culture, for plainly they lacked the culture of the 'obscurantists'. Laberthonnière himself had to admit that he had argued before he was well informed; this appears in the philosophical letters he was exchanging with Blondel.[3] The revolutionaries simply wanted a reform of culture; theirs was, indeed 'a movement towards something', a movement that rejected the site—which in any case they

---

[1] See Enrico Rosa, 'Uomini nuovi ed errori vecchi' in *Civiltà cattolica*, 1906, Vol. I, No. 1335 (24 January), p. 239.

[2] Ibid., p. 256.

[3] In the philosophical correspondence with Blondel already quoted; and see in particular their argument on Aquinas and Aristotle, and then, from the years 1919 to 1928, on the metaphysics of charity, pp. 241 ff.

either did not know or hardly knew—on which the scholastic building stood. In their refusal to see what they were struggling towards, they were consistent in saying that their 'profession of faith' presupposed a rejection of any rational construction, Thomistic or Scotistic or anything else; they were not so in their wish to make a break, having no means of fighting those who had a plan that was definite, however old. When the modernists grew angry at the way the Catholic hierarchy behaved towards them, they could hardly ever quote a criticism of their revolt that was in fact mistaken. All they could really criticize was the sort of serious disciplinary action (police-like, secret-agent style, etc.) taken in their case. They complained that they had been personally attacked, that their privacy and personal freedom had been struck at, but they could never refer to any mistaken doctrine. The fight took place on a moral plane, and the accusations were above all of a moral character. Was it too soon to accuse the reformers of an 'heretical' system? It was not; it might be said that they would never have one, and that this was why the Encyclical and the Pope himself spoke of modernism as a compendium of all heresies, and the exposure of their 'researches' in *Pascendi* always sounded like a rational violation.

'Of what use in the religious question can the fictitious distinctions of gnoseology and psychology be now?' Buonaiuti wondered, commenting on the philosophy of action in *Studi religiosi*. 'We now hear the most self-evident empirical statements doubted; distinguished scientists like Lechalas, Bergson, and Poincaré calmly sounding the knell of the exact sciences: thinkers seem to have become exaltedly suicidal . . .'[1]

This is rhetorical writing, much like that of the enemy Fr. Rosa, giving voice to a theoretical doubt. But whereas Fr. Rosa asked questions from his rock-like Thomistic position (and, since the expression of theological truth was anchored to this, it 'did not know' error), Buonaiuti proceeded in his opposite way with an equal serenity that could not fail to make a man who wished to describe the reformatory movement and had no wish to destroy its basis tremble with rage: 'What does the fantastic disappearance of an idol that has hypnotized too many souls matter to the inflexible laws of nature?' Buonaiuti continued. 'All the sceptical and brutal

[1] See Buonaiuti, 'La filosofia dell' azione', in *Studi religiosi*, May–June 1905, p. 214.

philosophy of monism and immanentism has worked for us. Does that surprise you? Men of little faith that we are! Does even history teach us nothing?'[1]

And this rage increased when, after all this confusion and the lighthearted description of the fall of some sacred cows, Fr. Rosa or his stand-in chanced to meet with utterances not unlike those that supported the refusal to admit that Tyrrell's condemnation was deserved:

> The difference between us and those who came before us in the varying scene of history lies in the greater store of wisdom and Christian light that weighs upon our souls like a plentiful meal waiting to be digested. . . . Philosophy has at last found itself. We are certainly not ill! *Only today* do we begin to understand *the full greatness of destiny* weighing on every human spirit.[2]

Both men refuse to understand, and in much the same way, just as those who were condemned refused to see it.

Tyrrell, in his famous 'Confidential letter to a Professor of Anthropology', written in 1903 but published only then and for the first time in the Italian press, expressed pretty clearly where the reformers were to be found, apart from the arguments that forced them out into the open and in retaliation to declare their own beliefs and to make the difficult path of research seem straightforward and definite. But von Hügel, in a letter to Loisy, whom he still considered a friend, but who was in fact remote and indifferent, possibly put it even better:

1. Authority. There is no authority exercised by men, however legitimate one might believe it to be, which has absolute rights or unlimited power . . .
2. The Church: the religious body. We have a clearer idea of its meaning than our opponents; we believe that a religious community is an organization whose members are jointly responsible in a communal life and activity . . .
3. Present reality: it is true that the Pope holds himself to be infallible, but we are right [here Loisy intervenes to criticize the letter: he feels that *they* are right according to Catholicism and that therefore he and von Hügel are no longer Catholics; whereas von Hügel feels that he himself and Loisy are among the few real Catholics who believe in the

---

[1] Ibid.
[2] See Buonaiuti, in *Studi religosi*, September–October 1904, p. 254.

perfectibility of Christianity, though there are few of them in the present hierarchy].

4. Life transcends our analysis. Science does not satisfy the needs of the soul and will never constitute a religion. The life of the soul requires an organized Church. The present crisis will not end with the complete desertion of the Roman Church and neither will the Church be able to remain a 'prison for the critical and rational mind, let alone for the modern enlightened conscience'. There will be the transformation, the purification needed by that spiritual life which after all has built the Church.[1]

The letter, in December of this year, 1906, concludes with a sad sentence: 'Je voudrais, par ma patience, mes lenteurs, mes sourdes douleurs, aider à cela.' And his old friend Loisy, sad once again (he had said his last Mass a month before), remarked on what they had done: 'Aider à la transformation de l'Église romaine, c'avait été notre rêve.'

[1] Letter from von Hügel to Loisy, December 1906, quoted in *Mémoires*, II, pp. 497–500, in a not completely faithful summary, judging by a similar letter sent by von Hügel to Tyrrell on 18 December; see *Selected Letters*, pp. 136–7.

PART III

16. *Rinnovamento:* Preparation

Rinnovamento, the first number of which appeared in January 1907, was long prepared for. In a sense, all whom von Hügel's religious and moral curiosity had affected were involved with it, all who in one way or another had a right to belong to the ideal group of souls in search of God brought together through his 'solitary, roving, weary' soul, as Clemente Rebora, a friend of the group, says in one of his poems. Von Hügel, together with Fogazzaro, must be considered its inspiration, the two great laymen of the reformatory movement; all the other contributors—with a few exceptions—had to be laymen, and were the co-editors: Antonio Aiace Alfieri, Alessandro Casati, and Tommaso Gallarati Scotti, whose names appear in the first large number.[1]

To this long, slow preparation (von Hügel's *la patience, les lenteurs et les sourdes douleurs*) we owe the fact that the first number seems to reflect the situation as it had been so far. In fact it almost seems to confirm all the suspicions and fears and even the irony which *Civiltà cattolica* had expressed about the Italian reformers, in particular when it dealt with the modernists of *Cultura sociale*. But their slowness in replying to the ecclesiastical hierarchy and its very definite denunciations, and in preparing *Rinnovamento*, might be interpreted otherwise—perhaps as an effort to win the interest of people generally indifferent to matters of religion; that is, laymen. This might, of course, seem yet another thing directed against the will and purpose of the official Church, but it was

---

[1] On *Rinnovamento*, apart from the works already mentioned (in particular Garin, Gallarati Scotti's *Life of Fogazzaro, The life of von Hügel*, the *Mémoires*, Buonaiuti's *Autobiography*) see Gallarati Scotti's commemoration on 5 December to the Press Club in Milan, published in the anthology *Saggi, Postille, Discorsi di Alessandro Casati*, edited by G. P. Bognetti and F. Arese, Milan, 1957, and, in the same anthology, Casati's commemorative speech on Stefano Jacini, p. 278, in which he calls Gioberti the inspirer of the time of free research, and considers the movement 'historically justified and much less foolhardy than it then appeared'. See also Gallarati Scotti's profile of Angelo Crespi in the latest *Dall'io a Dio*, Modena, 1950. *Rinnovamento* is also mentioned in letters to and from Amendola, in the collection of letters in *Il tempo della 'Voce'*, in Minocchi's letters, and in P. Scoppola's *Crisi modernista e rinnovamento cattolico in Italia*, Bologna, 1961.

not intended to be specifically critical; rather, it hoped to form a climate of opinion more favourable to 'speculations on the religious problem'. What *Civiltà cattolica* called the 'new men' could, either with Fogazzaro's 'prudence', or with von Hügel's Catholic ardour, deal with problems of textual criticism (Old or New Testament exegesis, the philosophy of religion); and this, which their sensitive consciences thought worth doing, would not merely help the clergy (who, like everyone then, were dealing with the famous 'culture of the clergy' and the dispute between the 'two cultures'), but would lead the indifferent laity to take an interest in questions usually left to the priest, and in particular to the priest in church.

Thus *Rinnovamento* appeared to be operating, or to have ranged itself, on two fronts. As far as the Church was concerned, it worked within it, seeking a reform of its structure, theology, and whole doctrinal machinery, for its authors felt that no aspect of doctrine, church practice, or even liturgy was outside the province of the laity as such, and, since they felt they were entitled to participate on the same level as the priests (some of whom had already been caught up in *Rinnovamento*, thus in a sense reversing the usual relationship of teacher and pupil), they wished to have a hand in the doctrinal or liturgical machinery. As far as the culture of the laity was concerned, they felt that the fact of being lay in no way diminished it, whatever form it took—philosophy, science, law; but they hoped to interest philosophers, scientists, and jurists in religious problems, in order to bring an end at last to educated people's sterile hostility towards religion, and misunderstanding of it. This had been happening in countries outside Italy for some years—France, in particular, and England, America, and Germany too. Why should Italy not take its part in the great movement to free philosophy from the narrow limitations of positivism? It would thus regain a sense of the great religious culture it had cradled in earlier centuries. And why should those who had inherited a new culture from the Risorgimento not take the two Italys that had emerged from political unification back to doctrinal unity?

But what was this 'lay culture' they wanted to inject religious thinking into, and by which they would finally be overwhelmed? A suspicion arises that they may have been as ignorant of it as they were (according to the Jesuits) of 'ecclesiastical culture'.

According to *Civiltà cattolica* the innovators or reformers were feverishly attacking the basis of doctrine while knowing nothing of the scholastic foundations on which, for centuries, it had been built: Leo XIII had wisely restored the prestige of scholasticism. They had personal links with this 'lay culture', admittedly. Casati was a friend of Prezzolini and Papini, who had brought out *Leonardo* in 1903; also in 1903, Croce's *Critica* first appeared, and Casati could claim to be a friend of Croce's as well. In Milan, Martinetti,[1] who was to write in *Rinnovamento*, was teaching, and many letters reveal other personal links, friendships, and alliances. But that was just it, the connections were all those of friendship, which some of the group, Casati more than the rest, and Gallarati Scotti, found valuable. But friendship and talk are one thing, effective participation in a movement, and an active feeling of working together, is quite another. The editors were young, well-educated, and belonged to aristocratic families; they were used to fine libraries, good literary style, unruffled patronage; and, in their villas and gardens and on the gentle slopes of their Lombard countryside, they had plenty of time for the reading and reflection their education and circumstances drew them to. Never for a moment did they doubt that they belonged to the ruling class, or that their most important task, strong in the experience their particular background had provided, was to ally the lay tradition of the Risorgimento with the reform of Catholicism. This meant working on two fronts, but on the inside of the movement for reform, that is on the inside of the Church. The fact that the Church rejected them or seemed to disapprove of their conduct did not worry their consciences in those days. They were spiritually nourished and comforted by frequent contact with enlightened priests, who were welcome at their villas and in their turn comforted and cheered in their everyday difficulties by generous friendship and lively conversation.

But what effective relationship was there between clerics and the laymen of *Rinnovamento*? Was there really a close link between the reform the religious were seeking to promote, and the culture the laymen meant to restore? Or was it just a temporary alliance? Partly it was just a misunderstanding, as reading the stout volumes of *Rinnovamento* gradually reveals. Buonaiuti, who under the

---

[1] See P. Martinetti, 'Il regno dello spirito' in *Rinnovamento* a. II (1908), No. 5–6, pp. 209–28.

pseudonym of Paolo Baldini wrote in it one of his most confused and forceful essays on the need for pragmatism (thus boldly and briskly starting the campaign he was later to conduct openly, under the same pseudonym, in the columns of *Nova et vetera*), had hardly anything in common with Casati or even with Fogazzaro, the inspirer; not even a pinch of the 'religious' in the traditional sense that links souls working for a common end. The laymen of *Rinnovamento* already considered Buonaiuti suspect; his mind might be admirable, his support sincerely desired, but they feared his violence on the one hand and on the other even his religious ideas, which were firmly based on his education as a Roman priest. Buonaiuti himself seemed to feel the cultural support of the laity was scarcely worth having—at least the cultural support of these particular laymen, who argued so subtly, yet believed so tepidly. He judged them on moral grounds, and in his autobiography—which is certainly not reliable as far as dates are concerned, but reveals his own particular sort of sincerity—he referred to Casati and the rest as 'men of letters', 'sensitive souls' who were friendly with heretics for a while and then went on to what was more to their taste, literature and diplomacy; and practically accused them of 'betrayal'.[1]

[1] See *Pellegrino di Roma*, p. 83: 'A friendship seemed to bind us that for my part I should never have abandoned, if on the other hand faith in the ideal of spiritual regeneration in Italy had been maintained; had this been done, we might have differed from time to time in matters of tactics and attitudes, but there would have been no room for deviations or, to put it bluntly, betrayal.' Casati, to whom Buonaiuti confided all his most intimate thoughts, because he then considered him 'alas, a faithful, trusted friend', made the mistake of seeing in Buonaiuti 'something that recalled the spiritual position of Henri Bremond'. Buonaiuti mentions this detail in order 'to show how little the editors of the Milanese *Rinnovamento* had realized the gravity and power of the crisis of modernism, into which they should have come as moderators, since, having chosen to take part in it, having had a close view of what we passionately felt and what the difficulty of our programme meant, they then withdrew and took up positions that were openly and cruelly opposed to our formidable programme. So much the worse for them.' See, too, how Buonaiuti judged Casati who 'soon left the shelter of Christian religious experience, as it was expressed in both orthodox and modernistic terms, and, mysteriously enticed by an easier spiritual situation, took up the tame, contradictory Hegelian idealism of which Benedetto Croce, to the detriment of all Italian culture ever since, was setting himself up as leader', his friends 'no longer firm and constant', and Gallarati Scotti 'a delicate and quixotic man of letters'. Buonaiuti's fiercest attack on Gallarati Scotti appears in the French (but not in the Italian) edition of his history of Catholic modernism (p. 109, in a note): 'Having moved on *ad meliorem frugem*, he did his best to obliterate the memory of the part he had played in *Rinnovamento* and found, like all apostates, that the best means of assuring the success of his

As to the second priest, Murri, who wrote without using pseudonyms, he too was more a guest than a contributor to the review. Murri followed his own ideas and wrote what he was publishing elsewhere, on matters of political inquiry, and used no special tone in writing for *Rinnovamento*. But when he had to take a stand on *Pascendi* he used *Rinnovamento* to drive home his own strict scholastic orthodoxy, and his refusal to consider himself one of those who were seeking innovations of doctrine. He was, indeed, one of the severest defenders of scholasticism against any effort to overturn it or to make a different philosophy of religion or a religion of the future; thus going almost scandalously against the whole cultural tone of the review.[1] His connection with *Rinnovamento* was almost entirely through Gallarati Scotti, and through him some aristocratic Milanese supporters of the Lega democratica nazionale: it was a sort of electoral alliance, based on a misunderstanding, but in this case the misunderstanding was not wholly the fault of either party.[2] Tyrrell's connection with *Rinnovamento* was a closer one, for Fogazzaro admired Tyrrell's mind and knew his work and character; but it was a one-sided relationship, for Fogazzaro wanted him to contribute—though they merely translated things he had written some time before and in addition cut them, censored them, and used them in a context Tyrrell did not know and would hardly have approved. *Rinnovamento*, in fact, wanted to draw on Tyrrell's experience, which was wholly different from theirs, gaining

repentance was to turn to his former companions, who, in spite of the necessarily uncertain outcome of such an all-embracing, revolutionary plan of action, waited for the most critical moment to expose themselves to danger.' Buonaiuti also quotes unfavourable comments on Scotti and his *Rinnovamento* group in personal letters from Tyrrell to him.

[1] See R. Murri, 'L'Enciclica Pascendi e la filosofia moderna' in *Rinnovamento*, a. 1, Nos. 1–10 (September–October 1907) and 11–12 (November–December).

[2] Gallarati Scotti was proclaimed Honorary President of the First National Congress of the Lega democratica nazionale, held in Milan from 15–17 September 1906, and gave the inaugural speech, in which he put forward a programme of independence from clerical politics and of opposition, not to genuine Christianity, but to a 'disguised theocracy that wished them to submit every act and every thought', not to the essence of dogma nor to the hierarchy in its divine mission, but to a 'distorted concept of authority that distorts souls and wishes to penetrate even national life' (see summary in the *Giornale d'Italia* of 18 September 1906). On the relations between Scotti and Murri, see de Rosa, *L'Azione Cattolica*, Bari, 1953; G. Spadolini, *Giolitti e i Cattolici*, Florence, 1960; but, in particular, P. Scoppola in a series of essays that appeared in the *Rivista storica italiana*, a. LXIX, No. 1 (March 1957), reprinted in the book mentioned.

what advantage they could from it and seeking to copy him in ways it is hard to justify. Tyrrell was much closer to the spirit of *Nova et vetera*, to Buonaiuti in particular, though it appears from letters that he feared the Roman group's violence and hoped their polemical ways would have no extreme results.[1]

Semeria was much more closely allied with *Rinnovamento*, for he was a great friend of von Hügel, as an unpublished correspondence, kept in the archives of the Barnabites in Rome, reveals; he was also in direct contact with Blondel, Laberthonnière, and many other religious and laymen. Indeed, von Hügel thought of giving Semeria the editorship of the review when Casati showed signs of giving it up (which he then did). Yet there is no official sign of him in the volumes of *Rinnovamento*; and besides, his great reputation as the moving spirit in charitable work during and after the First World War today seems rather foreign to modernism. Semeria took a very active part in the reforming movement in its early days, and in the field of exegesis and of philosophy: some letters he wrote to Blondel show he was an acute student and critic of the philosophy of action and of the so-called method of immanence.[2] These passionate interests of his are referred to in much that he wrote and in sermons; but both his writings and his sermons seem hasty and unelaborated, with information sacrificed to clarity. He took part in the famous journey to Russia that culminated in the visit to Leo Tolstoy; his friend Minnochi mentioned it in the *Giornale d'Italia*, and thus provoked (justified) criticisms from the Catholic press for the inanely deferential tone he used in speaking of Tolstoy, who, reading between the lines made it clear, had treated the two Italian priests with scant respect since, before receiving them, he had asked them to read what he had written on the abolition of the clergy.[3] But Semeria

---

[1] See in particular a letter to V, 3 May 1908: 'I think you will agree with me that modernism is corrupting rapidly into a popular revolt. The younger and cruder men have been exasperated by Pius X and have lost all patience with synthetic schemes. The *Lettere di un prete modernista* referred to in the last *Nova et vetera* means a change of programme, a possible schism; a this-worldliness of outlook that makes the whole thing banal and commonplace . . . I wrote an article for *Nova et vetera* in a moderating sense; but they asked me to alter it. I said they might alter it, but in that case I would not sign it . . . I don't believe we doctrinaires will be able to hold back these rebels' (in *Life*, p. 350).

[2] See letter from Blondel to Semeria of 19 August 1896 and 26 November 1900 in answer to a letter from Semeria, in *Lettres philosophiques*, pp. 91–5 and 215–18.

[3] See Minocchi's report in *Giornale d'Italia* of 14 August 1903. It should be

did not speak of the journey as enthusiastically as Minocchi. Indeed, when he was recalled home by telegraph to undertake a job that then seemed a punishment, he forfeited Minocchi's admiration, as far as it could be forfeited, by naming him responsible for everything that had been written and published about the visit. Semeria wrote a letter to Pius X which Bishop Bonomelli signed, asking for the 'non expedit' to be withdrawn, and was the recipient of Murri's letters on the culture of the clergy, which are probably still the clearest document from the early days of the movement for reform in Italy. We probably owe other anonymous writings to Semeria, other letters signed by other hands; they show how active he was, at least in the early years, though this activity was not enough to make him modernist in spirit. Like Buonaiuti, he was a priest and had, perhaps more than Buonaiuti, a definite idea of obedience. Gradually his culture had become a tool of apologetics, and he had studied Blondel, and Loisy too, not for their own sakes, but in order to use them in his preaching for purposes of Christian propaganda. And so, as far as we can judge from the evidence available, Semeria may be said to belong, with Minocchi, to the early, orthodox modernism, that of Leo XIII. He may have inspired the second phase, and was certainly a friend of those mainly concerned with it, but he was not active in its inner discussions and never took an active part against the Church. All this must have caused him great personal suffering, which must have been responsible for his almost sudden decision to give up his studies (even those that were useful as a tool of apologetics) when he left Italy, and to 'do good'.

Many private papers relevant to the history of Italian modernism in general and *Rinnovamento* in particular are still inaccessible, in particular many private papers which throw light on the relationships within the 'small Church'; and those available do not tell much more about the effectiveness of these alliances than is known from what officially happened—apart from revealing a general fear of persecution, shown in repeated calls for prudence and secrecy.[1]

remembered that *Civiltà cattolica* had had a long essay on the pseudo-Christianity of Leo Tolstoy in June of the previous year (series VIII, Vol. VII, No. 1249), from which arose the polemical 'Visita di due sacerdoti cattolici a Leone Tolstoi', *Civiltà cattolica*, series XVIII, Vol. IX, No. 1277 (August 1903).

[1] Semeria's letters to Minocchi, kept among Minocchi's papers by his family, which I have been able to consult, show this.

Other priests more directly connected with *Rinnovamento*, though their names do not appear in it, were Don Brizio Casciola and Fr. Gazzola. Fogazzaro and von Hügel often mention them in their letters as 'spiritual fathers', regular confessors of the young, teachers of the religious life. Without anything written on the subject, it is impossible to measure their influence. One of them was a parish priest in Milan, and a woman in his congregation kept copies of some of the sermons he gave at Sant'Alessandro. These do in fact mention the traditional themes which the reforming movement and *Rinnovamento* were concerned with, such as the culture needed to understand and discuss Christianity, the need not to consider the message of the Gospels as simplifying the difficulties of modern man too radically, and not to consider Christ as remote from the character of the modern world, so that a confession of faith will be radical and not a half-hearted commitment that is a matter of feelings alone, and so on. These sermons, admittedly, show signs of a spiritual climate not unlike that of *Rinnovamento*, in particular the parts written by Fogazzaro, just as some of the ideas expressed in an anthology edited by this group of friends and entitled *Paterno spirito* seem very similar. Nearly always moderate in tone, full of patient spirituality, and sometimes remarkably subtle, they are nevertheless isolated thoughts, whose influence on the Milanese reformers and their conduct it is impossible to judge.[1] Those who really inspired the group were von Hügel and Fogazzaro.

[1] See *Sermons given in Milan, S. Alessandro, in 1905* [but some dated 1904 and 1906] *by Father Gazzola, Barnabite, later persecuted and reduced to silence by the ecclesiastical authorities under the accusation of modernism, and shortly afterwards dead. These notes were collected by a follower (Signora M. Sofia Castiglioni, I believe).* This is handwritten on the first of three typewritten volumes which I have consulted. Fr. Gazzola was born in January 1856 at Periano in the vale of Trebbia. He entered the Barnabite order in 1876 and in 1885 was appointed parish priest of Sant'Alessandro in Milan. In 1889 he was sent away but recalled after only twenty-three days; in the summer of 1906 he was ordered to renounce his parish for good. He died in 1915. See Gallarati Scotti in the commemoration of Casati, already quoted: 'In those days a man was living in our city who had the highest spiritual gifts as priest and thinker, Fr. Pietro Gazzola, Barnabite, Provost of S. Alessandro, whose learning, doctrine, and glowing religiousness, composed of ardent ideas and the highest piety, towered over us all. There is no doubt that he had a profound influence on Casati; from being a follower of Rosmini in philosophy, he had surpassed him in his exploration of the new problems and new currents of ideas, and it was he who, in long, illuminating talks, turned the young man's soul, already torn by an inner conflict between religion and philosophy, to a wider interpretation of Catholic dogma. So much so that I

This was so, at least, in so far as the background, the original character, and the need for *Rinnovamento*'s existence were concerned. During the three years it appeared, however, it widened its scope and cannot be said to reflect a single point of view. Quite apart from differences of age and opinion among those who directed its policy and contributed to it, there was a reason for this in the very character of the movement for reform which *Rinnovamento* wished to express, and whose various aspects, perhaps, it hoped to bring together. It was not, as we have seen, a movement with any precise and recognizable characteristics, but a whole series of thoughts and studies, all with varying origins yet closely linked to the individual experience of those who were learning to use the theoretical tools of their particular field of

---

am not sure that *Rinnovamento* was not first inspired by him' (p. 13); and see also Gallarati Scotti's introduction to *Paterno Spirito, Pensieri*, Palazzo Mattei, Rome, 1918: 'Fr. G's preaching showed how his thought had long tormented him, and the proper certainty of a man who has found a solution. His knowledge of modern culture, as opposed to religious faith, put him in touch with denial, scepticism, and weak faiths. In his congregation at S. Alessandro there were not only convinced believers but a great many learned men, lay teachers and members of the ruling classes. Perhaps the preacher was aiming in particular at these intellectuals, and felt that in a large city words that fitted their needs should be heard' (p. xx). Certainly some of Fr. Gazzola's collected thoughts recall passages in *Rinnovamento*; for instance 'Catholicism is a life, first of all [compare this with the words in the introduction to *Rinnovamento*: 'In us Christianity is life'], and afterwards a doctrine' [Thought 32]; 'our theology is like Penelope's web; we keep remaking it continuously [. . .] our natural science will be thought childish prattle by our descendants; and we have woven this natural science into our theology; the cloth will be remade, but the weft remains; for the weft is made by the saints, not by theologians' (pp. 26–7), and a comparison might indeed be made between Fr. Gazzola's thoughts and Fr. Huvelin's warnings. On Don Brizio Casciola see Fogazzaro's letter to Agnese Blanck, of 8 December 1908 (in *Lettere scelte*, pp. 650–1): 'That priest is called Don Brizio Casciola. He is Umbrian. He became a priest in the seminary at Perugia. When he was very young he went to Rome, and there read very widely modern works in four languages. At the same time he gave himself up with enormous energy to works of social charity. Poor as St. Francis, he kept moving about, according to circumstances. Wherever he went he held meetings of educated people, of workers, and of gentlemen, to educate and heighten religious feeling in general and to uplift the spirit by means of literature that was both good and great. For some years he has been running a small farming colony of orphans and waifs, which he founded thanks to a rich friend's generosity. All he eats is fruit and vegetables; he leads a very hard life, and even does manual work. . . . This is the man, and he is unique. To me he is worth volumes of Christian apologetics, Christ is with him always; a religion that produces a man like Don Brizio cannot fail to be great and true.'

study. And all these ideas and studies were brought together and given a platform on which to express themselves; but while they were still soft and indeterminate and without any conceptual system or doctrinally exact means of expressing themselves. Nor were these studies moving in any single direction: some were taking place within the Church, some outside it, and not necessarily against it. And so, although it appeared too late in so far as the results of some modernists' ideas—Loisy's in particular—were concerned, and seemed unaware of where the modernists' studies were inevitably leading, although the ecclesiastical hierarchy already knew it (*Pascendi* was now well under way, though not completed), *Rinnovamento* showed or wished to show how full of energy the reformers' efforts had been, and how much they needed to take a stand on matters of conscience. But in the end it also made clear how some experiences and doctrines were incompatible; indeed, it might almost be called the ripe fruit of a movement that had been cut off at the roots, on the one hand, and on the other the beginning of a generically religious culture in Italy, which later came to nothing.

If one examines *Rinnovamento*'s three years, in the stout, severe-looking volumes, the motives that inspired it are quite clear from this distance. They were certainly heterogeneous. To sum them up, they were Catholic spirituality or literary mysticism, expressed by Fogazzaro; pragmatism, expressed by Calderoni and Vailati, who were laymen, and Buonaiuti, the priest; biblical criticism, dealt with by von Hügel and the very young Stefano Jacini; Catholic participation in politics, dealt with by Murri and Gallarati Scotti; and cultural news, which criticized affairs and ideas in religious Europe. *Rinnovamento* had, of course, other subjects it dealt with in its three years' existence, among them discussion, polemics; but these are the central ones on which the character of the review depended. Fifty years later the others it dealt with, though in no way foreign to *Rinnovamento*, do not seem to take their particular character from the context in which they appear, and do not need to be read as part of *Rinnovamento* in order to give their full meaning.

None of the subjects stands out from the rest, none dominates the review. What marks *Rinnovamento*'s three years is not a single philosophy or a single group prevailing over the rest, but particular events that can be dated exactly.

The first of these was the 'small council' of the modernists, held in Paris in January 1907. It was Loisy who called it a 'small council'. He was unwilling to participate in it, and left it to Sabatier to bring together an international group of dissidents inside the Church, who were interested in its reform—from the inside, of course. Such a meeting, Loisy felt, was already without interest for him. The chance for it came when Fogazzaro was in Paris, where he had been invited to give a lecture on his religious thought. He accepted gladly and lectured on 'The religious ideas of Giovanni Selva', and his lecture appeared in the second number of *Rinnovamento*, translated into Italian. Neither Tyrrell nor von Hügel was at the meeting; von Hügel telegraphed his *fraternelle sympathie* to the distinguished guest and 'the whole meeting'. In fact von Hügel feared that the Protestant Sabatier would try to turn aspirations for reform into a direct attack upon the Church of Rome, but on that occasion Fogazzaro seemed unaware that he was serving a particular cause and being used as a tool in a movement that transcended his own ambitions. His closest followers, and even the editors of *Rinnovamento*, reproached him for saying he was pleased with the way his ideas of religious reform had been received in a learned atmosphere, and supposed he had led men to a higher degree of spirituality (the spirituality shown in his novel), without pointing the Catholic hierarchy out as the enemy. But he seemed not to remember or to realize that his novel had been condemned, and that he had accepted the condemnation in 'silence', if not in obedience or explicitly admitting his own wrongs and errors. He was now speaking again: no longer 'sub specie fictionis', but at a public meeting of the reformers, outside Italy, indeed in France, which in those very years had explicitly declared itself against Catholic Rome. It was, of course, natural for Fogazzaro to get his own back on the authorities that had condemned him, by showing them his prestige abroad—and for his religious ideas, too; but it was equally natural that his behaviour was thought to contradict the renewal of the 'silent reformers'. And in fact, after expressing Giovanni Selva's ideas in Paris, Fogazzaro no longer expressed his own in *Rinnovamento*; nor did his 'The words of Don Giuseppe Flores' appear there, though it was to appear in his biography by Gallarati Scotti. 'In Paris I lived in *reasonable* Catholic circles and found unspeakable satisfaction in them; I saw the flower of Catholic France around me, applauding',[1] he wrote with ingenuous joy to Mgr. Bonomelli a few days after his triumph. But he seemed not to realize that these Catholics understood his hopes of reform rather better than he did, and from what he said chose not what referred to his spirituality, which the need for obedience and reserve meant must be treated with circumspection, but what in fact contradicted the official attitudes of the Church of Rome. Fogazzaro's friends obviously realized the ambiguity of his success much better than he did. From then on—and this is why the 'small council' can be said to have conditioned and changed the history of *Rinnovamento*—they gave up his particular reform, though not explicitly or officially, and left him to the short-lived hope of religious success in the international field. Internationally, Fogazzaro seemed to have become a kind of leader in the movement for reform, but his friends at home preferred to stay outside it, to look elsewhere for leaders and to develop autonomously, after their initial success, instead of going ahead in depth with their own studies. In a way the Fogazzaro Lectures show the public side of Fogazzaro's ambition, whereas *Rinnovamento*, which was promoted through the religious inspiration that had found its sincerest expression (apart from the many fruitful personal relationships) in *Il Santo*, developed in quite another direction, though never denying or ignoring Fogazzaro in the process.

The success of Fogazzaro's religious ideas among the reasonable Catholics of Paris and Geneva coincided with the appearance of the first number of *Rinnovamento*. Fogazzaro repeated his lecture in Geneva a few days after giving it in Paris. The clerical press then accused him of having 'protestantized' himself, but Fogazzaro deluded himself that, on the contrary, he had worried the Protestants with his loudly repeated professions of Catholicism. It was natural at such a time that *Rinnovamento*, in which an article of Fogazzaro's appeared called 'For the Truth' (the inaugural lecture to the Lectures that were to be held the following April), was immediately thought to be expressing his ideas of reform. The tone of the introduction seemed to confirm this: 'Weary of the familiar rhetoric of programmes and conventional promises . . . a few words that will immediately estrange the frivolous from what is undertaken as a duty . . . this is not a review for the

---

[1] See Fogazzaro's letter to Mgr. Bonomelli of 3 February 1907, quoted in Gallarati Scotti's *La vita*, p. 469.

general public . . . in us Christianity is life . . .'[1] The tone, perhaps, more than the contents planned: 'We maintain that nowadays the only possible apologetics is research itself.' Today the programme seems to be more expressed than inspired by Fogazzaro: those who thought of contributing to the renewal of Italian culture, which was still not centred enough on the spiritual, without which outward progress is worth little, seemed to be using the sort of language Fogazzaro had made his own, rather than actually sharing his values. Besides, Fogazzaro was the best known personality in the group; the others, and in particular the editors, who had given life to the review, though they shared his views on reform and imitated the heartfelt tone he used, really wanted to do something quite different. They were very young and were 'young gentlemen' (as a small book attacking Milanese modernism called them), whom it was much easier to treat with irony and scorn than to criticize. Of these, the only one to give himself away publicly had been Gallarati Scotti, 'led so much astray and so puffed up by the juvenile praises of his mind and culture', 'not merely official delegate of the Lega democratica nazionale, but eleventh-hour Christian Democrat.[2] Gallarati Scotti had in fact joined the League in May 1906 and had made the inaugural speech at the first national congress held in Milan in the following September. The fact that this young Milanese duke had joined caused some surprise, and his speech on ecclesiastical politics had made people suspect him of intemperance. Now, in the first number of *Rinnovamento*, he emphasized the stand he had taken so far by appearing openly hostile to the new Pope's cultural and political attitude, and by suggesting that an alliance between those working for innovations in the field of doctrine and those promoting revolutionary ideas in the field of political life might be necessary. That is, he was seeking to unite the two great revolutionary branches, as the enemies of every kind of reform already said was being done, thus going directly against Murri's wish to keep the two branches of reform completely separate. At least it would seem that this was what he particularly hoped to do. In the introduction to the news of religious life and thought, which appeared in the first number of *Rinnovamento*, he wrote:

[1] See *Rinnovamento*, a. I, No. 1 (January 1907), introduction.
[2] See S. A. Cavallanti, *Milano centro di modernismo?*, Tipografia pontificia San Bernadino, Siena, 1907, pp. 9 and 11.

The Church is going through one of the gravest times in its history . . . It is not a case of new schisms or new heresies, but of the very faith of thousands of consciences. It is a case of seeing if, in the face of the universal renewal of scientific thought, Catholicism will have the strength to assimilate it and to translate its dogma into our language . . . or if instead—rejecting the representatives of philosophy and religious science—it will refuse to adapt itself to the intellectual exigencies of present-day humanity, thus making a definite split between theology and contemporary thought, as its enemies wish.[1]

These statements were too serious for the irony with which they were treated; unless the critics preferred to treat them with irony because intemperance and serious suggestions were typical of the immature. Very likely these young men knew little about the renewal of scientific thought—Garbasso's article on thermo-dynamics which appeared in the first number did not mean much; and the universal renewal they were trying to impress on the Church seems to have coincided with the crisis in their own development. Sensitive young men are always subject to crises of the kind when they reach the threshold of maturity; for maturity seems to open out onto emptiness, since the science, whose victory they at once fear and desire, is seen in its most literary form—that is, in the form their positivistic education has suggested to them.

All the same, this clear expression of the connection between Catholic doctrinal and political reform corresponded to Murri's new undertaking to deal with doctrinal matters in his social programme, and thus in a way it justified his presence as a contributor to the first number of *Rinnovamento*. Since he was another suspect person, who had been present in Paris at Fogazzaro's triumph, Catholics increased their criticisms. Most violent, as usual, was the criticism of *Civiltà cattolica*, which did not wait until the end of January to announce the new publication,[2] and did not so much examine what the innovators were saying as simply call them to order. But it criticized the contributions of Fogazzaro and Gallarati Scotti, and the introduction, in which it discovered, as the *Rassegna nazionale* had done, a paraphrase of the 'paradoxical oddities' of the Abbé Laberthonnière, 'and of other rather muddled minds'.

[1] See T. Gallarati Scotti, 'Introduzione a "Cronaca di vita e di pensiero religi-osé" ', in *Rinnovamento* a. 1, No. 1, p. 68.

[2] See *Civiltà cattolica*, 1907, Vol. I, No. 1359 (January), p. 333.

These people take no account of the immense harm they do themselves and other ingenuous good souls. They look like lambs thirsting for truth and running to the fountain, whereas in fact they are wolves scattering the flock; they look like sowers who go eagerly out to the field, and there sow tares. So much fresh energy, so many fine mental gifts frustrated by pride, arrogance and lack of discipline that can bear no check! And is the new periodical in which they mean to mature these ideas of theirs called *Rinnovamento?* What will they renew but the sad examples that abound in ecclesiastical history of reformers without a mission? The title of the ancient Christian apocrypha would suit it better: *Acta Pilati.*

And in the March number:

Silent reformers, young apostles of love, you who love to speak of Christian charity, of Christianity that is life, of Catholicism that is religious experience, of the spirit of Christ felt in the heart 'as an immanent command to raise one's life', answer your conscience a little but not with a metaphor: you who feel so kindly towards the wicked, are you not afraid that you hate Catholics, your brothers, a little? Are you not especially afraid of damaging the cause of truth itself with the obvious insufficiency of your doctrines?[1]

These laymen 'without theology', these 'haughty' youngsters, *Civiltà cattolica* went on to say, 'imitate Pilate by arousing doubts yet waiting for no answer, and condemning many souls to certain scepticism and disbelief'. Yet a far greater sin, it continued, was that of 'those [who were] instigators and teachers of all these errors. As the Jews were to Pilate, so these [were] to the young they [had] led astray: "maius peccatum habent".'

'C'est la faute à Voltaire.' It was Loisy's fault, and Laberthonnière's, Buonaiuti's and Murri's, the fault, that io, of the clergy who had led astray these young, right-thinking aristocrats; as for Fogazzaro, who according to *Civiltà cattolica* was the most Christian of them all, he had been led astray by Klein, and by reading Tyrrell, Casciola and Semeria (these latter two unnamed).

In the same first number, Gallarati Scotti spoke of Tyrrell as the greatest English Catholic writer since Newman. 'A most delicate, subtle and affective spirit,' he went on, 'that, having assimilated criticism, gave it a religious meaning which, overcoming both dry scientific positivism and evanescent mysticism,

[1] See ibid., 1907, Vol. I, No. 1362 (March): 'Il rinnovamento di silenziosi riformatori', p. 729.

reconciles its warring actions in a higher truth.'[1] But when they spoke of Tyrrell it was not so much to make known his particular form of religion as to denounce the behaviour of the Church in putting his 'Confidential letter' on the Index. Of Tyrrell himself *Rinnovamento* wrote: 'He is an exquisite master of the mind who prefers to create human awareness rather than construct an architectonic system, who knows the reasons and language of the heart, the darkness and light of the mind, and the antitheses of the faith.'

Of the Church's action it wrote:

No one living in the bosom of the Church can imagine the impression of terror that such acts of theological violence and ecclesiastical absolutism may produce in the minds of those on its threshold, who cannot distinguish the essential Church from the Church whose forms are changeable and often disagreeable. And this impression would become even worse if, thanks to literal orthodoxy and the triumph of the most restrictive forms of Catholicism, all the liveliest and strongest minds who are seeking to retranslate eternal truths into contemporary language were taken out of the active clergy . . . a dangerous split between intelligence and authority would thus be made in the Church.[2]

So, once again, the Church must consider those souls on the threshold, must show its traditional prudence in order to avoid offending the hesitant chosen spirits that a favourable puff of wind might drop into its lap. It sometimes looks as if the silent reformers of *Rinnovamento*, or some of them at least, felt the whole trouble lay in the Church's inconceivable lack of taste, in a vulgarity or crudity that was in complete contrast with their own wellbred backgrounds and those of the learned priests they had known. They reproached the Church for not having read the latest book of literary criticism or philosophy or fiction, especially for not noticing the accusations made by the latest Nordic thinker, whose criticisms would have shown the Church the path it should take for its own reformation. The Church they were opposing was an ageing mother who failed to understand her growing son's flashes of brilliance, who insisted on handing him lists of laws and duties printed in ugly letters on still uglier paper; a home-grown,

---

[1] *Rinnovamento*, a. 1, No. 1, p. 77. Gallarati Scotti also said that Tyrrell, 'disciple of the great thinker [Newman] through his own spiritual education, lacked his gigantic ardour, his mathematical precision, his Michelangelesque form' (ibid., p. 77).

[2] Ibid., a. 1, No. 1, p. 80.

housewifely Church thrust into a backwater of history by the crisis of European awareness. Above all, it was a Church that hated what was difficult, whereas they understood only what was difficult, and what was difficult was theirs by right. What they were not much aware of, or seemed not to be, was the 'historical' meaning and gradual growth of something in civil life that conflicted with, if it had not actually absorbed, the cultural and political world in which they had been brought up. They did not see the ethics that were in keeping with the unitarian Italian state as an alternative to religious ethic. They seemed unaware of that new ethic, which was the opposite of the conservative ethic of Rome, since their two histories destroyed each other —an ethic of the state taking over from an ethic that was supranational or remote from what was happening to various peoples. Nor did they seem to realize that when Europe ceased to lead the world the Church must renew its spiritual links with the East, and must seek to keep some sort of hold over the fringes and boundaries of this spirituality, which had still not accepted its own firm concepts; or that the Church might lose a thousand hesitant followers in a state of crisis without losing any of its strength as a preserver of the past.

What the *Rinnovamento* group thought counted was individual crises, the elements of spirituality to be found in this or that thinker, which must not be lost. They felt they must nourish one another and cling together to form a Church that was renewed by intelligence, which might take over from the Church set rigidly in authority. But what escaped them, or seemed to, was the fact that the conflict was not proceeding in terms of intelligence and of authority: intelligence to them meant above all a culture of the various forms of religious experience, whereas authority meant above all the affirmation of a single truth in an exact, restricted, conceptual order. On the other hand, just as the terms State and Church could no longer be used to circumscribe or limit the struggle, and other concepts besides the class struggle were arising to illustrate it, so the terms of intelligence and of authority could certainly not take their place. This was already the case and it was to become more pronounced in the years ahead.

The question was: which was the single authority to be invoked; where was the one place in which truth could be found?

Was it the Catholic Church entrenched in centuries-old positions, abstract, unchangeable, unintelligible to the modern mind, unable to change over to the new, the true, and the 'modern', as changeable, uncertain, yet living experience was laboriously doing? Or was it intelligence alone, free from the orthodox, established interpretation of dogmas, free from submission, its ever-present foe, able to move from the depths of the unconscious to the sublimity of the mystical union, free from the divergencies of language, culture, logic and will? And what was all this supposed to defend? Or was it in order to understand a new reality better?

The reality of the Church of Rome. The *Rinnovamento* group thought the Church needed a reform; to them reform meant 'seeking in the very essence of Catholicism the lost flexibility of the truth to the varying genius of time and place'. Thus Gallarati Scotti expressed himself in one of the most illuminating essays that appeared in the review, 'The Catholic reform of Vincenzo Gioberti'. The reformer Gioberti had 'a similar conception of Catholicism [which] led him to exalt the function of the mind, of science, of the laity in the Church', to seek, 'an aristocracy of Catholic thinkers who might educate public opinion'.[1] The problem of democracy necessarily seemed fundamental at the time—that is, the way in which people who were not diplomatists, teachers, or politicians, who were totally unlike the old aristocracy, could take over positions of authority. It was not only in Italy, or above all in Italy, that this was happening: new ruling classes with very different backgrounds were appearing to show that radical, inescapable changes were necessary in relation even to the Church of Rome. At the same time the structure of clerical vocations was radically changing, and by looking at the background of the clergy the modernists could have found significant pointers to the future composition of the hierarchy they were then opposing. But what in fact the *Rinnovamento* group proposed was reform that consisted of an exceptional degree of lay authority, working especially in the field of thought and speculation, among philosophers, critics, and lay thinkers. Once more it was a case of intelligence against authority, but both conceived in a traditional way; whereas it could be said that intelligence and authority were altering radically. The *Rinnovamento* group did, in fact, find

[1] See T. Gallarati Scotti, 'La riforma cattolica di Vincenzo Gioberti', in *Rinnovamento*, a. 1, No. 11 (February 1907).

importance in the mystical element, to counterbalance the aristocratic element they found in Gioberti. 'What is missing, at the
basis of *Riforma cattolica*,' they wrote, 'is a profound Christian
experience, or even the concept of what the essence of Christianity is: the imitation of Christ, that it may be vital and renewing.'
Gioberti never knew 'that whole side of Christian life that is
mysticism, without which no real reform has ever been possible,
and never will be. For if we can optimistically dream of a new
springtime of Christianity,' *Rinnovamento* went on, 'we feel that
our hopes are sterile if we trust only in an intellectual movement
of critics and philosophers and do not think that religious feeling
must be renewed to its roots in love, in one of these great gusts of
awareness even the humble can take part in, and which found in
the Franciscan movement its gentlest, most meaningful type.'
    So it was to be the mystics who, together with the learned,
were to reform the Church. Mysticism for the humble, philosophy for the learned; would they, between them, form the ideal
Church, or would the mystics, going beyond her in Christ, deny
all authority? But mysticism as it is understood here is that of
Sabatier's *San Francesco*, 'gentle, meaningful', and not the least
bit historically likely (Minocchi, asked by Sabatier to study the
saint, seems to have revealed no other, more sincere, 'tribulations').
It is not the tougher, more vigorous mysticism of St. John of the
Cross, to whom the young Boine referred in the same number
with a very different sort of spirit and forcefulness. Rather it is
an attitude, a mystical attitude that can be found in Tyrrell, but
above all is caught in Fogazzaro's yearning. Thus it was all a case
of religious psychology, but nothing to do with doctrine.
    Yet since they were calling for reform, and denouncing the
vulgarity and even the terror of some of the Church's actions and
dispositions, the *Rinnovamento* group could not fail to consider
the problem of orthodoxy, could not avoid answering the questions
put to them by both laity and hierarchy. These might or might
not be straightforward questions (are you or do you still call
yourselves Catholics?), but in any case readers of *Rinnovamento*
—those few chosen souls offered a cure by a few other chosen
souls—were having things explained. And the answers, even
more than the questions asked, showed the *Rinnovamento* group
up clearly (with the exception of Buonaiuti and Murri, that is:
Buonaiuti never bothered with problems of the kind, and Murri

considered only problems of discipline). In reply to their critics—
the answer is anonymous, but one may suppose it was made by
Gallarati Scotti, with the help of Alfieri and Casati—the *Rinnovamento* group refused to declare themselves either orthodox or
heretical, refused to give any clear reply. In fact, they refused to
be questioned about their orthodoxy and about the orthodoxy of
others doing research like themselves. Orthodoxy (which might
be called faith) was the result of research, if the research resulted
in something that could be contained within a definite formula.
But research did not necessarily imply such a result; it was by its
own nature a way of life, that could be recognized as valid and
fruitful quite independently of any result it might have or of any
orthodoxy. As, in scientific research, there was no point in inquiring about the scientist's faith, so in religious research there
was no point in asking about the researcher's faith. This, if it
existed, was independent of the research; it belonged to the
private world of affections and connections and traditions that
might alter the course of men's lives but would not interfere with
their conceptual principles, which would always be free and, in
so far as their vocation, background, and faith itself were concerned, quite neutral. An astronomer would no longer be asked
to alter the results of his researches in the light of his faith, to
look at the sky with a believer's eye or cover his telescope lens
with a filter to change the structure of the universe. The freer
his eyes of earlier inner visions, and the more perfect his instrument, the better and more clearly would he see the laws that
governed the universe. Religious science should be studied with
as much neutrality, since the laws that guided it were analogous
to the laws of science, which the researcher discovered in the very
act of research and did not postulate beforehand, for fear of
changing the object of his study. The subject, that is the man
doing the research, might be, indeed could not fail to be, an
historical man, and therefore linked to affections, beliefs, and
psychological patterns; but the object of his research was in a
sense metahistorical or metaphysical. The conflict between science
and religion could be summed up in a simple declaration: the
science of religion is a science like any other, and those who study
it have the same rights and duties as those who work in other
disciplines.

This had further results—though the authors of the reply to

the critics did not specify them. In particular, the Church should not oppose a new discipline with definite questions. (In speaking of the Church, the Church of Rome was always implied, since all studies and all arguments were directed at it; though this was another contradiction the *Rinnovamento* group failed to mention.) In earlier times the Church had finally agreed to free physics, alchemy, and astronomy from her custody. This had in no way lessened its power, because once these disciplines had gained their freedom, they always ended up singing its praises as the mother of them all. And so now, in these difficult times, having learnt cunning from its own wisdom, the Church must recognize that the very science of religion (one might even say religion itself) might become a discipline like the rest; not one that stood up directly against her, but one that might in fact become a tool of the Church's power, once learned men, having developed within the Church, went prudently ahead in research that would open up new fields, and their incomplete findings would help man to perfect his knowledge of his own origins. Of course during this long period of study well-loved ideas and values thought to be eternal might have to be sacrificed. A certain price would have to be paid, but the result would be that the very idea of religion would be perfected. Instead of being a confused collection of myths, legends, and superstitions, it might reach the point where it could be formulated in exact, conceptually perfect terms. In this case educated men, who were now troubled by the Church's vulgarity, inventions, and errors, could finally discover a simple, indisputable truth, expressed in formulas like the indisputable formulas of science; like them, definitive, and, in a sense, objectively neutral.

Now, this particular contradiction might arise: that some historical research, conducted by an *historian*, that is, by a man linked to cultural traditions to his own psychological state, to circumstances of language, culture and so on, but who took no account of all these, since the object of his research transcended them and failed to presuppose them, would lead him to find or pick out an absolute, metahistorical value, purified in fact by the historical elements his research had gradually revealed. This element would be pure, and not subject to change: an essence precipitated in a number of compounds does not cease to remain pure in itself. This element was religion.

Well then, the Catholic Church should make itself the guardian, as it was the expression, of this essence of religion; or rather the Catholic Church should allow a few chosen spirits to settle the controversy by studying the essence of Christianity and thence the essence of religion. For if the Church were strong in its own truth, it could agree to have it proved outside the particular historical element in which, down the centuries, it had been considered. If, on the other hand, the Catholic Church appeared hostile to such studies in order to entrench itself in the historical forms that had supported it so far, its historical career might be cut short, and certainly its philosophical and 'religious' point would be lost. The science of religions would include Christianity among the historical forms in which this immutable essence had been incarnate; like other historical forms that had succeeded one another since man first realized his need to turn to a force that transcends him, but no greater than these others.

Why Christianity, and Catholicism in particular, should enjoy this privilege, why, that is, it should be final—both historically and in essence—was not clear to the contributors of *Rinnovamento* (as some of the consequences mentioned were not clear to them either). Very likely, and without meaning it ironically, the advantage of Christianity over the other historical forms in which the essence of religion was incarnate lay in that private, historical element, in all the traditions and psychological conditions the researcher thought it best to shake off when he went in for objective research. Thus the end of the research, or its conditioning character, having been rejected from the prelude, re-emerged in the masterly finale, and the skilful orchestration was not, it turned out, conditioned by the particular timbre of that favoured element, the solo instrument.

A reply of this kind, even if the consequences were not clearly defined at this point, could not satisfy the critics. A remark like: 'There is no point in examining our orthodoxy through what appears in this review'[1] was enough, on the one hand, to arouse suspicion or annoyance, in the atmosphere of suspicions, apostasies and calumnies; and, on the other, the ardent wish to distinguish between friends and enemies and to bring an end—even if crudely and temporarily—to the dangerous uncertainty in distinguishing truth from error.

[1] See 'Ai nostri critici', in *Rinnovamento*, a. 1, No. 11 (February 1907).

Others might choose, and might even make mistakes, but the *Rinnovamento* group would not even call themselves neutral. The Pope kept urging obedience to authority, and spoke plainly even if ignorantly; but they refused to accept that they had anything to do with orthodoxy, since they denied orthodoxy and even the fact that there was any possible conflict between orthodoxy and criticism.

And besides, the Pope had already had to reply, some time before this. On 17 April 1907, when he gave the hat to the new cardinals, Pius X made a violent speech in which subjects and expressions from his next encyclical appeared. The Church did not accept the innovators' proposals: it would not accustom itself to the new disciplines arising; it saw no chance of welcoming the science of religions and those who studied it. In short, Pius X rejected the whole movement, from within and from without:

... Alas, there are rebels who profess and spread in subtle form monstrous errors on the evolution of dogma [he said], on a return to the Gospels, which means, as they put it, divorced from the explanations of theology, from the definitions of the Councils, from the maxims of religious books; on the emancipation of the Church, but in a new way (these men do not rebel, for they do not wish to be cast out, but neither do they submit, for they will not give up their own convictions); and finally on the Church's need to adapt itself to the times in everything; in speaking, in writing, and in preaching there is charity without faith, which is tender towards unbelievers, and throws open the way to eternal ruin.

You can see clearly, oh Venerable Brethren, that We, who must defend what has been entrusted to Us with all our strength, are right to be troubled by this new attack, which is not a heresy, but the compendium and the poison of all heresies, which undermines the foundations of the faith and denies Christianity. Yes, it denies Christianity, because to these modern critics Holy Scripture is no longer the certain source of all the truths that belong to the faith, but an ordinary book; to them inspiration is confined to the dogmatic doctrines, but these are understood just as they please, so that it is not really unlike the poetic inspiration of Aeschylus or Homer. The legitimate interpreter of the Bible is the Church, but subjected to the rules of so-called scientific criticism, which is imposed on theology and enslaves it. As far as tradition is concerned, all is relative and subject to change, so that the authority of the Fathers is reduced to nothing. All these and a thousand other errors they propagate in pamphlets and reviews, in religious books and even in novels; and they wrap them up in ambiguous terms and cloudy forms which always allow them a way of escape in order to avoid open condemnation, yet ensnare the imprudent.

We count a great deal on your work, Venerable Brethren, in letting the bishops, your suffragans in your own districts, know who these sowers of tares are, in joining Us in the struggle against them, in informing Us of the danger to which souls are exposed, in denouncing their books to the Holy Office and meantime using the facilities allowed you by canon law, by solemnly condemning them; urged on in this by the high obligation you have assumed to help the Pope in the government of the Church, to combat error and defend the truth, even to the point of bloodshed.[1]

The bishops did not, of course, get to the point of bloodshed: but some of the modernist priests, not knowing quite whether they were defending truth or error, were martyrs of a 'modern thought' that had no idea what to do with them, and of a religious culture they often misinterpreted. Yet they were persecuted, their consciences and their persons were truly persecuted with a fury, a violence and a bitterness that seemed to belong to another more heroic and certainly more religious age. The persecution of the modernists, given official support by what the Pope had said, and already carried on in monasteries and seminaries, was really terrible; it was, as it were, much greater than those it was persecuting, as if the Roman curia had found in striking, cursing, and denouncing the strength it had lacked in preaching, in bearing witness to Christ, and in doing good.

Nor did the silent reformers of *Rinnovamento* get to the point of bloodshed. Once more they seemed undisturbed by what the Pope said. He spoke as harshly and violently as they spoke subtly and with learning; and, instead of a new university discipline, brought back the traditional vision of hell for the guilty and for unbelievers. Which, after all, meant them.

[1] Quoted in *Civiltà cattolica*, 1907, Vol. II, No. 1365 (April), pp. 358-9.

17. *Rinnovamento:* Condemnation and the end of the Alliance

On 29 April, Cardinal Andrea Steinhuber, Prefect of the Sacred Congregation of the Index, addressed a letter about *Rinnovamento* to Cardinal Ferrari, Archbishop of Milan. In it, having expressed his disgust at seeing 'a review clearly in conflict with Catholic teaching and the Catholic spirit,' he deplored 'in particular the way these writers [troubled] people's consciences, and the pride they [showed] towards the teachers of the Church, and almost towards its doctors'. It was sad, he continued, that among those who wished to take on the role of teacher in the Church and give lessons to the Pope himself, were some already known for what they had written in the same spirit, men like Fogazzaro, Tyrrell, von Hügel, Murri, and others.

And while such men deal so haughtily with the most difficult theological matters and the most important of the Church's affairs, the editors boast that it is a *lay, non-confessional* review and distinguishes between official and non-official Catholicism, between the dogmas of the Church as truths to be believed, and the immanence of religion in individuals. In short, there is no doubt at all that the object of the review is to cultivate a very dangerous spirit of independence from the Church's teaching, to encourage private judgement at the expense of the Church's own judgement, and to set itself up to prepare an anti-Catholic renewal of the spirit.

The letter therefore asked the Cardinal to warn the editor of the review 'to desist from so evil an undertaking, one so unworthy of a true Catholic,' and expressed the wish that 'as soon as possible' he would bring to the notice of the public the judgement of the Sacred Congregation of the Index.[1]

---

[1] Cardinal Ferrari, in a letter to the clergy of the Diocese about the letter from the Sacred Congregation of the Index, wrote: 'As you see, something is ordered and something requested: I had already fulfilled what the order required and pray that others will react to it with edifying meekness. . . . Of the errors of that letter I have written quite four times in the past two months: I will say only how much I am grieved by the thought that a few have thrown a sinister shadow over

The *Osservatore romano* of 3 May published the letter, and the Cardinal communicated its contents to the editors of *Rinnovamento* on 10 May. Three days later Alfieri, Casati, and Gallarati Scotti replied:

We, the undersigned, editors of the monthly review *Rinnovamento*, reaffirming the full submission of Catholics to the ecclesiastical authorities, express profound distress that intentions which have always been foreign to it and conflict with our sincere love for the Church have been attributed to our work, and deny as fully and explicitly as possible the charge that in it we are trying to assume the role of teacher in the Church.

But we do not believe we should stop publishing our review, since this would imply that we recognize the right of the Congregation of the Index to force the laity to cease scientific-religious, political, and social studies, which should be and should appear independent, in order to avoid justifying the accusation that only outside the Church can pure, calm mental work be pursued in freedom, using what methods it chooses and carrying on its research in tranquillity.

We are the first to admit the limitations and insufficiencies of our work, and so we expect objections and accept corrections. These may be scientific, in the name of wider, more certain studies; religious, in the name of a higher spiritual life; Catholic, in the name of a more authoritative expression of Christian truth. But we cannot give up thinking and expressing our thought; above all we cannot cease our work when it has just begun, before we have given the authorities themselves and the public of honest critics enough to judge us and our intentions justly.

Perhaps this attitude, which means that without pride but without weakness we claim for ourselves and for others the right to think and study with greater trust in the Catholic Church, may bring pain to some timid consciences, and may serve as a weapon for our enemies. But we hope it will be understood as an act of loyalty, all the possible consequences of which we have long considered, without personal involvement; and may thus show that the charity which demands obedience may also impose a humble but firm resistance that means we could not justify acceptance, either to our own consciences or to others.

We pray to God that this act of ours may show the fervent love we bear the Catholic Church, from which we never can nor wish to be parted.[1]

---

this diocese, in particular over the clergy, which nevertheless has no share in the censured journal, but has given and continues to give proofs of true submission and unshakeable attachment to the Holy See' (see text, in *Civiltà cattolica*, 1907, Vol. II, No. 1367, May).

[1] See *Rinnovamento*, a. 1, No. 5 (May 1907). Von Hügel associated himself spiritually with the editors' reply: see letter to Maude Petre, quoted in Michael

The two letters were published in *Rinnovamento*. But a third, in which the Archbishop of Milan replied to the editors, was not. No mention of it was made and this silence is significant:[1] it looks as if its accusations of pride and haughtiness in taking over the role of the teacher were disliked. Possibly the reason for this silence may be found in the fact that once more the editors were arguing over the point of the whole controversy, or rather over their relationship with the Church. If they wanted to maintain this relationship, their actions had a special meaning, their studies a purpose, the actual stand they were taking an object; if they intended to break it off, what they were doing in a sense meant nothing. And it seems the editors took no definite decision on the subject. Young, but perspicacious, they cannot have failed to realize that the nub of the whole question was their relationship with the Church. Their letter can be interpreted in two different ways: on the one hand, all their studies were intended for the Church, which had all their love, and from which they neither could nor would be parted; on the other hand, in thus defining both their research and its destination, they put themselves outside the Church by avoiding the disciplinary relationship that joined them to it, and showing they were not aware of being an integral part of it. The Church they referred to did not seem to be the Church that included them, but a part of the learning and teaching Church that listened to them, or should have done. This was the Church that needed reforming and seemed not to

de la Bedoyère's *Life*, p. 192: 'Those young fellows in Milan are acting *admirably*, like the chivalrous high minded gentlemen, and strong-souled, tough willed Christians and Catholics that they are—their answer to Rome is a very model of what such things could be'; but the whole letter should be read, since it shows how exactly von Hügel's thought coincided with that of his Milanese friends. He wrote to Tyrrell, too, on the occasion of the letter: 'We have evidently, once more, a piece of administrative rhetoric, something intended not to define a reality but to effect a situation' (ibid.). Cardinal Capecelatro, Archbishop of Capua, also associated himself with the letter, and expressed his disagreement with Cardinal Steinhuber's censure.

[1] See the text in *Civiltà cattolica*, 1907, No. 5 (October); particularly relevant is this part of it: 'It is impossible to understand such treatment of the Church while at the same time professing to love her dearly; just as it is impossible to understand the love a son professes for his own mother, who is a good mother and an excellent teacher, when he tells her: your orders are unjust, and I am putting up a "humble but firm resistance to them"; unless the Church he professes to love so much is quite different from the Church St. Ambrose meant when he said: "Ubi Petrus, ibi Ecclesia; ubi Ecclesia, ibi nulla mors sed vita aeterna." '

realize it needed it; nor did it recognize in these laymen a force that could reawaken it.

The man who spoke to them sadly was a bishop, their own bishop; the man who had warned them, although without naming them, some time earlier, was the head of the Church. The problem of his infallibility did not arise when the criticisms of the new heretics were discussed, but his authority must not be disputed. The Church which had spoken out against them, at its highest level, was the Church they professed to love, and their own Cardinal's words imply a filial relationship, which they ignored in their reply. Besides, they had personal connections with their pastor, which Cardinal Ferrari showed in his letter: his reluctance to take a stand and to mention the Holy Office's censure came partly from his wish to avoid scandalizing his flock, to which the editors of *Rinnovamento* belonged. But they still refused to take account of this Church which warned and condemned them; instead they kept addressing themselves to another Church that needed reform, and which they loved, nevertheless, immensely and wisely. It was not hard for the Jesuits of *Civiltà cattolica* to point out these contradictions; nor even for the laity, who by right were a part of modern thought. Perhaps even the inner group of *Rinnovamento* realized its own contradictions; yet it remained united through the very fact of sharing some of these contradictions and uncertainties.

As in the case of Loisy and Tyrrell, it was up to the Church to reject them, to declare them first outsiders, then enemies. The two priests had to be treated in a direct and personal way: it was not enough to include them in the general condemnation of a movement they belonged to: they had to be excommunicated by name. As far as the *Rinnovamento* laymen were concerned, the Church seemed not to have spoken. Only a few numbers of their review had appeared, and in these only a few essays really deserved strict scrutiny; so they felt it was too soon to incur disciplinary measures. Besides, they were young, and had taken only the first steps in some difficult studies: could they really have run into inexcusable errors already? All they asked was to be allowed to mature at their own pace, and cut their teeth on problems the Church had spoken out on. Then, if their work ran into errors, they should be judged, but not before. No one could really question their good faith, and if their training was at fault they were the first to admit it. As for presuppositions, they really had none: all they wanted was to deal with theology and biblical criticism as laymen. This was their only premiss: this was what they defended and stood out for.

Their studies were all destined, above all, for the Church—a Church considered in its history, in its essence, in its present political position; and all their efforts were aimed at improving and eventually correcting its present condition by bringing the laity into it as a new source of strength. But the *Rinnovamento* editors also intended to examine the religious and philosophical culture of their times and either consciously or unconsciously to find in it support for their aims. What *Rinnovamento* could be, and longed to be, was a critical training-ground; its predominant characteristic was, in fact, critical. This was why, although it welcomed the official speakers of the movement for reform, Tyrrell in particular, it was also anxious to reach what was new in philosophy, in criticism, and in historical studies. These new ideas might, the editors hoped, be drawn into the movement, yet they might at the time be considered outside it, and their values and discoveries must be made known and justified. *Rinnovamento* was fighting on two fronts: on the first, it was concerned with its current conflict with the Church, and here the pressure was mounting. Responsibilities had to be assumed, stands taken at once—and the editors, in spite of their culture, indeed because of it, did not really feel ready to do this. The second front was a matter of longer-term tactics: there was no need to make instant decisions, and more chance of thinking things over, of forming a proper critical opinion. For this reason the 'religious' history of *Rinnovamento* can be seen in two ways. The first means following its course against the background of events in international modernism in general and Italian modernism in particular: this is a tale of excommunications, of suspensions *a divinis*, of conflicts between individuals on the stand they should take towards the hierarchy. This hierarchy was now openly naming and condemning heretics, *all* heretics. The second way in which one can look at *Rinnovamento* needs no contemporary yardstick: it is a tale of statements, of the ups and downs of particular movements, of the alterations of opinion, this way or that. In it Calderoni's pragmatism, that appears in the second number, follows Fogazzaro's spiritual attitudes, and then comes nearer to Croce; and so it goes on, voices and movements of thought alternating, and none finally prevailing as characteristic of the group.

Inspiring this second front is Alessandro Casati.[1] In 1935 Croce dedicated his *Lives of adventure, faith and passion*, 'brilliant historical reconstructions' that recall 'fine hours travelling and studying in his dear, generous company', to him.

Rinnovamento published little by Casati: learned book reviews or critical reflections occasioned by the publication of works like Croce's *Essay on Hegel* or Prezzolini's *Red Catholicism*. These showed him as a well-informed, sensitive and intelligent critic, but were not enough to show where his preferences lay or in what direction his work was moving. Besides, Casati never wrote much, or lengthily. It was as if all his learning and culture brought him to the top of a blank page and no further, and prudence, laziness, or an abundance of leisure made him avoid expressing his own spiritual experiences, and leave to others the task of writing and making statements. Perhaps he put the best of himself and his personality into talk, into understanding, stimulating, and helping (financially at times) those who were involved in cultural life; into letters, and particularly into reading, considered not as an entertainment but as a duty.

The signed articles he contributed to *Rinnovamento* do not even show his exact attitude to modernism, and it would appear that he influenced his fellow-editors, Alfieri and Gallarati Scotti, to persevere in the work they had begun, to take seriously the responsibilities they had assumed: this, rather than seeking doctrinal innovations or certainties as a result of particular studies. When Casati dealt with Croce, Labriola, Bjørnson, or Hegel himself (even in his odd criticism of dialectic) he set them in the context of cultural history, Italian in particular, though in a European setting; he did not treat them as his masters. The mysticism he mentioned was a vital, indispensable element in the active idea of spirituality, not something to use explicitly in argu-

---

[1] On Alessandro Casati, apart from Gallarati Scotti's commemoration already quoted, see also W. Maturi's obituary in the *Rivista storica italiana*, LXVII, Naples, 1955, No. 3, pp. 475–6. See also Francesco Flora, *Alfonso Casati*, Milan, 1946, on the son who was killed in the Second World War (and whose letters to the family have been published, Ceschina, Milan, 1961); see judgements made in the letters of Amendola (quoted) and Prezzolini. Others (among them Croce, in his diary) mention Casati as a diplomatist. It is to be hoped that his letters will be collected and published.

ments, as a weapon of conflict or renewal. The fact that he dealt with the 'return to Hegel' or with Labriola's work, instead of other subjects and writers, is almost entirely a sign that his fine critical intuition saw what was of value, what was worth making known or defending; it showed no particular preferences and did not indicate any particular line of study. Or so at least it would appear. Buonaiuti's opinion of him, however, is hard to share fully. When he looked back on those years and in particular on the time he spent with Casati before the modernist conference at Molveno, Buonaiuti felt his friend was at the most merely curious about souls, or a diplomatist in the making, who for a while, being intellectually good-natured, was lingering among religious men in a state of crisis. As far as Buonaiuti himself was concerned, those years seemed almost a waste of precious time, which he, a priest already hunted by the Roman watchdogs, spent with literary unbelievers. Certainly the Roman Buonaiuti and the Lombard Casati had nothing in common; but not everyone censured Casati's detachment and gentlemanly prudence, or his culture, which had such different origins and aims from Buonaiuti's. To judge the Casati of *Rinnovamento* from his later diplomatic career is to misunderstand the special character of the Lombard aristocracy's moral background. Here, the reconciliation of the lay tradition of the Risorgimento with the religious renewal of the Church, of the formation of the ethical value of the State with the change in the hierarchical structure of the Church, meant serious, immanent problems, necessities and undertakings that required long and prudent consideration, with all values well in mind, or else overturned. Some contributors to *Rinnovamento*, Buonaiuti in particular, or Tyrrell, its guest writer, had a more precise feeling for the Church and its need of reform, and contrasted this feeling with the very different interests of their friends at the time, both then and in looking back on those days; but the Lombard aristocrats, Casati in particular, had, both through family tradition and by their own direct education, a more precise feeling for the State. And just as their feeling for the Church was changing, and they wished to make it a living instead of a hierarchical Church, so their vague feeling for the State was evolving in the structure of the parties and through the pressure of the popular movements; and they must have been conscious of both changes, even if they did not advance them. Of them all, Casati seems most aware of the whole movement in which he was taking part as an expression of, above all, a moral change, which would find its necessary conclusion in the structure of the State. Perhaps he was the only one of them all to understand this. For this reason, his cultural curiosity, his learning, his busy stint as editor, seem not much more than a prudent, wearisome preparation for something else. And perhaps this is why, in referring to the spiritual journey of his friend Stefano Jacini, a contributor to *Rinnovamento*, he sought to attribute to him a lack of satisfaction in the mere work of research, which was in fact his own.[1]

On 15 April Don Romolo Murri was suspended 'a divinis'. The reasons given for this were interviews he had given to journalists and never retracted, letters sent to the *Corriere della Sera* on the religious crisis in France, and, possibly the main reason, two articles which appeared in the January and March numbers of *Rinnovamento* of the parliamentary function of the Socialist Party after the congress of Rome, and on the radical party and programme in Italy. He was the first to be struck, but:

. . . it was not, as in Loisy's case, a matter of the relationships between criticism and theology, nor, as in that of Tyrrell, who was already deprived of the Mass because he refused to have his private correspondence censored, a case of the native and inalienable rights of a human individual in the face of authority . . . it was a matter of the competence of the ecclesiastical authorities in political and social matters, and therefore a matter of defining how far this extended, in such matters, without disturbing the essential ideas of two societies and the varied forms of human activity.

It was Buonaiuti who thus interpreted the condemnation in his *Letters of a modernist priest*, and one can share it.[2] As for Murri, when he was questioned about his intentions in the *Corriere della Sera*, he replied by telegraph:

I have nothing to say: I am a priest, and a priest I remain, respecting the authorities, faithful to all my duties. I have sacrificed long sad years to my love of truth and of the Church, I explain the sharp conflicts at the present time of profound crisis for Catholicism, I always maintain—in spite of any particular deficiencies I may have—that the standards behind my criticism and action will give religious society new vigour

[1] See A. Casati, 'Commemorazione di Stefano Jacini', in *Saggi*, op. cit.
[2] See *Lettere di un prete modernista*, Rome, 1908, p. 177.

and will make it more fruitful and efficacious in civil life; I plead for the tacit sympathy of all free believers.

Thus—but once again *Rinnovamento* seemed not to realize it—Rome took its final stand, and the innovators were at last rejected. The movement had had three ideal phases: Loisy's, the exegetical; Tyrrell's, the mystical; and now, the political. All three phases, however much the reformers may previously have disagreed among themselves, were now drawn together in a joint condemnation. All that the contributors to *Rinnovamento* had left, if they wanted to escape, was a vague 'cultural modernism', and, if they wanted to take their researches elsewhere, the neutrality of science and philosophy. If they wished to continue studying religion, they must frankly and definitely appear as heretics or rebels. In order to chart their future course of action, they decided to meet at the Congress of Molveno.[1] Everything urged them to hasten—a plea to Pius X called 'What we want', by a group of Roman priests, and more than this the first decree of doctrinal condemnation, *Lamentabili sane exitu* on 3 July, and the placing on the Index of Le Roy's *Dogme et critique* on 26 July. Molveno was probably the last time the reformers met with common hopes, the finishing post which all must reach after their effort to achieve unity over so long a time, in several places and with diverse faiths. After it the history of modernism becomes scattered into isolated cases of struggle, resistance, submission, or yielding. After Molveno each man chose his own way and continued along it, firmly or less firmly convinced, but knowing he was quite alone. In any case, when they left Molveno, feeling certain that the restoration under Pius X would now throw them into confusion, the reformers found waiting for them, as precise and pitiless as their aspirations had been vague and uncertain, the encyclical *Pascendi dominici gregis*.

[1] The reports on the Congress of Molveno by various people who attended differ noticeably; but each man was trying to justify his own behaviour rather than reconstruct what was said and done at that admirable final meeting. Thus Buonaiuti in his *Pellegrino di Roma* and Gallarati Scotti in his *Vita del Fogazzaro* implicitly recognize that any kind of alliance became impossible at such a meeting, and this was so forever. Unfortunately von Hügel's diary says nothing significant about the Congress (at least the extracts used by his biographer do not), nor is it described elsewhere, except in reports by Sabatier (*Les modernistes*, p. lii, malignant and frivolous) and Houtin (*Histoire du modernisme catholique*, p. 177). On which see Buonaiuti's comment in the original French edition of his history of modernism (n. 1, p. 109, suppressed in the Italian edition).

Chronology

1864 8 December
Encyclical *Quanta cura*, accompanied by the *Syllabus*, a collection of eighty erroneous propositions already condemned by Pius IX in documents, decrees, and addresses, among them proposition LXXX, which was particularly noteworthy: 'The Roman Pontiff can and must come to terms with progress, liberalism, and modern civilisation', taken from the allocution *Iamdudum cernimus* of 18 March 1861.

1868 29 February
Promulgation of 'non expedit'.

29 June
Bolla di indizione of the Ecumenical Council (Vatican Council).

1869 8 December
Work of the Vatican Council, suspended 20 October 1870, begins.

1870 18 July
Approval of the Constitution: *Pastor aeternus* on papal infallibility.

1871 Charles Darwin: *The Descent of Man*.

1878 20 February
Leo XIII (Gioacchino Pecci, 1810–1903) elected Pope.

1879 4 August
Encyclical *Aeterni Patris* on the study of the philosophy of St. Thomas.

1880 In Florence the first number of the *Rassegna nazionale* appears. Louis Duchesne (1843–1922) publishes the *Bulletin Critique*, to which he asks Alfred Loisy (1857–1940) and Friedrich von Hügel (1852–1925) to contribute.

1884 Von Hügel's first journey to Paris, where he meets Mercier, Ollé-Laprune, A. de Mun, d'Hulst and, in particular, Huvelin and Duchesne.

1888 7 March
Leo XIII condemns forty propositions taken from the works of Antonio Rosmini.

1889 H. Bergson: *Essai sur les données immédiates de la conscience*.
In Padua, under orders from the Holy See, Giuseppe Toniolo sets up the Catholic Union for Italian studies.
The Barnabite Father Gazzola, 'le plus grand curé de la ville', according to Loisy, denounced by the Holy Office and exiled

from Milan, is recalled on account of a protest from his parishioners, both nobles and middle-class.

1890 J. M. Lagrange (1855–1938) founds the École pratique d'études bibliques in Jerusalem.

Auguste Sabatier (1830–1901): *La vie intime des dogmes*. Alfred Loisy: *Histoire du Canon de l'Ancien Testament*.

1891 22 February

Antonio Fogazzaro (1842–1911) lectures on 'A recent comparison between the theories of St. Augustine and Darwin on the Creation', at the Venetian Institute of Science and Letters.

15 May

Encyclical *Rerum novarum* on the condition of the workers.

July

F. von Hügel: *Notes addressed to the very Reverend H.I.D.R. upon the subject of Biblical Inspiration and Inerrancy* (first published work).

Loisy publishes: *Histoire du Canon du Nouveau Testament*, discussing lessons held at the Institut catholique.

1892 At the International Scientific Congress of Catholics held in Paris the question of the non-authenticity of the Pentateuch (whose authenticity is to be decreed by the Biblical Commission in 1906) is raised. Other congresses are held in Paris (1888 and 1891), Brussels (1894), Fribourg (1897), and Munich (1900). One is planned to take place in Rome in 1903 but not held, as thought unsuitable.

Publication of the *Revue biblique*, edited by J. M. Lagrange, begins. Publication of *L'Enseignement biblique* begins. 'Certainly nobody will be surprised to see us applying the historical and critical method to biblical knowledge. It is not because we are losing sight of the supernatural character of the Scriptures, or of the dogmatic principles which are the infallible guideline of exegesis; we are only complying with the exigencies of the present time.' (In the programme, published in the January–February number, reproduced in the first edition of *Études bibliques* (1894), and not in those that followed.)

Death of Ernest Renan (1823–92) on 7 October.

G. Semeria (1867–1931) attends the lectures of Antonio Labriola at the Ateneo romano.

1893 January

The first number of the *Revista internazionale di scienze sociale e discipline ausiliarie*, edited by Giuseppe Toniolo and Salvatore Talamo, appears, a journal that proposes 'to illustrate the value of the Christian social order and to follow the marvellous movement of ideas and action that nowadays battles generously all over the world for the health of universal civilization and for the true greatness of Italy', and goes on to say that 'a journal with this aim can be produced only by men who are profoundly Catholic, who totally subordinate science to faith and profess meek and unconditional obedience to the teachings and authority of the Church'.

25 January
In the *Correspondant* Monsignor d'Hulst publishes an article on the various schools in theology, which draws attention to teachings of Loisy (mistakenly placed in the *école large*).

2 March
At the Collegio romano Antonio Fogazzaro lectures on *The origin of man and religious feeling*; this, which, with other lectures (*A recent comparison* (1891), *On the beauty of an idea* (1892)), is bitterly attacked by *Civiltà cattolica* (15 and 31 October, 1893), which Fogazzaro answers in 'Pro civilitate', an open letter to the editor of *Nuovo Risorgimento*, Professor L. M. Billia (Vol. IV, no. 2).

During this year in Paris the French translation of the *Mystery of the Poet* is published by Perrin.

May
The Rector of the Institut catholique, Monsignor d'Hulst, tells Loisy that his course on biblical exegesis is to be suspended for a year. M. Fillion of San Sulpice, pious and uncritical, whose pupils were unable to attend the courses at the beginning of the year, takes over.

3 November
750 copies of *L'Action* by Maurice Blondel (1861–1941) published; the edition was sold out by September 1895.

18 November
Encyclical *Providentissimus Deus* on Biblical studies.

November
First meeting of von Hügel, Monsignor Mignot (1842–1918), and Loisy, 'a memorable date in the history of Catholic modernism', according to Loisy, who suspends the publication of *Enseignement biblique*.

1894 H. Bergson: *Matière et mémoire*. The first number of *La Quinzaine*, founded by Paul Harel from 1896 and edited by Georges Fonsegrive (1852–1917), appears.

The directors of the Opera dei Congressi, under the direction of Giuseppe Toniolo, set out their *Programme of Catholics in the face of socialism*.

In the *Dublin Review* (October 1894) von Hügel's first article appears: 'The Church and the Bible, the two stages of their inter-relation' (the second and third were to appear in the same review in April and October 1895), a comment on the encyclical *Providentissimus Deus.*

1895 A new series of the *Annales de philosophie chrétienne*, founded in 1829 by Augustin Bonnetti, is under the editorship of Charles Denis, with the participation by Maurice Blondel and Lucien Laberthonnière (1860–1932), who in effect is its editor from 1905. They were condemned in 1913.

Meeting in Rome of Giovanni Semeria, von Hügel, and Blondel; Blondel is received in a fatherly way by Leo XIII; von Hügel sends the Pope a short dissertation on the validity of Anglican orders. The first number of *Vita nova*, a university review founded and edited by Romolo Murri (1870–1944), appears; proposing 'because of the special conditions of the present time, to turn its attention in particular to the study of social questions'.

1896 Publication of the *Revue d'histoire et de littérature religieuses*, 'purement historique et critique', edited by Loisy, begins. Von Hügel contributes financially to launching it.

January and July
Blondel publishes his 'Lettre sur les éxigences de la pensée contemporaine en matière d'apologétique et sur la méthode de la philosophie dans l'étude du problème religieux', in the *Annales de philosophie chrétienne.*

In Florence, on 10 March, the publication of the fortnightly *Rivista bibliografica italiana*, directed by Salvatore Minocchi (1869–1943), begins.

Von Hügel, through the mediation of Duchesne, director of the French school at Palazzo Farnese in Rome, is received by Leo XIII on 7 March. Two days previously he had read a paper to the Society for Biblical Studies, directed by Faberi, in the presence of Fracassini and Eugenio Pacelli.

Italian Catholic University Federation (F.U.C.I.) founded in Rome; linked, with the Congresso di Fiesole, to the Opera dei Congressi.

1897 Felix Klein (1862–1953), friend and correspondent of Fogazzaro, publishes his *Vie du père Hecker*, French translation of W. Elliot's biography, the programme of 'Americanism' in France.

Congress IV of Catholic Scientists at Fribourg, attended by Minocchi, J. M. Lagrange, Blondel, and Semeria, who reads a paper by von Hügel on the Hexateuch ('The historical method and its application to the study of documents').

Auguste Sabatier: *Esquisse d'une philosophie de la religion d'après la psychologie et l'histoire*, the first and fundamental 'modernistic' text, according to *Civiltà cattolica*, and an important influence on Loisy, as he admitted.

October

First meeting between von Hügel and George Tyrrell (1861–1909), who in the same year had published *Nova et vetera*, according to M. D. Petre his first real book. Von Hügel shows Tyrrell Blondel's *Lettre*.

1898 Lucien Laberthonnière publishes 'Le dogmatisme moral', an essay that, according to Gallarati Scotti, had a strong influence on Fogazzaro.

1 January

First number of Romolo Murri's *Cultura sociale* appears; with articles by F. Invrea, Igino Petrone, Luigi Caissotti di Chinsano, and others, including Semeria. Murri's programme declares: '. . . what used to be a defensive programme is now spreading out into a much more definite and varied one, which includes public and social life in a new and Christian light'.

The Holy Office proclaims the Johannine comma 'authenticum textum'.

George Tyrrell publishes *Hard Sayings*, Blondel *L'illusion idéaliste*. At Pisa, Giovanni Gentile publishes his degree thesis on Rosmini and Gioberti.

15 December

The works of Hermann Schell (1850–1906) are put on the Index: *Catholic dogma* (in six volumes); *Catholicism as the beginning of progress*; *The divine truth of Christianity*; *The modern age and ancient faith*; *A study of the history of culture*.

Loisy, under the pseudonym of A. Firmin, publishes an article on Christian development according to Newman.

1899 22 January

Testem benevolentiae, Apostolic letter from Leo XIII on Americanism, sent to Cardinal Gibbons, Archbishop of Baltimore.

8 September

Depuis le jour, Leo XIII's Encyclical addressed to the French clergy, 'precondemnation' of 'premodernism'.

At Turin, Romolo Murri and G. B. Valente outline the programme of Christian Democracy. Marcel Hébert (1851–1916) publishes *Souvenirs d'Assise*, which, according to Houtin, was to inspire some pages of Fogazzaro's *Il Santo*.

Von Hügel's first meeting with Henri Bremond (1865–1933), who already corresponds with George Tyrrell.

George Tyrrell's article on Hell, 'A perverted devotion', appears in *The Weekly Register*, and causes his removal from Farm Street, the famous Jesuit church in London.

1900   A. Harnack (1851–1930) publishes *Das Wesen des Christentums*.

In *Critica sociale*, Claudio Treves appeals to the Italian clergy to make 'a sincerely democratic Catholic party'.

24–28 September
Fifth (and last) International Scientific Congress of Catholics at Munich; Blondel, Duchesne, Batiffol, and Semeria take part.

1 November
The 'Manifesto to Italian catholics', written by Murri, in *Domani d'Italia*.

Pastoral letter from the English Catholic hierarchy on *The Church and liberal Catholicism*, which reasserts a clear distinction between the *Ecclesia docens* and the *Ecclesia discens*, an important matter in later modernistic discussions.

12 December
Loisy starts his free lectures at the Sorbonne.

1901   18 January
Encyclical *Graves de Communi* on popular Christian action.

In Florence *Studi religiosi, a critical and historical review to promote religious culture in Italy*, is launched under the editorship of Salvatore Minocchi. In the July–August number an article by von Hügel on Loisy appears.

In May and June, von Hügel meets Tommaso Gallarati Scotti and Monsignor Achille Ratti in Milan.

July
Albert Houtin (1869–1926) meets Loisy. The report of their meetings (published posthumously by Sartiaux) angers Loisy and makes him start work on the draft of his *Mémoires*.

The constitution of the Biblical Commission is announced; among its members are D. Fleming, Gismondi, Fracassini, and Amelli.

In Rome the *Giornale d'Italia* starts publication, giving a good deal of space to the examination of religious controversies.

In the December number of the *Bulletin* of Tolosa Monsignor E. Mignot publishes an essay on 'La méthode de la théologie', according to Loisy one of the first declarations of Catholic modernism.

1 November
In the Florentine *Rassegna nazionale* Fogazzaro publishes his poem *Alla verità*.

Giovanni Semeria, who lectured at Vicenza on 'The Gospel and criticism', publishes *The first Christian blood* (Pustet, Rome).

3 December

Leo XIII makes Rome and the suburbicarian dioceses readopt Bellarmino's *Catechism* in a slightly revised edition.

1902 27 January

Instruction from the Holy Office on popular Christian or Christian-Democratic action in Italy, sent by Cardinal Rampolla, Secretary of State, in the Pope's name, to all the regular clergy of Italy, together with the new edition of the Statute and Rules of the Opera dei Congressi; in an appendix: Programme of popular or Christian-Democratic action.

French translation of Harnack's *Das Wesen des Christentums* appears. From this year onwards, Giovanni Semeria contributes to *Studi religiosi*.

March

Houtin publishes *La question biblique chez les catholiques de France au XIX siècle*; Loisy, who appears in it as orthodox, had urged its publication.

24 August

Romolo Murri gives a lecture on 'Freedom and Christianity' to the Christian-Democratic Committee of San Marino; the Vicariate calls it 'reprehensible, worthy of censure'.

27 and 29 August

Bitter argument between Cardinal Giuseppe Sarto, patriarch of Venice, and Romolo Murri, occasioned by a letter from the Cardinal against Murri's article 'The Fall of Venice', and in favour of Count Paganuzzi, President of the Opera dei Congressi. Rampolla, Secretary of State, writes to Cardinal Sarto, saying that 'the Holy See deplores the way this priest has gone, and is seriously worried as to what can be done to bring him back to better judgement'.

21 September

Death of Don Davide Albertario (1846–1902), editor of the *Osservatore cattolico*, in Milan.

26 September

Civiltà cattolica declares itself authorized to state publicly that *Studi religiosi* has no ecclesiastical approval, though it was asked for.

30 October

Decretum *Vigilantiae* for the institution of the Biblical Commission.

November
Alfred Loisy publishes *L'Évangile et l'Église*. First letter from Tyrrell to Loisy (20 November).

8 December
Encyclical *Fin dal Principio*, sent to the bishops of Italy, on the education of the clergy: 'Since the beginning of Our pontificate We have borne in mind the grievous state of society and have not been long in recognizing that one of the most urgent tasks facing the Apostolic see is that of looking carefully into the education of young priests'.
Leo XIII also sends the bishops of Italy the letter he sent to the clergy of France.

1903 17 January
Cardinal Richard of Paris condemns Loisy's *L'Évangile et l'Église* because it is such as to 'seriously disturb the faith of the laity in the fundamental dogmas of Catholic teaching'.

July
Salvatore Minocchi and Giovanni Semeria, with a letter of introduction from Paul Sabatier, visit Leo Tolstoy. A description of the visit, written by Minocchi, in the *Giornale d'Italia* on 14 August, provokes a sharp rebuke from *Civiltà cattolica*. Semeria is recalled to Italy by telegraph.

20 July
Death of Leo XIII, aged 93, in the 25th year of his reign.

4 August
Election of Pius X (Cardinal Giuseppe Sarto, 1835–1914) to the papacy.

4 October
Encyclical *E supremi apostolatus cathedra*, which expounds the Pope's programme with St. Paul's words: 'Restore all things in Christ' (*Instaurare omnia in Christo*), in which he mentions 'lying science which lays the way open to the errors of rationalism and semirationalism'.

5 October
Alfred Loisy publishes *Autour d'un petit livre* and a second edition, 'revue et augmentée', of *L'Évangile et l'Église*.

10–13 November
Nineteenth Italian Catholic Congress held in Bologna. With Grosoli elected in place of Paganuzzi, the younger element prevails. Luigi Sturzo takes part in the Congress.

16 December
The following books by Alfred Loisy are put on the Index: *La religion d'Israel*; *Études évangéliques*; *L'Évangile et l'Église*;

Autour d'un petit livre: Le quatrième Évangile. In his letter to Cardinal Richard, on 19 December, Rafaël Merry del Val, nominated Secretary of State the previous November, writes: 'The very grave errors in these books are mainly in connection with: early Revelation; the authenticity of the facts and teachings of the Gospel; the divinity and knowledge of Jesus Christ; the Resurrection; the divine institution of the Church; the sacraments.' The following books by Albert Houtin are also put on the Index (23 December): *La question biblique chez les catholiques de France au XIX siècle* and *Mes difficultés avec mon évêque.*

18 December

Motu proprio of Pius X, *Fin dalla prima* on popular Christian action.

Maurice Blondel publishes: *Principe élémentaire d'une logique de la vie morale.*

Harnack's *Das Wesen des Christentums* translated into Italian by A. Bongioanni, published by Fratelli Bocca of Turin.

The publication of *Leonardo*, edited by G. Papini and G. Prezzolini, begins.

The publication of Benedetto Croce's *Critica* begins.

Baldassarre Labanca's *Gesù Cristo* published.

Rules laid down for the Commission for promoting biblical studies are published.

1904   2 February

Encyclical *Ad diem illum*, for the fiftieth anniversary of the promulgation of the dogma of the Immaculate Conception.

16 February

Italian translation of von Hügel's article on Loisy, which appeared in *The Pilot* on 9 January, published in the Florentine *Rassegna nazionale.*

In three numbers of *La Quinzaine* Maurice Blondel publishes his essay 'Histoire et dogme ou les lacunes philosophiques de l'exégèse moderne', dated Aix, 20 November 1903.

11 March

A letter from von Hügel on Loisy, in reply to an article by B. Labanca, published in the *Giornale d'Italia*; this newspaper and the *Corriere della Sera* announce the coming condemnation of *Action* and Loisy's excommunication.

In the June number of *La Quinzaine*, von Hügel publishes his 'Du Christ éternel et de nos Christologies successives', on Blondel's essay, and partially supporting Loisy; counter-reply from Blondel in the same journal through his friend the Abbé Wehrlé.

21 July
The Milanese Christian Democrats meet and propose to organize themselves into an autonomous national association, while some of the leaders in Rome, at Romolo Murri's, decide to set up Italian Christian Democracy, an autonomous movement under the title of 'Lega democratica nazionale'.

28 July
The promotion Committee of the Opera dei Congressi dissolved.

30 July
Diplomatic relations broken between France and the Holy See. The term *modernism* appears, probably for the first time, in *Miscellanea*, edited by U. Benigni, and since then is used in polemical writing, until adopted by the Pope in the Encyclical *De modernistarum doctrinis* (September 1907), better known as *Pascendi*.

Lettres romaines appears anonymously in the *Annales de philosophie chrétienne*.

Italian translation of William James's *Varieties of Religious Experience* by G. C. Ferrari and Mario Calderoni published by Fratelli Bocca of Turin.

The International Congress of Free Thought held in Rome in September, attended by over 3,000, including 1,500 Italians.

Henri Bremond, mainly responsible for making Newman's thought known in France, leaves the Society of Jesus, without any apparent disagreement.

Ernesto Buonaiuti (1881–1946) publishes his essays 'Neothomism and the University of Louvain', and 'Spencer and his work from the religious point of view', in *Studi religiosi*. In the December number of *Studi religiosi* Semeria publishes: 'A method and a model of Christian Apologetics' on George Tyrrell's *Lex Orandi*.

1905 15 April
Encyclical *Acerbo nimis* 'on the promotion of Christian doctrine'.

16 April
Edouard Le Roy (1870–1954) publishes his essay 'Qu'est-ce qu'un dogme' in *La Quinzaine*.

26–30 April
International Congress of Experimental Psychology held in Rome, attended by James, Fano, de Sarlo, Morselli, Lombroso, Papini, Tarozzi, etc. Papini reads a paper: 'Influence of the will on knowledge'.

15 May
Pius X receives Salvatore Minocchi and praises his work.

11 June

Encyclical *Il fermo proposito*, addressed to the bishops of Italy, for the setting up and development of Catholic Action, a lay association for Catholic religious propaganda to the outside world.

14 June

The *Compendium of Christian doctrine* appears with the support of Pius X, a 'one and only' catechism that, apart from a few small changes, uses the text approved for several years by the bishops of Piedmont, Liguria, Lombardy, Emilia, and Tuscany.

3 July

Vote taken in the French Chamber on the law to separate Church and State in France (a law later passed on 9 December 1905).

August

Third international Congress of Liberal and Progressive Christianity held in Geneva; Albert Houtin attends.

27 October

The first number of *Demain, politique, social, réligieux, organe hébdomadaire de critique et d'action* appears in Lyons; contributors are Fogazzaro, Minocchi, Murri, Semeria, and Giulio Vitali.

5 November

Antonio Fogazzaro's *Il Santo* published by Baldini and Castoldi in Milan.

E. Buonaiuti publishes his essay 'For the Philosophy of Action' in *Studi religiosi*.

Lega democratica nazionale founded in Bologna; it proposes 'to bring together thinking and mature young proletarians with the object of working together—through study and personal effort, in Catholic and professional associations, through the spread of ideas, written or spoken, through political action and in other suitable ways—in order to make the public activity of Catholics democratic, to defend the workers' interests and see to their political education, and to advance economic, intellectual, and moral life in Italy'.

The publication of the *Rivista storico-critica delle scienze teologiche*, the first numbers edited by Father Giuseppe Bonaccorsi, the later by Ernesto Buonaiuti, begins.

1906   January

Extracts from the 'Confidential letter to a Professor of Anthropology' by George Tyrrell, who the following months is expelled from the Society of Jesus (7 February), published anonymously in the *Corriere della Sera* in Milan.

11 February
Encyclical *Vehementer nos*, a solemn protest against the anti-religious legislation in France, urging Catholics to try by legal means to preserve the Catholic tradition of France.
George Tyrrell says his last Mass.
5 April
Fogazzaro's *Il Santo* put on the Index. It had appeared in a French translation in the *Revue des deux mondes* from 15 January to 15 March.
Lucien Laberthonnière's *Essais de philosophie religieuse* and *Le réalisme chrétien et l'idéalisme grec* also put on the Index.
May
T. Gallarati Scotti joins the Lega democratica nazionale, whose journal, *Azione democratica* is published early in the month in Bologna.
27 June
The Biblical Commission decrees the Mosaic authenticity of the Pentateuch, a decision contrary to the conclusion expressed in von Hügel's essay. Von Hügel answers in a pamphlet, *The Papal Commission and the Pentateuch.*
26 July
Encyclical *Pieni l'animo*, the first official sign of doctrinal ferment and reform spreading among the clergy. Priests and deacons are forbidden to join the Lega democratica nazionale, deacons under pain of being forbidden Holy Orders, priests under pain of suspension *ipso facto a divinis.*
July
Rivista di cultura, edited by Romolo Murri, appears in Rome.
15 September
First national Congress of the Lega democratica nazionale in Milan; inaugural speech by T. Gallarati Scotti, interventions from Murri and Cervini. A plan is formulated to keep independent of the official line in clerical politics and to oppose 'a disguised theocracy that seeks our submission in every act and every thought', and 'a distorted concept of authority which misleads souls and seeks to interfere even in national life'.
September
George Tyrrell publishes *A Much-Abused Letter.*
Buonaiuti visits Loisy at Garnay.
1 November
Loisy says his last Mass.
1907 January
The first number of *Rinnovamento* appears in Milan; edited

by Aiace Antonio Alfieri, Alessandro Casati, and Tommaso Gallarati Scotti.

18 January

In Paris Fogazzaro gives his lecture on 'Les idées réligieuses de Giovanni Selva', repeated on 30 January at Geneva, published in *Demain* at Lyons on 8 February, and in *Rinnovamento*, also in February.

15 April

Don Romolo Murri is suspended *a divinis*.

17 April

At a consistory for the creation of new cardinals, Pius X denounces 'rebels who profess and in cunning ways spread monstrous errors on the evolution of dogma, on a return to the Gospel . . . We must with all our strength defend what has been handed down to us . . . in the face of this attack, which is not a heresy but the poisonous sum-total of all heresies, attacks the very foundations of the faith, and seeks to destroy Christianity.'

24 April

Fogazzaro gives the inaugural lecture of his Fogazzaro Lectures at Turin.

29 April

The Congregation of the Index writes to Cardinal Ferrari of Milan about *Rinnovamento*, asking him to appeal to its editors 'to desist from their infamous work, unworthy as it is of a true Catholic'.

13 May

Reply from the editor of *Rinnovamento*.

15 May

Quello che vogliamo (*What we want*), open letter from a group of Roman priests.

22 May

Counter-reply from Cardinal Ferrari.

29 May

Answer from the Biblical Commission on the author and historical truth of the Fourth Gospel.

May

The first cyclostyled numbers of the *Corrispondenza romana*, Monsignor U. Benigni's organ of information.

3 July

Lamentabili sane exitu, decree of Inquisition condemning sixty-five propositions dealt with in various works on ecclesiastical subjects, the majority of them Loisy's.

26 July
The following placed on the Index: 'Dogme et critique' by Edouard Le Roy, *La crise du clergé* by Albert Houtin, and the review *Coenobium*, published in Lugano.

August
An argument, which later became public, between George Tyrrell, the Prior of Storrington, and Cardinal Ferrata, on the right of censoring correspondence.

27, 28, 29 August
Meeting at Molveno, in which the *Rinnovamento* group take part: von Hügel, Buonaiuti, Don B. Casciola, Mari, Piastrelli, Fogazzaro, Murri, and Fracassini.

8 September
Encyclical *Pascendi dominici gregis* on the modernist doctrines.

September–October
In *The Times* of 30 September and 1 October George Tyrrell publishes 'The Pope and modernism', two articles which had already appeared in the *Giornale d'Italia* of 26 September. This was the first time the modernists had taken a stand with regard to the Encyclical.

In the *Grand Revue* of 10 October Tyrrell publishes 'L'Excommunication Salutaire', and is forbidden the sacraments (the article is dated 18 May 1905, however).

28 October
In Rome *Il programma dei modernisti, Risposta all'enciclica di Pio X 'Pascendi dominici gregis'* appears anonymously.

29 October
The Pope excommunicates its authors, both writers and anyone else involved in its publication.

6 November
Cardinal Ferrari forbids *Rinnovamento* to be bought or read, under pain of suspension *a divinis ipso facto* for priests.

18 November
Motu proprio 'Praestantia Scripturæ' on the Pontifical Biblical Commission's decrees and on the penalties for those who ignore pontifical prescriptions against the errors of the modernists.

23 December
Cardinal Ferrari excommunicates fully the 'editors, directors, authors, and collaborators of the review *Rinnovamento*'.

Studi religiosi and *La Quinzaine* cease publication.

T. Gallarati Scotti gives up his co-editorship of *Rinnovamento*.

1908 January
Nova et vetera, fortnightly organ of the International scientific-religious Society, appears in Rome.

Vita religiosa, a Catholic monthly review, 'created by some *Studi religiosi* writers', but in fact founded and edited by Salvatore Minocchi, appears in Florence.

23 January
Salvatore Minocchi is suspended *a divinis* for a lecture on Genesis given on 19 January in Florence.

31 January
Alfred Loisy publishes *Les Évangiles synoptiques* and *Simples réflexions sur le décret du Saint-Office 'Lamentabile' et sur l'encyclique: 'Pascendi dominici gregis.'*

10 February
Catholici: lendemain d'encyclique, a French modernist's answer to the encyclical, appears in Paris. Loisy publishes the last number of the *Revue d'histoire et littérature religieuses* (dated September to December 1907).

14 February
The Archbishop of Paris, M. Amette, Cardinal Richard's successor, publishes an ordinance forbidding the clergy and faithful of his diocese, under pain of serious penalties, to read, buy, sell or possess *Le Programme des Modernistes* (French translation, published by Nourry), and, under pain of excommunication, to read, possess, print, or defend *Les Évangiles synoptiques* and *Simples réflexions*. Most of the bishops think it unsuitable to forbid *Le Programme*, but the order is supported by eleven archbishops, among them Monsignor Mignot.

18–27 February
Discussion in the Italian Chamber on religious teaching in schools, on a motion of Bissolati.

7 March
Nominative excommunication of Alfred Loisy.

March
Lettere di un prete modernista, published by Libreria editrice romana, appears anonymously in Rome.

14 April
Alfred Loisy publishes *Quelques lettres sur des questions actuelles et sur des événements recents.*

F. von Hügel publishes *The Mystical Element of Religion*, his first great work.

George Tyrrell publishes *Medievalism*, an answer to Cardinal Mercier.

6–8 September
II National Congress of the Lega democratica nazionale, at Rimini.

October
Meeting between Bergson and Loisy, whose candidature to the Collège de France Bergson supports, showing affinities between his thought and Loisy's in similar fields.

December
Nova et vetera ceases publication.

20 December
The first number of *Voce* appears.

1909 January
At Gualdo di Macerata, Murri's *Rivista di Cultura* appears again, and the Cardinal-vicar at once pronounces a severe decree against it. The first number of the *Rivista di filosofia neoscolastica*, edited by Giulio Canella and Agostino Gemelli, appears in Florence.

13 January
Romolo Murri's *I problemi dell'Italia contemporanea*, Vol. I: *La politica clericale e la democrazia* is put on the Index.

2 March
Loisy is elected to the Collège de France, to the chair of History of Religions.

22 March
Romolo Murri is excommunicated, nominatively and personally, for having accepted election as a deputy of the left (14 March).

21 April
Encyclical *Communium Rerum*, for the eighth centenary of St. Anselm, in which 'the sowing of errors and perditions, given, through the unhealthy mania for what is new, the name of modernism', is again condemned.

6 June
Works by the following put on the Index: Joseph Turmel, Guillaume Herzog (a pseudonym of Turmel's), Romolo Murri *Battaglie d'oggi*, in four volumes; *La vita religiosa nel cristianesimo*; *La filosofia nuova e l'enciclica contro il modernismo*), Sostene Gelli (a pseudonym of Tyrrell's).

30 June
Biblical Commission's reply on the historical character of the first three chapters of Genesis.

15 July
Death of George Tyrrell.

27–31 October
III Congress of the Italian Philosophical Society held in Rome,

under the presidency of Giacomo Barzellotti, at which Minocchi gives his lecture on 'Religion and philosophy'.

5 November
The Pontifical Biblical Institute inaugurated in Rome; this was announced in the apostolic letter *Vinea Electa* of the previous 7 March

December
Rinnovamento ceases publication.

1910 5 January
Commento, a bi-monthly cultural review edited by Romolo Murri, appears in Rome.

January
The first number of the *Revue moderniste internationale* appears in Geneva.

Loisy's *Revue d'histoire et de littérature religieuses* starts publication again.

March to May
Ernesto Buonaiuti and Father Enrico Rosa, S.J., argue bitterly in *Civiltà cattolica* and the *Rivista storico-critica delle scienze teologiche*.

April
Loisy publishes his essay 'Jésus ou le Christ', in the *Hibbert Journal*, and it is republished the same month in *Coenobium*, which takes a referendum on the problem; this may be considered Loisy's first important statement of his break with Christianity, and in the essay he takes up the subject (and the inspiration) of Reitzenstein's book on the hellenic mystery religions (1910), which was to be developed in the volume *Les mystères païens et le mystère chrétien*.

1 May
Biblical Commission's reply on the Psalms.

26 May
Encyclical *Editae saepe* in honour of St. Charles Borromeo, which, by mentioning some of the Protestant personalities, provokes outbursts in Germany, and starts up accusations against the Modernists again.

26 June
Motu proprio of Pius X, who settles a formula for the oath to be used by those taking a degree in Holy Scriptures.

25 August
Apostolic letter *Notre Charge Apostolique*, condemning the French movement of *Sillon*.

Congress of 'Progressive and Liberal Christianity' in Berlin (mentioned by Antonio Banfi in *Voce*).

1 September
Motu proprio by Pius X, *Sacrorum antistitum,* which settles a formula for the anti-modernistic oath.
7 September
The *Rivista storico-critica delle scienze teologiche,* edited by Buonaiuti, and the manuals on religious knowledge promoted by it, put on the Index; among them Buonaiuti's *Saggi di filosofia e storia del Nuovo Testamento.*
III Congress of the Lega democratica nazionale held at Imola.
Public retirement of Tommaso Gallarati Scotti.

1911   Murri expelled from the Lega democratica nazionale.

Index